ESSENTIAL MAWDUDI SERIES

ISSUES IN ISLAMIC SOCIETY & STATE

Sayyid Abul A'lā Mawdūdī

Translated and Edited by
Ahmad Imam Shafaq Hashemi

General Editor
Prof Anis Ahmad PhD

THE ISLAMIC FOUNDATION

Issues in Islamic Society and State

First published in England by
THE ISLAMIC FOUNDATION
Markfield Conference Centre,
Ratby Lane, Markfield, Leicestershire,
LE67 9SY, United Kingdom
Email: publications@islamic-foundation.com
Website: www.Islamic-foundation.com

Quran House, PO Box 30611, Nairobi, Kenya

P.M.B 3193, Kano, Nigeria

Distributed by
KUBE PUBLISHING LTD
Tel: +44 (0) 1530 249230
Fax: +44 (0) 1530 249656
Website: www.kubepublishing.com

Cataloguing-in-Publication Data is available
from the British Library

ISBN 978-0-86037-602-6 *Casebound*
ISBN 978-0-86037-696-5 *Paperback*
ISBN 978-0-86037-707-8 *Ebook*

Cover Design: Nasir Cadir
Typesetting: S4Carlisle
Printed by: Imak, Turkey

Contents

Transliteration Table

Arabic Consonants

Initial, unexpressed medial and final:

ء	ʾ	د	d	ض	ḍ	ك	k
ب	b	ذ	dh	ط	ṭ	ل	l
ت	t	ر	r	ظ	ẓ	م	m
ث	th	ز	z	ع	ʿ	ن	n
ج	j	س	s	غ	gh	هـ	h
ح	ḥ	ش	sh	ف	f	و	w
خ	kh	ص	ṣ	ق	q	ي	y

Vowels, diphthongs, etc.

Short:	ـَ a	ـِ i	ـُ u
Long:	ـَا ā	ـِي ī	ـُو ū
Diphthongs:		ـَوْ aw	
		ـَىْ ay	

Foreword

Social scientists study society from different perspectives. Anthropologists try to understand how a so-called primitive culture evolves into more refined and modern cultural practices. Sociologists look into internal dynamics and interfaces between social institutions like family, social customs, traditions, law and belief patterns. Psychologists try to understand human behaviour and how the human mind responds to different stimuli, how memory works and perceptions are formed and behavioural change takes place. Political scientists try to find out power sharing between various stakeholders in a political order, while economists try to understand and predict the economic behaviour of man, market trends, the factors responsible for development and resource generation and distribution.

Religious studies in the West or the East normally follow a historical methodology and look into evolution of religious institutions at a macro level. They also study at micro level various components of a religion, like dogma, worship, festivals, rites and rituals, etc. Islam in its nature presents a slightly different phenomenon. Unlike other religions, it is not a set of theological notions, rites and rituals or a matter of certain ways of worship. Assuming Islam is a religion like other faiths becomes a primary stumbling block in discovering the true image of Islam. In Islam, individual, society and state are organically linked together. Separation of one limb from the total body of the Faith leads to a basic methodological flaw, and consequently the end result of research may sound logical but may not be true and valid. A study of society and state in Islam therefore calls for an objective and holistic methodology which should not subscribe to the existing reductionist social science methodology that predominates in the west.

When Islam is studied from an orientalist perspective, the main concern of a scholar is philological or ethnographic. Historical and cultural or religious studies have their own basic assumptions, drawn from an evolutionary approach. Therefore the researcher looks into pre-Islamic Arab society and traditions in search of finding the origin of Islam in pre-Islamic customs, traditions and faith patterns. Effort is made to relate Islamic teachings with tribal traditions and customs. Most legal studies claim that Islam only sanctified and gave a normative status to the Arab *jāhilī* or pre-Islamic tribal legal practices (hand amputation, stoning to death, etc.). Most qualitative analyses indicate the evolution of Islam from a polytheistic tradition to a henotheistic and ultimately monotheistic tradition. Application of the historical evolutionary methodology also leads researchers to conclude that just as Christianity had its historical roots in Jewish tradition, similarly conceptual roots of Islam are to be found in Christianity and Judaism. Since the research methodologies used treat Islam as no more than a 'religion', therefore with all sincerity conclusions drawn may appear logical but may not be true and valid.

When looked from a holistic-phenomenological perspective, Islam is not a religion in its popular meaning. It is a way of life. Its worldview provides guidance in how human beings relate themselves with their Creator God, Allah *subḥānahu wa ta'ālā*; how they should relate themselves with the universe and mankind. It also tells them how to build a society along global divine/ethical values; and how a political order should work in order to provide justice, fairness and basic human rights to people. Being comprehensive, the Islamic worldview has no conflict between *dīn* (Islam as the way of life) and *sulṭāh* (the authority of the state), rather *dīn* and *sulṭāh* make an integrated totality without becoming a theocracy.

A major methodological flaw in the social science methodology, when applied to the study of society and state in Islam, is its reductionism. The research design is based on basic methodological assumptions of psychology, sociology, economy, political sciences, anthropology or a positivist empirical concept of knowledge, truth and ultimate reality. An obvious example is the materialistic-Marxist methodology which reduces all human activities to a material dimension. Similarly, application of psychological methodology reduces man to a conglomerate of psychic disorders, abnormalities, instincts, drives and hungers. Study of society, from an economic perspective, reduces all human activities to their economic dimension, utility and gains. The totality of human beings and society appears missing from these micro studies. Islam being a total way of life deserves to be studied with a holistic perspective and not from a reductionist perspective. This does not mean we overlook economic, psychological or sociological dimensions. It only means using a comprehensive methodology which may approach Islam as a unified body of knowledge, society and state. When studied for an empirical qualitative sociological or historical methodology, Islam can only lead us to its being reduced to a social or historical phenomenon. A holistic comprehensive methodology which may not subscribe to a pre-determined notion of knowledge, truth and reality alone can help us in understanding the total message of Islam.

Islam, the youngest in the Abrahamic religious tradition, puts enormous emphasis on man's role in society. The fact of the matter is that while recognizing man's individual ethical responsibility and accountability, it visualizes man as an actor in history and a key player in social change. This should not lead one to think that Islam considers personal ethical excellence and spirituality as secondary. The point that needs to be highlighted is: Islam wants personal development and spiritual excellence to be achieved through an individual's pro-active social involvement. The objective of Islamic spirituality is not individual salvation or liberation at the cost of withdrawal from society and rejection of the 'worldly'and 'material' in order to excel in spirituality. An authentic Prophetic Tradition (Hadith) calls all this earth as *masjid* (mosque). Iqbal, elaborating on the Hadith, says:

> The Ultimate Reality, according to the Qur'an, is spiritual and its life consists in its temporal activity. The spirit finds its opportunities in the natural, the material, the secular. All that is secular is, therefore, sacred in the roots of its being. … There is no such thing as a profane world. All this immensity of matter constitutes a scope for the self-realization of

> spirit. All is holy ground. As the Prophet (peace be upon him) so beautifully puts it: 'The whole of this earth is mosque'. The state, according to Islam, is only an effort to realize the spiritual in a human organization.[1]

In other words, the Qur'anic and Prophetic view of society and state does not accept separation between the so-called sacred and the profane; society, individual as well as state represent an organic unity founded on *tawḥīd*.

This organic relationship between society and state is a distinction of the Islamic tradition. In most secular ideologies, society and state may enter into conflict. The Marxist concept of society and state is a classical example of this clash, conflict and a dialectic which leads to, at least at a theoretical level, an unending process of thesis, antithesis and synthesis culminating theoretically in a classless society. Islam looks on society and state from a totally different perspective. The Qur'anic anthropology does not accept the evolutionary development of man from a sub-human to a human state. The Qur'an does not accept a concept of god who creates by trial and error. Nor does it believe in a god who after having created all that is in the universe needs to retire. Allah *subḥānahu wa ta'ālā* is the Visionary Planner (*al-Musawwir*), the Caretaker (*al-Ḥāfiẓ*), the Nourisher (*Rabb*) and the Ultimate Creator (*al-Khāliq*), who creates out of nothing. He has created man as such as an independent being, not a by-product. Man is created in the best constitution (*aḥsan taqwīm*) with a clearly defined objective of being Allah's *Khalīfah* or vicegerent on earth. The Qur'an dispels the confusion that man was supposed to be a permanent resident of heaven who fell from Allah's Grace and was sent down as a punishment. This Jewish and Christian concept of man's fall and original sin has no place in Islam.

Recognizing man's individual ethical responsibility and accountability, Islam visualizes a dynamic role of man in society. It rejects the concept of spirituality at the cost of abandoning social,

---

[1] Muhammad Iqbal, *The Reconstruction of Religious Thought in Islam*, edited by M. Saeed Sheikh (Lahore: Institute of Islamic Culture, 2009), p. 123.

economic, political and cultural activity. It is also important to note that individual, society and state are all organically related together in the *tawhīdī* paradigm of the Qur'an and the Sunnah. *Tawḥīd* is the core of Islamic teachings. Islam wants a manifestation of *tawḥīd* in the behaviour of an individual as well as in social development and activities and in the exercise of authority by the state. There is no power struggle between the three and all draw their moral and legal authority from the core teachings of *tawḥīd*. This is the primary principle on which the individual's personality, society and state are founded. *Tawḥīd* synergizes the attitude and behaviour of the individual, society and state. Consequently, the power struggle that exists in non-*tawḥīdī* societies and states does not find way in an Islamic *millah*. The individual, society as well as state are to ensure realization of *tawḥīd* in the state policies, strategies and socio-economic and legal institutions. The major issue, in the context of history, however, has been a *de facto* deviation of state from the ideal *khilāfah* to monarchy or a departure from the primary principle of *tawḥīd*. Nevertheless, throughout the fifteen centuries, the society and individual have remained committed to the principle of *tawḥīd* or sovereignty of Allah in most social and personal matters. Man's destiny and realization of a just, fair and balanced (*'ādil*) society and state remain recurring themes in the Qur'an.

The Qur'an, while dilating on the purpose of man's creation, mentions that before He created man, Allah *subḥānahu wa ta'ālā*, informed the angels about His plan. They were told that man will be empowered with ethical judgment, as Allah's *Khalīfah*, and shall be guided by the divine revelation (*waḥiy*) on how to live a successful life in this world. Since the destiny of man, before his coming into being, was disclosed to a group of angels, i.e. to be Allah's vicegerent on earth, the Qur'an totally rejects the notion of man's fall, inheritance of sin and ultimate redemption through an ordeal of crucifixion. It also renounces living a life of celibacy in order to enhance spirituality. The Islamic view of man also transcends the western and eastern concepts of his identity on colour, racial, ethnic and linguistic basis of nationhood. Its universalistic approach considers humankind as a single family or community (Ummah). '*Human beings, We created you all from a male and female, and made you into nations and tribes so that you may know one another. Verily the noblest of you in the sight of Allah is the most Allah-conscious of you. Surely Allah is All-Knowing, All-Aware*'.[2] Here the Qur'an highlights four important aspects. First, the whole of humanity, with variety of colour, language, physical features, has a common parentage. Therefore, no one can claim superiority over the other on the basis of genetics, colour, race, ethnicity or language. Second, creation of tribes and nations is by design for the purpose of distinction and not for discrimination. Third, one important purpose of human creation is socialization (*ta'āruf*). Last but not least, what makes a person noble in the sight of Allah is his observing *taqwā* or ethical and moral conduct and behaviour and not his colour, race, or language. Islamic society is therefore a *taqwā*-conscious society where Allah-consciousness, His love as well as fear of losing His favour, is the motivating force behind every single act. Man's economic, political, social and cultural activities are motivated by the desire to seek Allah's pleasure.

Living in a family life and building a society where *ma'rūf* (good) prevails while evil (*munkar*) is marginalized – if not totally eliminated – is an obligation and *raison d'*être of the *Ummah Muslimah*. Family thus becomes the building block of society and civilization. Its ethical foundations are enshrined in the Qur'an and are reflected in values of truth (*ṣidq*), honesty (*amānah*) equity and fairness (*'adl*) and virtue (*birr*). Virtue, or *birr*, a core Qur'anic value, is defined by the Qur'an in terms of believer's social responsibility. It says:

> *Righteousness (virtue or* birr*) does not consist in turning your faces towards the east or towards the west; true righteousness consists in believing in Allah and the Last Day, the Angels, the Books and the Prophets, and in giving away one's property in love of Him to one's kinsmen, the orphans, the poor and the wayfarer, and to those who ask for help, and in freeing the necks of slaves and in establishing prayer and dispersing the zakat. True righteousness is attained by those who are faithful*

---

[2] *Al-Ḥujurāt* 49: 13.

> *to their promise once they have made it and by those who remain steadfast in adversity and affliction and at the time of battle (between Truth and falsehood). Such are the truthful ones, such are the Allah-fearing (*muttaqun*).*
>
> [*al-Baqarah* 2: 177]

This *āyāt*, one of the longest of the Qur'an, elaborates the meaning of *birr*. It touches on the core meaning of authentic *'aqīdah* i.e. belief in Allah *subḥānahu wa ta'ālā*, the Creator, in His Messengers, in Angels, and the Books; observance of devotions like prayer or *ṣalāh*, zakat etc. At the same time it underscores importance of social responsibility as an obligation and duty of a believer. It exhorts a believer to spend on relatives, orphans, the poor and the wayfarer and those who ask for help. It further underscores that virtue and piety means spending on the liberation of slaves besides establishing system of prayer and zakat. It also points out that *birr* also means to be steadfast in times of test and trial. Those who observe the attitude of *birr* consequently are called the truthful ones (*alladhīna ṣadaqū*) and Allah-fearing (*al-muttaqūn*).

The above *āyah* indicates that the focus of Qur'anic teachings remains on realization of good, ethical and just behaviour at the community (*jamā'ah*) level, therefore *birr*, *taqwā* and *ma'rūf* are not a matter of individual quality. The Qur'an wants to create a dynamic global Community and society, an Ummah conscious of its social, moral and legal obligations. In order to forge this Ummah it creates from within society a *jamā'ah*, a group of committed persons, who enjoin good and forbid wrong. The Qur'an calls such persons truly successful.[3] Consequently, the Ummah, the Muslim community, has been made collectively responsible for dissemination of good and forbidding evil and wrong: '*And it is thus that We appointed you to be the community of the middle way so that you might be witness to all mankind and the Messenger might be a witness to you.*'[4]

---

[3] *Āl-'Imrān* 3: 104.

[4] *Al-Baqarah* 2: 143.

What makes Muslims an Ummah, therefore, is not its physical, genetic or ethnic character but its being a mission-oriented community. It enjoys consensus of minds and hearts through its faith in the divinely revealed values and ideals. It also responds to internal and external challenges with a common concern. The Ummah, whether in Morocco or Canada, in Indonesia or in New Zealand, globally shares in its heartbeat and response to issues that relate with its basic values and norms. Irrespective of space and time, its devotion to the Qur'an and the Prophet (peace be upon him) remains unchanged. This unity of hearts, constructs a consolidated society and community, as pointed out by the Qur'an in several places: '*The believers, both men and women are allies (*awliyā'*) of one another. They enjoin good, forbid evil, establish prayer, pay zakat and obey Allah and His Messenger. Surely Allah will show mercy to them. Allah is All-Mighty, All-Wise.*'[5] The bond, therefore, which fabricates the Muslim society and ultimately global community, is two-fold. First and foremost, accepting Allah consciously and the Prophet (peace be upon him) as final authority in all public policy issues, personal, socio-economic and political matters. Second, to join hands in realization of *ma'rūf* (good) and in forbidding *munkar* (evil) in society. Prayer and zakat in this context are tools for achieving this objective as expressed elsewhere in the Qur'an: '*and establish prayer. Surely prayer forbids indecency and evil.*'[6] Cooperation in *ma'rūf* and fighting against evil, immorality, indecency, corruption and wrong makes it an ideal ethical Islamic society, a pro-active, ethical and moral force. Its emphasis on moral behaviour helps in marginalization of unethical practices, extremism and violence in society.

This social dimension of Islamic '*aqīdah* (faith) and its implications are often not properly comprehended by the Muslim elite as well as by those who study Islam from an empirical social science methodology. Islam visualizes man precisely as a socially-responsible ethical being. Even areas regarded as personal space are viewed by it in a social context. In Islam, none of the '*ibādāt* (singl. '*ibādah*, acts of worship)

---

5 *Al-Tawbah* 9: 71.

6 *Al-'Ankabūt* 29: 45.

can be conceived, purely on an individual level. Prayer, as mentioned earlier, is obligatory in public congregation for men, while women are advised to have their congregational as well as individual prayer at home without any loss to the reward from Allah *subḥānahu wa taʿālā*. Similarly, the month of fasting is observed collectively all over the world by Muslims, and hajj (pilgrimage) is only performed collectively. No one can perform hajj individually but in a congregation. Zakat, which is not a tax but *ʿibādah* and one of the five pillars of Faith, is to be collected by the state and distributed according to the categories fixed by the Qur'an. If the Islamic state, for any reason, does not exist or fails to play its role, the Muslim society must develop an independent social institutional support system consisting of honest and trustworthy persons who collect zakat and distribute to those in society who deserve it. In brief, this essential social dimension of zakat, *ṣalāh*, *ṣawm* and hajj indicates that *ʿibādah* is not simply a quest for personal piety or making the individual self perfect, but it leads to man's total social involvement, interaction and development, which helps in fine-tuning of the individual as an agent of social change. Ultimately it leads to realization of *maʿrūf* and elimination of *munkar* in society through a state mechanism.

Those who approach Islam with a pre-conceived notion that like other religions it is a faith which requires its followers to observe certain devotions and prayers, rituals and ceremonies, miss the most distinct aspect of Islam. It is not a faith in the conventional understanding of the term but a way of life, a guidance (*hidāyah*) in the vital aspects of man's ethical conduct in society. It is therefore more than a matter of personal salvation or spiritual elevation. Like other religions, Islam does have a system of *ʿibādāt* (devotions), but their philosophy, form and objective is totally different. It is not a faith confined to personal salvation or individual spiritual transcendence. The very concept of *tazkīyah* (purification, growth, development, progress) of *nafs* (self) and *rūḥ* (soul) is linked with social responsibility, civic engagement, social change and social development. Zakat of *nafs* and *māl* (wealth, resources) or purification of self and its development is achieved therefore through active involvement, participation and engagement in socio-economic upliftment, in order to seek Allah's Pleasure.

Giving of zakat is not only on wealth but on knowledge, experience and wisdom, to be offered as a right of people of the community and in order to have one's own growth and development.

Prayer is traditionally understood in religions of the world as meditation and personal devotion. In Islam it is essentially a social and collective activity. The Qur'an calls for establishment of *ṣalāh* (*iqāmah*) and not just offering prayer in seclusion. It has to be offered in congregation in a *masjid* – collectively in a public space – even if a home is designated for this purpose in case a dedicated mosque does not exist in an area. At the same time, extra prayers (*nawāfil* and *sunan*) can be performed, preferably in privacy. *Ṣalāh* is not only an encounter of the whole congregation with Allah but has deep educational dimensions. It creates social cohesiveness, a sense of belonging, equality, mutual assistance and brotherhood. It also educates the congregation at a micro level, how to select their leader in the mosque, and at a macro level in their political life. Society in this respect becomes the building blocks that evolves and moves toward the realization of state.

Islamic society brings together different stakeholders under one umbrella of brotherhood of faith and makes a conscious effort to eliminate classifications based on colour, ethnicity, language, caste and economic or political affiliation. It has no room for a 'VIP culture' of a feudal and ruling class. In the ideal society created in Madinah, the emoluments for the *Khalīfah* (from Abū Bakr, 'Umar and 'Uthmān up to 'Alī) was the same as that of an ordinary citizen. As *Khalīfah* they enjoyed no legal immunity nor any special treatment. Yet the writ of the state governed by them was recognized all over the territory of the Islamic State and beyond. Society in the Islamic scheme of life means connectivity, mutuality and interpersonal relationship. This is based not only on sharing in economic, political or personal benefits but in a bond of brotherhood (*ikhā'*), just and fair behaviour (*'adl*), fulfilment of rights and obligations (*ḥuqūq wa 'l-farā'id*) and cooperation in good (*ma'rūf*) and disassociation from evil and wrong (*munkar*). This society has been pluralistic. It consists of *Ummah Muslimah*, or the community of the believing Muslims, who enjoy full religious, ethical, economic and social liberty. They play an important role in the development of a conducive and peaceful environment. Since an Islamic state is by definition promoter and protector of Islamic values and culture, it is only logical to assume that only those citizens and members of society who own these values can qualify to hold key positions in its political structure. This does not stop those who may not subscribe to Islam as their faith and ideology from playing an active role in society.

Islamic society, to sum up, is a classless, colour-free, ethics-centred, just, fair and equitable society. It assigns high priority to family, education, health care, ecology and the human rights of its members. It is pluralistic and not theocratic but committed to the realization of Allah's Sovereignty in all domains of life. It enjoins ethical practices and frustrates immorality and corruption. Its institutions get strength from the state and the state gets its inspiration from its citizens. Even when an ideal Islamic state is not in operation, Islamic social institutions and society at large reflects and communicates Islamic values to the coming generations.

The state in Islam, to begin with, has three-fold responsibility. First and foremost, to create space for the individual to act consciously, responsibly and ethically in a social framework. Second, to ensure that society does not get corrupted, polluted and degenerated. Third, to ensure the policies of state are fully in line with the two non-variable principles of Islam: the Qur'an and the Sunnah of the Prophet (peace be upon him). The development of state and society are not exclusive but are organically related and synergized. Therefore, the whole discourse on social change in society, whether it comes from top down or bottom up or whether individual transformation should precede social change leading to ultimately political change, is irrelevant and based on a typical exclusivist, evolutionary mind-set. In Islam, development of individual, society and state takes place concurrently and not in isolation or in a vacuum.

The *raison d'être* of man's creation is his being deputed on earth as *Khalīfah*, or vicegerent. Its justification is expressed in the Qur'an in one single word, i.e. the Sovereignty of Allah: '*Don't you know that to*

Allah belongs the sovereignty of the heavens and earth: and you have not beside Allah any friend or helper.'[7] The Qur'an clearly states the purpose of man's creation on earth is none other than realization of Allah's commands in society and state: '*Behold your Lord said to the angels: "I will create a vicegerent on earth."*'[8] It also refers to the Messengers sent to reform society not just as 'preachers' but persons with legal and political authority to adjudicate in disputes and establish Allah's writ on earth: '*O David, We have indeed made you a vicegerent on earth: so judge you between men in truth (and justice).*'[9] Individual, society and state are thus organically related to each other and there cannot be a separation at conceptual or practical level between them, though in terms of their ideal realization the first two, i.e. the individual and society, may exist independent of a state in some exceptional and given situations. Wherever such a phenomenon exists it has a natural desire to manifest itself in political change. The ideal situation, however, remains when all three have a concurrent growth and development, even under a so-called western secular political system in a Muslim country or in a Muslim minority context.

Statehood in Islam is not a later institutional development. It is an integral part of the holistic Islamic vision of life. It cannot be separated from the very concept of Islam as *dīn*, as illustrated in the Qur'an:

> *Allah has promised to those of you who believe and do righteous deeds that He will surely grant them in the land* khilāfah *(vicegerency, political authority) as He granted it to those before them; that He will establish in authority their* dīn, *which He has been pleased to choose for them; and that He will replace with security the state of fear that they are in: 'They will worship Me (alone) and associate none with Me in My divinity.'*
>
> [*al-Nūr* 24: 55]

7 *Al-Baqarah* 2: 107.

8 *Al-Baqarah* 2: 30.

9 *Ṣād* 38: 26.

Three vital aspects are highlighted in this Qur'anic statement: first when believers act righteously, following the ethical teachings of the Qur'an and the Prophet's Sunnah, they qualify for *khilāfah* as a gift bestowed upon them as well as earned by them. Second, *Khalīfah* is not simply a political title. It means a paradigm shift from a state of oppression, insecurity and injustice to a divinely-guided system founded on equity, justice, peace and security. Therefore, *khilāfah* symbolizes realization of basic human rights of the citizens of an Islamic society and state. Last, but not least, the new order is not a theocracy but a realization of the principle of *tawḥīd* in personal, social, economic, cultural, legal and political space in human institutions.

In the Qur'an, the term *dīn*, used to denote Islam, carries a comprehensive meaning. While Islam itself is defined by the Qur'an as True and Straight Way of life, *al-Dīn al-Qayyim*, the Qur'an specifies 'dīn *in the sight of Allah is al-Islam*.'[10] It further elaborates: '*This day I have perfected for you, your* dīn *and have bestowed upon you My Bounty in full measure, and have been pleased to assign for you Islam as your* dīn.'[11] Elsewhere, the Qur'an makes it explicit that *dīn* is not limited to prayers, fasting, zakat, or *'ibādāt*. It calls for a total quantitative change in human behaviour in economic, political, social and other human interventions. It is a totality and not a matter of observing some religious practices: '*Believers enter wholly into Islam and do not follow in the footsteps of Satan for he is your open enemy.*'[12]

Having defined Islam as *dīn*, the Qur'an also clearly mentions its domain which includes political authority. The Qur'an refers to three earlier Prophets, *Sayyidunā* Dawood, Sulayman and Yusuf, who established political order and realized Allah's sovereignty on earth. Specific references are made in the Qur'an to the realization of Allah's sovereignty by His Messengers. In the narration of Bānū Isrā'īl, the Qur'an talks about Prophet Dawood (David) as combining in his personality both in Prophethood and political power: '*O David, We have indeed made you Vicegerent (*Khalīfah*) on earth, so judge*

[10] *Āl-'Imrān* 3: 19.

[11] *Al-Mā'idah* 5: 3.

[12] *Al-Mā'idah* 5: 3.

you between men in truth and justice).'[13] Prophet Solomon makes a supplication to establish a political order based on Divine Guidance, peace and justice: '*My Lord, forgive me and bestow upon me a kingdom such as none other after me deserve. Surely you are the Bounteous Giver.*'[14] A more elaborate narrative tells us about exercise of political authority by Prophet Joseph. Before he took over the highest public office in Egypt, he shared his vision of Allah's sovereignty with fellow prisoners: '*Fellow prisoners! Is it better that there be diverse lords, or just Allah, the One Irresistible. … All authority to govern rests only with Allah. He has commanded that you serve none but Him. This is the Right Way of life.*'[15]

The Qur'anic view of *dīn*, being comprehensive, includes not only principles of state but it makes state responsible for the proper observance of prayer, implementation of the system of zakat, realization of *ma'rūf* or ethical behaviour,[16] and elimination of wrong (*munkar*). It also makes the state responsible for the implementation of Shariah law. The legal dimension of *dīn* is well elaborated in the context of implementation of criminal punishment for immorality: '*Those who fornicate whether female or male (bachelor) – flog each one of them with a hundred lashes. And let not tenderness for them deter you from what pertains to Allah's* dīn, *if you do truly believe in Allah and the Last Day.*'[17] This *āyah* and others that deal with *ḥudūd* make it explicit that *dīn* is much more than devotions and prayers. It includes specific directions on criminal justice as well as on economic, political and social justice, needed for sustainability of a just social order. Restoration of law and order in society, realization of the writ of the Islamic state is another meaning of the term *dīn* used in the Qur'an: '*Keep on fighting against them until mischief (*fitnah, *oppression, injustice, insecurity) ends and* dīn *prescribed by Allah prevails.*'[18] Here, realization of *dīn* stands for elimination of corruption, exploitation and oppression from society.

[13] *Ṣād* 38: 26.

[14] *Ṣād* 38: 35.

[15] *Yūsuf* 12: 39–40.

[16] *Al-Ḥajj* 22: 41.

[17] *Al-Nūr* 24: 2.

[18] *Al-Baqarah* 2: 193.

Again it is not confined to personal relation with Allah *subḥānahu wa taʿālā*.

The divide between state and 'religion' which exists in most of the world religions has no place in Islam. Looking on it from a philosopher's perspective, we refer again to what 'Allāmah Muhammad Iqbal (1877–1938) said:

> The essence of *tawḥīd* as a working idea is equality, solidarity and freedom. The state from an Islamic standpoint is an endeavour to transform these principles into space and time forces, an aspiration to realize them in definite human organization. It is in this sense alone that the state in Islam is a theocracy, not in the sense that it is headed by a representative of God on earth, who can always screen his despotic will behind his supposed infallibility … All that is secular is therefore sacred in the roots of its beings. There is no such thing as a profane world. All this immensity of matter constitutes a scope for the self-realization of spirits. All is holy ground, as the Prophet so beautifully puts it 'The whole of the earth is a mosque' … The state according to Islam is only an effort to realize the spiritual into a human organization.[19]

Sayyid Abul A'lā Mawdūdī (1903–1979) and 'Allāmah Muhammad Asad (1900–1992) both endorse Iqbal's views on the nature of Islamic state. Sayyid Mawdūdī said:

> According to the Qur'an, the vicegerency of Allah is not the exclusive birth-right of any individual or clan or class of people: it is the collective right of all those who accept and admit Allah's absolute sovereignty over themselves and adopt the Divine Code, conveyed through the Prophet as the law above all laws and regulations: 'Allah has promised such of you as have become believers and done good deeds that He will most surely make them His vicegerent in the

[19] Iqbal, *Reconstruction of Religious Thought in Islam*, p. 123.

> earth' (*al-Nūr* 24: 55). This concept of life makes the Islamic *Khilāfah* a democracy, which in essence and fundamentals is anti-thesis of the theocratic, the monarchical and the papal forms of government, as also of the present day western secular democracy."[20]

'Allāmah Asad observed: 'Since every adult Muslim has the right to perform each and every religious function, no person or group can legitimately claim to possess any special sanctity by virtue of religious functions entrusted to them. Thus the term "theocracy" as commonly understood in the West, is entirely meaningless within the Islamic environment.'[21]

The Islamic state is essentially an extension of Islamic society founded on the ethical principles of *ma'rūf* (good), *'adl* (equity and fairness), *ḥaqq* (truth), *amānah* (trust), *shūrā* (counselling), and *maṣlaḥāh 'ammah* (public good). The guiding principles of the state reside in the Qur'an. First and foremost is the realization of Allah's sovereignty (*hākimīyyah*) on land through His *khilāfah*. Second, selection of the most capable persons who are trustworthy (*amīn*), and who are *umanā'* (trustees) of the masses and take care of their interests. Third, appointment of officers and state functionaries are made on the basis of merit (*ahlīyah*) and not on the basis of linguistic, tribal, ethnic or racial considerations. There is no place for hereditary succession in the Islamic political system. Meritocracy has to be strictly observed. Fifth, independence of the judiciary is one of the vital principles, and last but not least is the welfare of the people. The state has to ensure security, sustenance, and progress of its citizens. Its policies have to be people friendly and in line with the objectives of the Shariah.

The Islamic state as well as society is obliged to protect the rights of its citizens. These include: (1) Protection and promotion of the life

---

[20] Sayyid Abul A'lā Mawdūdī, *Islamic Law and Constitution*, edited and translated by Prof Khurshid Ahmad (Lahore: Islamic Publications Ltd, 1980), pp. 218–219.

[21] Muhammad Asad, *Principles of State and Government in Islam* (Gibraltar: Dar al-Andalus, 1980), p. 21.1

of every citizen irrespective of gender, faith, colour, age or language; (2) right to conscience including practice of *dīn*, religious freedom and security; (3) equal, easy and free access to justice; (4) right to protection of property; (5) right to act rationally; (6) protection of honour; (7) right to enjoin good and forbid evil; (8) freedom of association; (9) legal protection against wrongfully hurting religious feelings, insult of religious personalities or desecration of places; and (10) the right of the needy and the poor to be provided with basic necessities in order to achieve economic sustainability.

Due to limitations of space we cannot give a conclusive run down on the rights of citizens in an Islamic society and state. However, this brief discourse makes some effort to indicate that the Islamic state is based on participatory decision making (*shūrā*), and the election of competent persons (*ahl*) for public office on the basis of merit and not because of hereditary succession or the theocratic claims of a privileged clergy. Islamic political order is democratic in its essence. It does not accept western secular democracy as its ideal, because of its obvious conflict with the principle of Allah's sovereignty.

The contemporary western discourse on Islam and the Muslims appears predominantly a matter of distorted perceptions, apprehensions, pre-conceived images, misgivings and confusion – such as the Islamic state means theocracy and Islamization means fundamentalism. As indicated above, the Islamic state is not theocratic. There is no provision in Islam for clerics who may control affairs of state and enjoy infallibility. Similarly, adherence to the Qur'an and the Prophetic Sunnah and Hadith in no way can be termed fundamentalism for three obvious reasons. First and foremost the Qur'an calls for rejection of a dogmatic, closed-minded approach. It calls for critical thinking, evidence-based research and a deep study of *dīn*. Practically on every single page the Qur'an exhorts its readers to conduct rational, scientific research in order to create new knowledge. The Prophet (peace be upon him) in his often quoted Hadith underscores the importance of *ijtihād* and expresses his own and Allah's pleasure when Ma'ādh ibn Jabal *raḍiyallāhu 'anhuhā* indicates use of *ijtihād* in order to solve emergent issues and problems. It was due to their intimate interaction with the Qur'an and the Prophetic Tradition that Muslim scientists, physicians, chemists, engineers, pharmacologists, astronomers and geographers, along with historians, philosophers and legal thinkers came up with numerous original ideas and inventions. They gave the world a rich civilizational tradition.

Second, the Prophetic endorsement of *ijtihād*, when deputing Maʿādh ibn Jabal as the governor of Yemen, also dispels the common myth that the door of *ijtihād* was closed and now the time has come to re-open it. How can a person who claims to follow the Prophet (peace be upon him) act against his explicit endorsement of *ijtihād* and consider it as needed no more? The presence of hundreds of Qura'nic exegesis, commentaries on Hadith and research works on *fiqh* (law) and *kalām* (theological discussions) is evidence to continue the tradition of critical thinking in the Islamic history of ideas and culture.

Third, the explicit condemnation that the blind following of the forefathers of the Qur'an leaves no room for traditionalism or simply following the practices of the elders. '*When they are told to follow the (Revelation) that Allah has sent down, they say: "Nay, we shall follow the ways that we found our fathers (following)." What! Even if it is Satan beckoning them to the Penalty of the (blazing) Fire?*'[22] Only those views of the elders can be considered which are based on evidence from the Qur'an or the Sunnah. The call to Islamize simply means reconstruction of Islamic thought on the basis of Islamic epistemology. Needless to say, our concept of what is truth, right, knowledge and wisdom is directly linked with the epistemological paradigm we adhere to. The western thought, founded on Greek philosophical assumptions, secular world view and materialistic or utilitarian concept of society and state cannot offer an appropriate model of governance for a people who have their own set of values and norms.

Sayyid Abul A'lā Mawdūdī is perhaps the most influential twentieth century Muslim political thinker and strategist, whose writings

[22] *Luqmān* 31: 21.

were not only well received in Pakistan but also had a deep impact on the educated youth in Sudan, Egypt, Syria, Iraq, Jordan and in Southeast Asia during his own lifetime. His approach of a systematic, constitutional and democratic process of social change also influenced the thought process of western-educated Muslim intellectuals.

Sayyid Mawdūdī's simple but logical, rational and persuasive writings offer an alternative paradigm to young intellectuals. He calls for a return to the Qur'an and the Sunnah and to come up with *ijtihādi* solutions for modern social, economic, political, legal and cultural issues. His going back to the Qur'an and the Sunnah was misconstrued by secularists and the feudal elite who were brought up in a capitalist educational and social tradition. They thought that he was a traditionalist.

According to him, the contemporary capitalist economic and political system is exploitative and unfair to the underprivileged in society. Both systems violate basic principles of *'adl* (equity and fairness) of Islam. The failure of contemporary capitalist economic and financial institutions was further reflected in the recent global protests in over one hundred industrial capitals of the world, which indicates humanity needs a better alternative to this declining economic order.

Islamic social order, according to Sayyid Mawdūdī, has the capacity to substitute the present order with a fair and just order based on global divine ethical values of *tawḥīd*, *'adl*, *taqwā*, *ma'rūf*, *ṣidq* and *ḥaqq*. The systematic methodology of the Prophet (peace be upon him) of building the Islamic personality and character of his Companions led to the creation of a consolidated society with a deep commitment to brotherhood. This became the basis of a welfare state in Madinah. The ideal society of al-Madinah al-Munawwarah was a manifestation of peace within and peace without. It provided security to both the Muslims and non-Muslims; both enjoyed human rights without any discrimination. This moral and ethical revolution, adequately achieved by the Prophet in the Islamic State of al-Madinah, provides a model for peaceful realization of society and state in the Muslim majority situation as well as guidance where Muslims may not form a majority. State is a logical necessity, nevertheless if the state is not easy to be realized, civil society itself can assert its moral and ethical force in implementation of a peaceful and fair social order.

Dilating on the organic relationship between the individual, family, society and state, Sayyid Mawdūdī provides evidence from the Qur'an and the Sunnah on the universality of Islamic principles of society and state. Islamic social and political order was not a product of the Arabian environment. It had its roots in Divine Guidance, which was sent to guide the whole of mankind. Islamic Shariah's objective was to Islamize the Arabs and use them as carriers of its universal principles to the rest of the humanity. Islam never wanted to Arabize the people of the world. Its objective was to Islamize the Arabs and the whole of humanity.

The Universality of Islamic Principles of social justice, peace, fairness, equality of mankind and transcendence of ethical good, makes these values globally applicable. They are as relevant to a Muslim majority context as to a situation where Muslims may not be in a decision-making majority. Even when a given situation may not allow the Muslims to establish a political order, they have an obligation to strive for individual, familial and social behavioural change. The Qur'anic ethical principles of *ma'rūf* (good), *birr* (virtue) *ḥasanāt* (good deeds) *'adl* (equity and justice) and *salām* (peace and security), when realized in personal, familial and social life, result in an upright, socially responsible and ethically proactive social order. It brings blessings to each and every member of society irrespective of their colour, race, ethnicity or religion.

In the case of Muslim majority areas, Sayyid Mawdūdī shows that the borrowed social and political ideas and ideologies have failed in creating a harmonious and fair social order. He advocates for the Islamic alternative. The conceptual consistency and coherence in his ideas and his optimism helps the reader believe in the viability of this new ethical order. His short essays in the book under review indicate his depth of understanding of the issues and the relevance of his ideas in contemporary scenarios.

These essays were written by Sayyid Abul A'lā Mawdūdī originally in literary Urdu. Brother Shafaq Hashemi has done a remarkable job in capturing the spirit of Sayyid Mawdūdī's writings and conveying the contents in a pleasant English version. Wherever necessary the text has been slightly abridged and edited. This volume is a part of the Islamic Foundation's ongoing *Essential Mawdūdī* series. *Wa ma tawfiqi illa bi Allah.*

Prof Dr Anis Ahmad[*]

---

[*] Prof Dr Ahmad is Meritorious Professor of Comparative Ethics and Religions and Vice Chancellor at of Riphah International University, Islamabad. He is also Editor-in-Chief of the quarterly journal, *West and Islam*, published in Islamabad. He can be contacted at anis@anisahmad.com, or anis.ahmad@riphah.edu.pk.

Translator's Preface

The society and state that Islam seeks to establish are unique in all respects. These are the institutions which ensure the growth and development of individuals as free and responsible citizens of a free state; where their basic rights are guaranteed; where there is no distinction of caste, colour or creed; where no Arab has an edge over a non-Arab, a white over a black; where there are no *Brahmans* or *Shudras*; where everyone is equal before the law so long as he or she does not violate the fundamental rules and principles which form the foundation of the Islamic State. Islam is known to have blessed the world with the first-ever model of a truly ideal welfare state – a state where the ruler and the ruled enjoyed the same status; where the head of State, the *Caliph*, had no especial privilege or *Divine Right* making him above the law or empowering him with extraordinary prerogatives and *immunities*; where, in the words of *Sayyidunā* Abū Bakr, the ruler was strong with the strength of his fellow citizens and weak with their weakness; and to whom the mightiest among them was the weakest so long as he did not secure from him the usurped rights of the oppressed as demanded by the norms of Islamic law and social justice; and the most downtrodden among his people was the strongest so long as he was not elevated to his due status in the society and state. Such an egalitarian society and state were among the greatest gifts of Islam to humanity.

The Golden Era (*Khayr ul-Qurun*) of *Sayyidunā* Rasūl Allah and his four Rightly-Guided Caliphs (may Allah's peace and mercy be upon the Prophet, his illustrious family and Companions and all those who followed their glorious model) stand out in human history as the ever-shining examples of a superb personal conduct, benign rule and ideal governance and statecraft. It is not difficult to know from the authentic and properly-recorded data available in the Qur'an, the Sunnah and books of Islamic history, how an Islamic state should be governed, on what pattern the Islamic society should be raised and groomed and in what way the personal conduct, social attitudes, manners and morals of a believer be safeguarded to make them different from others and exemplary in all respect.

Unfortunately, the last two centuries of colonial domination virtually denuded the world of Islam of the great legacy of its glorious past and created for it practically insurmountable odds in all fields of social existence, including education, culture, economy, politics, law and administration. Under such circumstances, the rise of eminent thinkers, reformers and scholars like Sayyid Abul A'lā Mawdūdī on the intellectual horizon was nothing short of a blessing from the All-Merciful Lord, and in light of the guidance available to us in his writings we now find ourselves hopefully in a position to proceed further ahead to regain our lost glory. Sayyid Mawdūdī lived and died for Islam, and to illuminate for us the pathway to eternal bliss and herald the Muslim nation into an era of Islamic resurgence from East to West. He has written so much on so many aspects of Islam that it is quite difficult to compress all his writings within a single volume and under a single title.

This book, I*ssues in Islamic Society and State*, is based on some selected essays of Sayyid Mawdūdī which he contributed in his epoch-making journal *Tarjuman al-Qur'an* and delivered as radio talks during the crucial period from the 1930s to the 60s, and which were then published in the popular volumes of his articles *Tanqīhāt*, *Tafhīmāt*, and *Nashrī Taqrīrein* (a collection of his radio talks). The book is designed to offer thinking minds the answers to some critical questions regarding Islam and the Islamic social order and provide essential information on some of the issues that have faced the Islamic state and the society, and provide the way forward for the world of Islam to a better future. Carefully edited and annotated, it is divided into two Parts: Part One containing twelve articles on *Islam and Society* and Part Two with around two dozen articles, arranged under different titles and sub-titles, relating to *Islam and The State*. The book is a joint production of the Institute of Policy Studies, Islamabad and the Islamic Foundation, Leicester, UK, as part of their joint venture: *Islam and the West: The Essential Mawdūdī* series.

I would be failing in my duty if I do not acknowledge here, with a deep sense of gratitude, the inspiration and guidance that I received from Prof Khurshid Ahmad to make this work possible, which is, in fact, a small segment of a series in the pipeline. He is the leading light behind this ambitious project, and to me personally always a source of strength and inspiration.

May Allah *subḥānahū wa taʿālā* bless our efforts with the desired results in this world and the Hereafter and pardon us for all omissions and commissions in our humble endeavours.

Ahmad Imam Shafaq Hashemi*

* Mr Shafaq Hashemi is a former Information Group Officer and Diplomat. He is also a known linguist, poet and writer and is now a Senior Research Fellow at the Institute of Policy Studies, Islamabad.

PART ONE
Islam and Society

1 *Ijtihād*: The Dynamic Force*

The basic objective of both revival and revolution, whether in the socio-political field or in the realm of religion, is to correct the wrong. There is a fundamental difference, however, between the motives and modus operandi of the two. The revival is preceded by a process of dispassionate thinking and critical scrutiny of the given situation. Well-meaning souls coolly and thoroughly examine the objective reality, determine the causes of corruption, assess its extent, try to evolve steps to retrieve the damage and then use the corrective force only to the extent inevitable to remove those causes and improve the situation. On the contrary, revolution has its genesis in a seething anger and burning urge for revolt. The process of violent change lets one wrong replace another. The intemperance that upsets the situation is countered by yet another intemperance, which destroys the good along with the bad. There is no doubt that a revivalist also has to do what a revolutionary does; both target only the rotten part of the body to remove the rot. The difference, however, is that the revivalist, like a seasoned surgeon, first gathers his data about the exact nature and extent of the damage needed to be corrected and then proceeds to operate using his knife only to the extent needed. He has the balm ready simultaneously for the wound. The revolutionary, on the other hand, goes headlong to operate. His burning passion for revolt hardly gives him the opportunity to differentiate the right from the wrong. He has hardly any time to think of a heeling balm and when that time comes, if at all, it is already too late.

When the situation gets too bad, the suffering people generally lose patience and also their sense of balance to let them think

---

* *Tarjumān al-Qur'ān*, July 1934.

coolly of remedial measures. Such situations, therefore, often lead the revolutionary movements to go for a violent change, instead of a sustained campaign to improve and revive. Serious conflict erupts between the 'conservatives' and the 'progressives', which adds more fuel to the raging fire of anger and revolt. Both these groups move to the extreme limits of obstinacy and defiance and thus both immensely damage the cause of truth and righteousness. On the one side, extreme force is used to defend the wrong instead of the right, and on the other, attack is launched on everything irrespective of its being right or wrong. On their victory, the revolutionaries destroy everything of the old order, whether good or bad. The revolution marches on like a flood and indiscriminately sweeps away everything in its path. It wakes up to the need of reconstruction only after having caused enormous destruction. The revolutionary mind-set, however, has its own peculiar inhibitions. Efforts are made to do away with everything inherited from the conservatives. Everything of the old order, howsoever correct it might be, becomes to them an anathema.

Thereafter, the tortuous road to reconstruction passes through various phases of trial and error. When the revolutionary mind-set is eventually tired of its experimentations, it is only then that it discovers the road map of moderation. This is a road map that a revivalist is expected to always have before himself from the very starting point. The position of the revivalist and the revolutionary is best explained by the following Persian adage (in verse)!

هر چه داناکند، کند نادان　　　لیک بعد از خرابئی بسیار

What the wise one does, the simpleton does too,
But only after having wrought much damage!

The best example of the revolutionaries' predicament in our modern times is that of the Bolshevik Revolution. When the corrupt social order of Czarist Russia became intolerable to the local population, it gave rise to a revolutionary movement. Europe's socialist and democratic ideologies started attracting the Russians. The Czarist authority in turn used every tool of repression to crush popular sentiment and safeguard its vested interests. This caused the seething anger of the revolutionaries against royal despotism and the unjust distribution of wealth to spill over into the entire fabric of Russia's centuries-old civilizational system. Lenin emerged in Moscow as the re-incarnation of Karl Marx (1818–1883). The Czar was dethroned and along with him was destroyed each and every segment of the old socio-political, economic, cultural and religious legacy of the past. Following this wholesale destruction, attempts were made to establish a new social order based on socialist ideology. Bolsheviks devoted all their energies in attempts to remove every trace of the bourgeois legacy. They even went to the extreme of 'banishing' God from Soviet Russia. With the passage of time, however, a saner constructive approach finally took over the revolutionary madness and Bolshevik extremism gradually returned to the point of moderation.[1]

Similar extremism was witnessed during the French Revolution. The revolutionary zealots there also tried to destroy all the good and the bad of the old order and to evolve and introduce new revolutionary concepts and formulas. But the chaotic upsurge left France in a state of turmoil and it took quite some time to achieve the level of political, social and civilizational moderation and stability that we find in France today.

---

[1] That point of moderation came too late however for Soviet Russia. On December 1946, when the Soviets were at the apex of their glory as the world's second super power, Sayyid Mawdūdī made a remarkable statement, which reflected his futuristic approach and depth of insight as a great visionary, political thinker, and reformer:

> The forces that today belong to the secular camp will, one by one, break away and join the camp of Islam. A time will come, then, when Communism will live in the fear of its very survival in Moscow itself, when capitalist democracy will shudder at the thought of defending itself even in Washington and New York, when materialist secularism will be unable to find a place even in the universities of London and Paris, when racialism and nationalism will not win even one devotee even among the Brahmans and the Germans. [Sayyid Abul A'lā Mawdūdī, *Shahādat Ḥaq* '*Witnesses Unto Mankind*', translated by Khurram Murad (Leicester: The Islamic Foundation, 1986), p. 42] – Editor.

Turkey presents yet another example of revolution, where attempts were made to transform overnight, almost by a magic wand, a whole nation into another. While rushing through the surgical operation, the healthy parts of its body were also removed, along with the rotten ones, and in their place new limbs were imported from Europe and transplanted. The revolutionaries went to the extent of replacing the old brain by a new one, imported complete with its new headgear. But as time passes, the Turks are now growing to realize that everything old cannot be discarded as bad and all that is new should not be taken at its face value. They have, therefore, retracted in many cases from the extremist course to the path of moderation and equanimity.[2]

Whatever has been said here is in context with the revolutionary crisis now on the rise among the Indian Muslims. Before the negative fallout of this crisis starts showing, we would like to counsel both the 'conservatives' and the 'progressives' to check their steps and ponder for a while [to avoid falling headlong into the morass of social chaos].

Today, the situation in British India is as bad as it was, or is, in Turkey and elsewhere in the Muslim world. A particular group, in whose hands our religious leadership has been for centuries, has turned Islam into something monolithic and static. It is perhaps since the sixth or seventh century Hijrah that this group has refused to change its calendar. In their scholastic philosophy they do teach that the world is ever-changing, but practically speaking they have kept their eyes shut from the changes taking place in time and space. Today the worldly situations, thoughts, trends and ideologies have undergone total transformation and the socio-political issues and problems are no more the same now as they were before. Our traditional religious leaders, however, still regard themselves as though they were living in the same environment of five–six centuries back. They have remained unmoved by the new changes and challenges and instead their efforts have been to prevent their community from bravely facing the challenges of the time. They have in fact tried to draw it backward from every forward move. These efforts did succeed for a while, but

---

[2] Thus, we find twenty-first century Turkey to be so different from what it was in 1934, when the author could foresee its retraction from the 'extremist course' – Editor.

such success can never be everlasting. No community can live in isolation. In its interaction and dealings with the world it is bound to be influenced by fresh ideas and emerging issues. If the community leaders fail to remain in the vanguard of such changes and lead it correctly through the thorny pathways of the new developments, it eventually becomes the community's responsibility to throw away the yoke of their leadership from its aching shoulders.

The root cause of the malaise facing us today lies in fact elsewhere. Our religious leadership has been so much involved in side-issues that they lost track of the real ones. The side-issues then replaced the principal ones, from where cropped up thousands upon thousands of offshoots, which eventually came to be regarded as true Islam, though mostly of no relevance to Islam at all. The edifice of the Nation of Islam (*Al-Ummah al-Islamīyyah*) was raised on a well-defined order wherein the Qur'an occupied the top most position, followed by the Sunnah of *Sayyidunā* Rasūl Allah (peace be upon him) and then *ijtihād* [the inductive method of *scholarly interpretation of juridical issues in light of the guidelines provided for the purpose by the Qur'an and the Sunnah*]. Unfortunately, however, this order was reversed to the effect that *ijtihād* by the jurists of a particular period was given the top most position, followed by the Sunnah and then lastly the Qur'an. It is actually this reversal of the original order in the last six–seven hundred years that has led to the current stagnation and turned Islam into a static and undynamic entity.

No one can deny the eminent position held by the leading commentators of the Qur'an (*mufassirīn*), the scholars of the Prophetic Traditions (*muḥaddithīn*) and the founders of various schools of Islamic jurisprudence (*a'immah al-fiqh il-Islāmī*). Their contribution in promoting the Islamic Sciences and profound projection of the Islamic Message and Mission is undoubtedly immense. They used the faculties of reason and insight to delve deep into the Qur'an and the Sunnah and draw conclusions and formulate details concerning various laws and precepts. Their scholarly interpretations thus serve as a guide and help to the Ummah. Those cannot, however, become in themselves the original source and founthead of legislation. Our eminent jurists were great *mujtahids* (scholars of juridical issues), but their *ijtihād* can in no way become a permanent statute or abiding principle because of the limitations of time and space circumscribing human knowledge and intellect.

Allah alone is free from the limitations of time and space. He is the Ultimate Source of Knowledge and it is His Knowledge that is not the least affected by the changing times. The Qur'an and the Prophet of Islam (Allah's peace and blessings be upon him) are the glorious receptacles of the Divine Knowledge and Wisdom and hence they alone can be the source from where the seeker of knowledge can always get the required wisdom, thoughts and precepts for guidance according to the needs of all times and situations. As long as the *'ulamā'* and religious scholars continued gathering enlightenment and knowledge from this pristine source, and resolving theoretical and practical problems of their age through their carefully researched deductions (*ijtihād*), Islam continued marching on with the time. When, however, this process stopped and was replaced by blind followership (*taqlīd*), and the views of the old legists and scholars were accorded the sanctity similar to that of the texts of the Qur'an and the Sunnah, Islam's intellectual progress came to a grinding halt. The exponents of the Islamic sciences and torch-hearers of the Divine Knowledge, thus, unfortunately became bogged down in the labyrinths of peripheral issues. Instead of leading the world into the new vistas of thought and action, they were content with engaging their talents in frivolous matters. This eventually gave rise to factional conflicts and there emerged different sects and factions. Those belonging to a different sect or school of thought were generously labelled as kafir (unbeliever). It was such a sad spectacle to see the spirit of love, brotherhood, compassion, communal harmony and solidarity, which had been the hallmark of the Muslim social milieu, giving way to those very characteristics which the Qur'an ascribes to unbelievers and hypocrites.

What we are witnessing in our society today is the result of the backward swing of that pendulum. When the Muslim intelligentsia noticed that their religious leadership was not properly performing the duty of the community's guidance and instead of taking them forward was dragging them backward, they started getting out of the *'ulamā'*'s control and like an army under no one's command wandered all over. There was a group of Muslims that attributed all blame for the fumbles and foibles of those self-appointed champions of religion to Islam itself. They considered religion as the biggest hurdle in the way of their progress and openly preached against it and in favour of following the example of the advanced nations of the world. There was yet another group that took upon itself to abuse and malign the *'ulamā'* and religious leaders, as if by abusing them they were serving the cause of Islam and Muslims. A section of the self-anointed scholars of Islam started pruning the religion itself. There were some who cast aspersions against the eminent scholars of the past, while others took the Prophetic Traditions in their stride. There were also those who went to the extreme of venturing to introduce amendments even in the Qur'anic injunctions. Some zealots thought in terms of separating the state from religion because they believed that religion should be restricted to the sphere of beliefs, rites and rituals, leaving aside the state's mundane matters.

Thus, a number of groups rose to avowedly change the prevailing situation. Yet they were not so much for revival as for revolution. They did not bother to coolly analyze what had actually gone wrong; where lay the root cause of the malaise and how could it be effectively cured? Theirs was all a guesswork, but the surgical operation continued at will without ascertaining the exact nature of the disease and the extent of surgery required.

That is the reason why we are often forced to counter the radicals more fiercely than the conservatives, though we agree with them in principle about the need to bring about a change in the prevailing situation. We are at the same time very keen to replace society's stagnation by dynamism. That does not mean, nonetheless, to abandon or deviate from the true Islamic path for the sake of 'modernization'. We cannot similarly approve of any attempt to amend or add in matters of religious significance without any serious research and true Islamic scholarship. It is similarly not proper to unwittingly dismantle the magnificent structure which the eminent Muslim jurists (*fuqahā'*) and religious leaders of the past raised with so much hard work and dedication. It would be obnoxious similarly to reject the entire treasure house of Ahadith (Prophetic Traditions) on one pretext or the other, or bring about any amendment in the Word of God. All these are measures not of reform but more of perversion and damage.

The only cure for the malaise afflicting the Muslim Ummah today is to set right once again the order that has been reversed. Let the Qur'an assume the position of leadership and preeminence that has always belonged to it. Let Ahadith occupy the place given to them by no less a person than *Sayyidunā* Rasūl Allah himself, as well as by his Companions and *Ahl al-Bayt* (members of his family). (Allah's blessings, peace and mercy be upon the Prophet, his illustrious Companions and the glorious family.) Let the great contribution made by the Muslim jurists, theologians, commentators and transmitters of the Prophetic Traditions be given the same status as is their due. Let us make the best use of this great legacy and keep in place the things not needed to be changed. Let us also keep in mind at the same time that the scholarly works of our *fuqahā'*, *mufassirīn* and *muḥaddithīn* do not occupy the position of a permanent statute, nor have their books made us independent of the need of studies and reflection in the Qur'an and the Sunnah and the doors can never be closed for direct access to them.

The moment we restore this reversed order, the Islamic trail will start blazing once again. As discussed, the principal cause of the present stagnation is that the locomotive that pulls the train has been detached and placed behind. The driver has also been removed from his position and put somewhere in the back seat, while in our simplicity or ignorance we think that the front bogie can itself move and keep the train going forward.

The task of restoring the reversed order, however, needs to be carried out with full patience and perseverance. There is no need of any anger or haste. Whatever has happened did not happen intentionally. Nobody can blame any particular group of religious scholars for being responsible for the present state of stagnation and hampering the onward march of Islamic knowledge. This is the result of the general decline the Muslim Ummah is facing since around the last ten centuries in its political, military, economic and civilizational process. This decadence has not only adversely affected the World of

Islam's spirit of jihad (organized struggle against the forces of evil), but also their capability of *ijtihād*. The Muslims' outlook has changed not only regarding the various issues they face in life, but also about their religious and academic matters, and gradually a spectre of decay has set in unnoticed on all their intellectual faculties. Neither the *'ulamā'* nor their followers can be blamed for this sad development. Nothing positive can either be achieved by just laying blame on any particular quarter, or revolting in anger against the current malaise. The only way to redeem the situation is to coolly reflect on it and try to discover the root causes of the present state of affairs and then sagaciously change it for the better.

2 The Civilizational Crisis*

Every nation consists broadly of two classes: the masses and the elite. The masses, though great in number and the mainstay of its manpower, lack the qualities of intellectual leadership. They are endowed with neither sufficient knowledge nor financial power, nor do they have the status and position of eminence or the authority of government in their hands. Therefore, their job has never been to lead the nation but just to follow those who are there to lead. They are not the ones who make and carve out their way but those who tread the path prepared for them. It is the elite class that prepares the way and then leads the people on the track prepared for them. This privileged group is supported in their every action and approach by the power of their brain, wealth, status and strategy. The people, on the other hand, have to willy-nilly toe their line. Hence, it can rightly be said that the real strength of a nation lies not in its masses, but in its elite. It is due to them that nations rise or fall. Their right approach keeps a nation on the right track and if they go astray the whole nation goes astray. When good days dawn upon a nation, it produces an elite who follow the right path themselves and keep their people also on the right track:

وَجَعَلْنَٰهُمْ أَئِمَّةً يَهْدُونَ بِأَمْرِنَا وَأَوْحَيْنَآ إِلَيْهِمْ فِعْلَ ٱلْخَيْرَٰتِ وَإِقَامَ ٱلصَّلَوٰةِ
وَإِيتَآءَ ٱلزَّكَوٰةِ ۖ وَكَانُوا۟ لَنَا عَٰبِدِينَ ﴿٧٣﴾

> *And We made them into leaders to guide people in accordance with Our command, and We inspired them to good works, and to establish Prayers and to give zakat. They worshipped Us alone.*
>
> [*al-Anbiyā'* 21: 73]

* *Tarjumān al-Qur'ān*, February 1935.

Conversely, when bad times come for a nation, its elite become corrupt and their misdeeds and decadent manners ultimately cause the whole nation to go corrupt and decadent:

وَإِذَآ أَرَدۡنَآ أَن نُّهۡلِكَ قَرۡيَةً أَمَرۡنَا مُتۡرَفِيهَا فَفَسَقُواْ فِيهَا فَحَقَّ عَلَيۡهَا ٱلۡقَوۡلُ فَدَمَّرۡنَٰهَا تَدۡمِيرٗا ﴿١٦﴾

When We decide to destroy a town We command[1] *the affluent among them, whereupon they commit sins in it, then the decree (of chastisement) becomes due against them and thereafter We destroy that town utterly.*

[*Banī-Isrā'īl* 17: 16]

The 'Qur'ānic' term for the misguided elite is *mutrafin*, which means those enjoying affluence and the good things of worldly life. According to the testimony of Allah *subḥānahū wa ta'ālā*, it has always so happened that the class of *mutrafin* indulges in acts of moral depravity, profligacy, tyranny, and transgression and then the whole population gradually becomes afflicted with vice and a decline in manners and morals. Who can challenge this testimony of the Lord? We know by the example of our own people that society's degeneration began with the decadent manners and morals of its elite. In their self-indulgence as a class they started playing with the injunctions of the Islamic Shariah in a conscious effort to get away from its discipline. Like the Pharaohs and Caesars, the elite of the Muslim society turned the bondsmen of Allah *subḥānahū wa ta'ālā* into their own bondsmen. In place of God-worship they promoted the worship of royalty and regality. They taught their people to bow in humility and servitude to their own ilk instead of the Almighty. Committing acts of profligacy in their gorgeous dresses and elegant palatial mansions, they glamourized the most sinful and criminal activities as the most sought after for their people. They devoured

[1] The Lord facilitates the well/meaning for even a greater good and the corrupt to indulge in more corruption and thus bring about their own doom. This has been the Sunnah (Way) of the Lord; and '*You will find no change in Our Way*'. (*Banī Isra'īl* 17: 77) – Editor.

ill-gotten wealth, setting an ugly trend for those around them. They used their knowledge to misguide, their wisdom for mischief, their brain for deceit and intrigues, their wealth to buy the people's loyalty, their authority in government for repression and tyranny and their power for self-aggrandizement. Their personal example forced the people to resort to all sorts of unfair means to reach their goals. These unfair means included sycophancy, bribery, deceit, fraud, intrigues, etc. In short, our elite class was blessed by the Lord with so much of His bounties, which unfortunately they all misused. In this process they debased themselves and along with them the society as a whole.

This has been going on for centuries and the malaise of moral corruption has been sapping at the vitals of the Muslims' strength as a nation and distinct community. In spite of that extremely sad situation, however, the heart of a common Muslim has remained aglow with the light of faith. Practically he may not have been strictly observing the injunctions of religion, but from the inner core of his heart he has been devoted to Allah *subḥānahū wa taʿālā* and His Messenger (Allah's peace and blessings be on him). He has been emotionally attached to the Islamic Shariah in spite of its violations in practice. What Islam proclaimed right has continued to be regarded as right, though practically the wrong has been followed everywhere. Nobody has dared challenge what Islam had declared right as wrong and wrong as right, or discard the mandatory as obsolete and the forbidden as lawful.

The reason for this was that in spite of the overall weakness in faith and perversion of conduct, the otherwise decadent civilization has remained firmly based on the foundations raised by Islam. Though much damage was caused by the imported Greek and Persian philosophies, they could not bring about any drastic change in the Muslims' approach to life, let alone their total deviation from Islam. In spite of considerable digression under external influence from the well-defined pathway of religion, the fundamentals which formed the basis of the Islamic civilization and culture have continued to be firmly rooted in the Muslim psyche. Similarly, in spite of so much deterioration in the education system, the Islamic sciences have continued to occupy a prominent place and no educated member of the Muslim society could be expected to be without at least the basic knowledge of the Islamic Shariah and the social norms and traditions of Islam. Though the firmness of the Shariah's grip on the Muslim's day-to-day life is no more as it used to be, the Muslims' collective affairs are still governed by it. In short, Islam's impact remains very deep on the Muslim community's manners and morals, thoughts and actions in spite of the rampant weaknesses and deviations.

With the loss of political power and government during the eighteenth century, our privileged class of *mutrafin* realized that they were about to lose their social status, privileges, power and pelf and there was no way for them to escape the loss unless they switched their loyalties from their own society and people and equipped themselves with the Western values, culture and system of education. This marked a total change in their attitude, and the Colonized lost their sense of direction and gradually their frame of mind, viewpoint and inclinations all became rudderless. Their U-turn from Islam to Westernism was the only way out for their survival as a privileged class. Under the changed circumstances, the sense of shame and guilt, which was initially felt over any deviation from the Islamic injunctions, gradually gave way to apathy and then to unabashed violations of Islamic norms and values. The non-conformist attitude became a fashion and a sign of modernity. The overall attitude of our Westernized lot is now well past the limits of shame and could be the precursor of an open revolt. Those who violate the Islamic injunctions have become so emboldened now that instead of feeling ashamed or apologetic, they make fun of those who remain firmly devoted to Islam and its teachings. It appears as though the culprit is not the one who is violating the Islamic law, but those who observe it with all sincerity. Today, the religious-minded Muslims, especially if they are educated, are being made to feel embarrassed on performing Islamic duties. Human errors discovered in a person who observes Islamic injunctions are blown out of all proportion to show that those committed to their religion are more prone to such faults, as if the main reason for human foibles or flaws of character is nothing but one's being a devout Muslim.

This rebellious trend is confined not only to the proper observance of the Islamic duties like *ṣalāh* or *ṣawm*, but to almost all walks of life. Allegiance to Islam and observance of Islamic injunctions are denigrated as *mullaism*.[2] Today, the term *mullaism* has come to stand for a combination of social weaknesses like ignorance, narrow-mindedness, orthodoxy, obscurantism and irrationality. The nickname 'mulla' is given to a Muslim who is firm in his belief and practice and whose commitment to his religion is unshakable. Thus, as an attribute the 'mulla' is synonymous today to the 'uncivilized', 'uncultured' and 'retrogressive' – someone who is a misfit in society. It has become the worst abuse one may hurl against anybody, thanks to the 'coloured' lackeys of 'colonial Imperialism'. The anti-Islam bias has come to such a level that a premise advanced on rational ground, or with reference to an author from the West, at once becomes almost an article of faith. Yet, if the same thing is presented with reference to Islam, the Muslim mind gets bogged down in doubts and misgivings of different sorts.

Until recently, only our menfolk were prone to this anti-Islam virus and Muslim women were safe from its adverse effects. We could heave a sigh of relief that at least the sanctuary of the Muslim home (haram) remained a safe haven for the civilizational and cultural values of Islam. One of the principal reasons for the Islamic prescription of hijab for the Muslim women has been to provide them with such safe havens so that the bosom from where the Muslim baby gets its first nourishment may remain radiant with the light of faith and the cradle from where is to rise the future citizen of the Muslim society was fortified against the forces of apostasy, immorality and misconduct. The Muslim household that offered the environment for grooming a

[2] The terms *mulla*, *mawlavī* and *mawlānā* were actually titles of the graduates of various levels from the institutions of Islamic learning, like their modern day counterparts of the Bachelor, the Master, and the PhD. These evoked a sense of pride in their holders as well as the society that nurtured those institutions. The Colonial rule and the onset of western cultural disaster played havoc with the Islamic society and the abodes of Islamic sciences, with the result that those exalted titles gradually assumed a derogatory and abusive connotation. Presently, the terms fundamentalism and fundamentalist have replaced mulla and mullaism – Editor.

baby into an upright man thus remained unpolluted by such rampant unhealthy trends. The institute of haram was, in fact, an impregnable fortress of the Islamic civilization and its ultimate sanctuary, where the Islamic social order could find shelter if it was ever repulsed and had to seek safe haven for retreat. Unfortunately, however, this very fortress is now showing signs of cracks. The virus of westernization has reached inside our homes. Our Anglophile *mutrafin* are bent upon dragging their womenfolk out of their homes to infect them with the poison with which they themselves are already anointed. Our girls are now being sent to the same institutions which had taught our boys how to revolt against Islam, Islamic socio-cultural values and traditions.

The phenomenon of westernization of Muslim women appears to be the last of a series of steps designed to de-Islamise the Muslim society. It is no more an apprehension, but something that can easily be noticed by a discerning eye. The Muslim woman can now be seen moving around in her attractive outfit, wearing make-up in public, in an open violation of Islamic norms and ethical values. She goes to clubs, attends parties at hotels, rubs shoulders with men in public places and graces shopping centres in all her fineries. And the worst part of it is that instead of feeling guilty on openly violating the ethical norms of Islam, she is made to feel elated. She tries, on the contrary, to denigrate the upholders of the values of modesty and virtue. At first, the lady of the house refused to give up hijab as she was mindful of the teachings of her religion. When forced by her husband, she had to reluctantly come out in the open, but always felt the prick of her conscience over the piercing eyes that followed her unabashedly. She never for once enjoyed the fun and frolics beyond the four walls of her house, because she knew that the 'freedom' beyond was at the cost of losing Allah's Pleasure and the 'captivity' within the citadel of her home was the guardian of her real freedom. The change of attitude among our womenfolk has been brought about very cleverly by using the tactics of both persuation and force. This has systematically caused a secular trend to take over a section of our womenfolk, which is definitely a very sad development. Let us ponder for a while and think that if the generations which were bred and brought up in a relatively better environment by God-fearing mothers lose that environment, then what future lies for the new breed, reared by westernized parents? Can we expect from the children brought up in a westernized atmosphere, the children whose innocent gaze is no more familiar with the icons of Islamic values and culture, whose ears may have heard nothing about Allah and His Messenger and the clean slate of whose heart and brain has recorded only the imprint of western culture, can we expect them to grow up emotionally and intellectually as true Muslims, both in their acts and deeds?

In its first stage, a crime lies heavy on the heart of the one who commits it. Such a person feels disturbed by a sense of guilt. The crime may be punishable as demanded by its nature. It can also be condoned through repentance and expression of remorse as it may as well be attributed to human weakness. In its second degree, a crime may become something normal and the person committing it may have no sense of guilt, which only means his disrespect and apathy to the law. In its last stage, the crime becomes a way of life. Then, the defaulter has no respect for the law under which he is governed and tries to justify his conduct as permissible, or rather desirable according to a different legal code. He even goes to the extent of deriding his own legal system. To him all those are wrong who abide by the law that holds him liable for punishment. Such a person is guilty not only of violating the law, but also of sedition and revolt against the society's established legal norms and code.[3]

Every sane person knows that when someone reaches that last stage, he is no longer loyal to society's legal code, though he may be hesitant to openly declare his rebellion. It is extremely audacious, however, for him to think that he can remain a member of the Muslim community

---

[3] An authentic Hadith of *Sayyidunā* Rasūl Allah (peace be upon him) puts it metaphorically in a beautiful way. It tells us that when the believer commits a sin the first time, a black spot appears on his heart. If he repents and corrects his conduct, the spot disappears and his heart is polished; but if he does not and the sin increases, the spot keeps on increasing till it covers the whole heart. (*Abwāb al-Zuhd* [Chapters on Asceticism] narrated by Abū Hurayrah, 4244; *Sunan Ibn Mājah*, pp. 360–361) The experience shows that once a person reaches that stage, he loses sense of balance and cannot differentiate between right and wrong – Editor.

in spite of his wilful violation of Islamic injunctions, derision of the Islamic Shariah and denigration of those who faithfully adhere to their religion. On the one hand, such a person treats things declared unlawful by the Qur'an and the Sunnah as lawful, and on the other unabashedly claims to be a true Muslim. Who can vouch for the veracity of such a claim? Can belief and disbelief coexist? Is it possible for allegiance and revolt, devotion and derision, obedience and disobedience to go hand in hand?

Islam means total submission to the Will of the Lord and absolute allegiance to His Command. There is no true submission and allegiance without faith (*īmān*) and the first and foremost demand of *īmān* is that the believer (*mu'min*) should at once forego all his options the moment a decree from the Lord reaches him in a particular case. His immediate reaction should always be: 'We hear and we obey':

إِنَّمَا كَانَ قَوْلَ ٱلْمُؤْمِنِينَ إِذَا دُعُوٓاْ إِلَى ٱللَّهِ وَرَسُولِهِۦ لِيَحْكُمَ بَيْنَهُمْ أَن يَقُولُواْ
سَمِعْنَا وَأَطَعْنَاۚ وَأُوْلَٰٓئِكَ هُمُ ٱلْمُفْلِحُونَ ﴿٥١﴾

> *When those that believe are called to Allah and His Messenger in order that he (the Messenger) may judge their disputes among them, nothing becomes them but to say: 'We hear and we obey.' Such shall attain true success.*
>
> [*al-Nūr* 24: 51]

This act of submission is not out of any compulsion. It is instead a most willing and voluntary submission to the injunctions of the Lord and His Prophet (Allah's peace be upon him), without the slightest reservation or constraint within one's heart. If one submits outwardly but feels constrained within, one is not a *mu'min*, but a *munāfiq* (hypocrite):

وَإِذَا قِيلَ لَهُمْ تَعَالَوْاْ إِلَىٰ مَآ أَنزَلَ ٱللَّهُ وَإِلَى ٱلرَّسُولِ رَأَيْتَ ٱلْمُنَٰفِقِينَ يَصُدُّونَ
عَنكَ صُدُودًا ﴿٦١﴾ ... فَلَا وَرَبِّكَ لَا يُؤْمِنُونَ حَتَّىٰ يُحَكِّمُوكَ فِيمَا شَجَرَ بَيْنَهُمْ
ثُمَّ لَا يَجِدُواْ فِيٓ أَنفُسِهِمْ حَرَجًا مِّمَّا قَضَيْتَ وَيُسَلِّمُواْ تَسْلِيمًا ﴿٦٥﴾

> *When they are told: 'Come to that which Allah has revealed, and come to the Messenger,' you will notice the hypocrites turning away from you in aversion. ... But no, by your Lord, they cannot become true believers until they seek your arbitration in all matters on which they disagree among themselves, and then do not find the least vexation in their hearts over your judgement, and accept it in willing submission.*
>
> [*al-Nisā'* 4: 61 and 65]

A person who blatantly refuses to obey the Divine injunctions, and follows precepts other than those decreed by Allah *subḥānahū wa ta'ālā* and His Messenger (peace be upon him) cannot be a true believer, though he may continue to register himself as a Muslim in his country's census record. One may remain a Muslim even after committing sin, provided he feels guilty over his sinful act and willingly accepts Shariah as the law governing his life as a Muslim. But a person who insists on his sin being no crime, and instead takes pride in whatever he does while deriding those who observe in letter and spirit the injunctions of the Qur'an and the Sunnah as retrogressive and obscurantist, he cannot be a Muslim. One should, therefore, decide carefully and in all earnestness before embarking on a satanic course of no-return, if one prefers to remain a Muslim in all sincerity, or is reconciled to bartering one's soul away to the devil.

By the grace of Allah, Muslims, in general, are free so far from such a rebellious trend. They have in their hearts the same love for Allah and His Messenger (peace be upon him) and the same respect for the Shariah as their predecessors had. A fair degree of the observance of Shariah may also be noticed among them. The most alarming signs of the dangers ahead are, however, the designs of our power-wielding elite class to gradually convert the Muslim masses to their promiscuous trend. With all the resources of the state in their hands, they can easily subvert public manners and morals, project the secular culture of the West as a symbol of progress and tarnish the image of Islamic values and traditions as retrogressive. If our *mutrafin* do not reform, and continue their deviation from the right path, it may not be too late for the Muslim community to go astray and then justify Allah *subḥānahū wa taʿālā*'s writ in such an eventuality:

وَإِذَآ أَرَدْنَآ أَن نُّهْلِكَ قَرْيَةً أَمَرْنَا مُتْرَفِيهَا فَفَسَقُوا۟ فِيهَا فَحَقَّ عَلَيْهَا ٱلْقَوْلُ فَدَمَّرْنَـٰهَا تَدْمِيرًا ﴿١٦﴾

When We decide to destroy a town, We command the affluent among them, whereupon they commit sins in it, then the decree (of chastisement) becomes due against them and thereafter We destroy that town utterly.

[*Banī-Isrāʾīl* 17: 16]

3 The Current Malaise of the Muslim Community and its Cure[*]

Every social order, with whatever goal and objective, needs two basic characteristics to establish, consolidate and make itself a success. The first essential characteristic is that the fundamental principles that govern a particular society must be firmly rooted in the hearts and minds of its individual members and they must give these the importance they deserve. Secondly, every member of the society should individually and collectively have the necessary quality of allegiance and ownership. This means that whoever is made its leader must be properly respected and obeyed. The leader's orders should be carried out in letter and spirit; the rules and regulations made by him be sincerely and honestly observed; and all transgressions strictly avoided. These preconditions are inevitable for the success of any social order. No system, be that military, civil, political, social, or religious, can be established, maintained, or achieve its goals and objectives without proper observance of these two essential characteristics.

Human history is a witness to the fact that no movement was ever launched and sustained with success with a bunch of insincere, hypocritical and disobedient followers. Let us have a look at the world around us today. Can we think of an army that does not owe allegiance to the state, nor follows its chief's commands, whose soldiers refuse to observe discipline, are reluctant to rise on the bugle for parade or on the caution of their commander? Can anybody call such a crowd of recruits an armed force? Can they be expected to emerge successful on the battle front? What should we say of a state where citizens have no respect for the law; rules and regulations are flouted freely; its secretariat has no discipline; and functionaries do not carry out the

* *Tarjumān al-Qur'ān*, December 1934.

orders of their superiors? Can we expect a state with such qualities of its citizenry and officials to survive and sustain for long? We may very well see the examples of contemporary history's Germany and Italy.[1] The world is aware of the formidable strength gained by Hitler and Mussolini. But we should not lose sight of the factors behind their success. As mentioned earlier these factors are: (i) commitment to their faith and (ii) allegiance to the command. Nazis and fascist groups would have never emerged so strong and successful had their faith in their principles and objectives not been so firm and allegiance to their leadership not so resolute and unflinching.

As a universal truth that knows no exception, the qualities of faith and allegiance are the mainstay of every social order. The more the element of faith and the sense of allegiance (*īmān* and *al-sam'a wal-tā'ah*) are perfect, the stronger and more effective will be the order and its ability to achieve its objectives. Conversely, the weaker the faith and spirit of allegiance, the weaker will be the order and its ability to achieve its objectives. It is absolutely impossible for a social order or collective system to retain its vitality and sustain its growth once it becomes infected by the malaise of hypocrisy, ideological confusion, insolence, disobedience and indiscipline.

Let us now look at the predicament of the community that calls itself 'Muslim'. Unfortunately, today every kind of hypocrisy and duplicity that one may think of is found abundantly within this community. The Muslim society now includes even those who are skeptical about the fundamentals of their religion and freely propagate their skepticism. Those who openly express their disgust and distaste for religion and religiosity and prefer concepts and ideas borrowed from unbelievers also masquerade as Muslims. We have amongst us also those who give precedence to the rites and rituals of the *jāhilī* origin (pagan days of the Age of Ignorance), over the injunctions of the Qur'an and the Sunnah. We have in the community the deviants who slight the teachings of their religion just to please the anti-Islamic forces. There are those as well who are ready even to harm major Islamic causes for

[1] That was the time when Germany and Italy were the rising stars of Western Europe – Editor.

their petty personal gains, those who care for their individual interests more than those of their community. This is a matter of grave concern that with the exception of a small segment of steadfast and Islamically oriented Muslims, the majority of our community unfortunately consists today of opportunists and religiously misguided people.

This is the situation so far as the quality of faith is concerned. Now, let us look at the state of *al-sam'a wal-tā'ah*, or allegiance. One may notice a general distaste for religion among a powerful segment of our society today. The call for Prayer rises from the mosques, but these people remain generally unconcerned, as if they do not know the meaning and purpose of the call. Only a small number proceeds to the mosque, while a good number remains engaged in their routine. Ramadan, the month of fasting, dawns upon them, but very few care. They continue eating and drinking in public and instead of feeling ashamed of this flagrant violation of Islamic norms, they would rather wish to put those to shame who observe the sanctity of the month. Then, there are those who do keep fast, but only as a ritual and not with any sense of obligation, or because they think it good for health. They are also oblivious of its real significance and demands and indulge in activities not sanctioned by Allah *subḥānahū wa ta'ālā* and His Prophet. Zakat and hajj are observed to even a lesser degree. The negligence about what is halal and what is haram is also on the rise.

The Muslim community today faces a situation of suppression and cultural subjugation all over the world. Even in the countries where Muslims have their own governments, they are not free of the alien cultural, intellectual, and economic domination. They suffer from ignorance, poverty, and backwardness. They have reached the lowest level of moral degeneration. The qualities of trustworthiness, truth, and sincerity of purpose, for which they were once held in the highest esteem, have gone from them to others and these have been overtaken by the traits of treachery, falsehood, deceit, and misconduct. They are no more gifted with the characteristics of piety, love and fear of God and nobility of character. They are gradually losing the sense of pride, honour and concern for their community. They have no disciplinary order among their ranks. Those who once lived and acted in unison and total harmony, find their hearts divided, unity shattered, and their steps moving in different directions. They seem to have lost the ability to jointly work for a common cause. They stand crestfallen in their own eyes and in the eyes of others. Other nations of the world have lost confidence in them. Their strength as a nation and community is getting weaker and weaker and their cultural and civilizational superiority is almost a thing of the past. In spite of a gradual increase in the rate of literacy and in the number of graduates, postgraduates and foreign qualified persons, as also the gradual rise of their affluent classes, those who own palatial buildings, the latest models of cars, and occupy positions of power and pelf are morally so weak that they inspire no respect and awe in others and the future looks even more bleak.

There can possibly be just two reasonable options for a person regarding his religion, culture, or community system. If he enters the fold of a particular religion, culture or community, he must have full faith and observe completely the relevant laws, rules and regulations. Alternately, if he cannot, he should avoid entering its portals in the first place and having done so should gracefully make an exit. Rationally speaking, he has no third option. There can be nothing more unreasonable for him than showing disregard to the basic rules and regulations of a system that he claims to follow. He is not expected to wilfully violate the law and exempt himself from its applicability. A person suffering from such duplicity cannot avoid the growth of hypocritical traits within himself and the expulsion from his heart of the healthy traits of sincerity of purpose, warmth of feeling for everything noble, and firmness of resolve for a higher objective in life. The noble attributes of devotion, dutifulness, observance of law, and dedication to the higher values in life can find no inroad within his person. He will, thus, render himself incapable of being a useful member of any social order. Whichever party or organization he joins with such weakness and flaws of character, he will be a curse for it. Whatever system he enters, he will make it topsy turvy; any civilization he gets into he will be as despicable for it as germs of leprosy; and he will deface and defame any religion he follows. It is better for such a turncoat to stop claiming to be a Muslim and join the group he deems fit for himself and about which he feels sure to sincerely observe its discipline. An unbeliever, who is faithful to the religious and cultural norms of his community and observes them sincerely, is much better than a 'hypocrite Muslim', who is a 'Muslim' just in name.

Those were definitely at fault who sought panacea of the Muslim community's collective malaise in Western education, modern culture, economic improvement and attainment of their political goals. Those who uphold the view even today are equally wrong. By the Almighty Lord, the Muslim society will continue to suffer from humiliation and weakness, as is the case today, even if each and every member of society obtains a master's degree; becomes a PhD or barrister; is westernized from top to toe; and secures all available seats and positions of authority in government and local councils. The current downward slide will continue so long as the society is infected with the cancer of *nifāq* (hypocrisy); has no regard for what has been enjoined to each member as mandatory; and is given to disloyalty and rebellion against Islam and Islamic ideals.

If we are to rise and prosper as a powerful and well-respected community, we will have to create within ourselves, first of all, the attributes of faith and allegiance. Without this, we will be worth nothing, neither as individuals nor as a community. The moment we inculcate these traits, we will then become a cohesive force capable of living a life of dignity, holding our heads high in the comity of nations. As a disorganized and disjointed lot, whose individual members are sick morally and spiritually, we can never be in a position to rise and face the well-organized and powerful nations of the world. Can a stack of hay, howsoever huge, ever stand as a castle?

The worst enemies of Islam and Muslims are those who are busy spreading irreligiousness and disloyalty in the community. The presence of such enemies within the Muslim Ummah's body politic today is more dangerous than that of unbelievers, because they are engaged in attempts to dynamite the society from within. The hypocrites would like the Muslims to fail in this world and the Hereafter. They are those about whom the Qur'an forewarns:

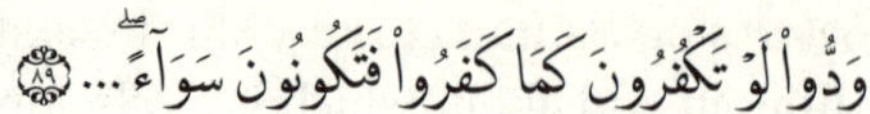

They wish that you should disbelieve just as they disbelieve so that you may all be alike.

[*al-Nisā'* 4: 89]

The best thing that can be done to save the community from their mischief is that every sincere Muslim who is keen to remain firm in his faith and social conduct must not have a relation of trust with them: فَلَا تَتَّخِذُوا مِنْهُمْ أَوْلِيَآءَ (*Do not, therefore, take allies and close associates from them*). The eventual punishment of such double-faced agents of un-Islam, who try to destroy the Muslim society from within, is to wage a war against them in order to be able to regain the pristine glory it lost due to their influence.

4 The Rise and Fall of Nations*

The universal principle, which Allah *subḥānahū wa taʿālā* has laid down in the Qur'an about the divine scheme of things, is that the Lord does not inflict punishment on any community in general so long as it is willing to mend its ways:

وَمَا كَانَ رَبُّكَ لِيُهْلِكَ ٱلْقُرَىٰ بِظُلْمٍ وَأَهْلُهَا مُصْلِحُونَ ﴿١١٧﴾

And your Lord is not such as would wrongfully destroy human habitations while their inhabitants are righteous.
[*Hūd* 11: 117]

The destruction of communities does not always mean their decimation or turning their habitations upside down. One form of destruction is that the unity of a nation is shattered, its collective strength is broken, or it is subjected to bondage, persecution and humiliation. In light of the above principle, so long as a community continues following the path of goodness and virtue and does not deviate into the sideways of vice, corruption, disobedience and rebellion, thus committing crime against itself, it is spared of destruction and Allah's wrath. In keeping with this universal principle, punishments inflicted on communities have been graphically mentioned in the Qur'an, along with description of specific crimes that invited the Divine Wrath on them. The purpose of these narratives is that the people should be forewarned about the harvest they are bound to reap of whatever they are sowing now:

* *Tarjumān al-Qur'ān*, April 1935.

فَكُلًّا أَخَذْنَا بِذَنۢبِهِۦ ۖ فَمِنْهُم مَّنْ أَرْسَلْنَا عَلَيْهِ حَاصِبًا وَمِنْهُم مَّنْ أَخَذَتْهُ ٱلصَّيْحَةُ
وَمِنْهُم مَّنْ خَسَفْنَا بِهِ ٱلْأَرْضَ وَمِنْهُم مَّنْ أَغْرَقْنَا ۚ وَمَا كَانَ ٱللَّهُ لِيَظْلِمَهُمْ
وَلَـٰكِن كَانُوٓا۟ أَنفُسَهُمْ يَظْلِمُونَ ﴿٤٠﴾

So We seized each for their sin. We let loose upon some a violent tornado with showers of stones; some were overtaken by a mighty Cry; some were caused to be swallowed up by the earth, and some We drowned. Allah would not wrong them, but it is they who wronged themselves.

[*al-'Ankabūt* 29: 40]

The second aspect of this Divine Tradition is that the cause of destruction is never individual acts of vice or corruption, but the collective sin of a community and its social degeneration. This means that individual failings of character and misdeeds, however great those might be, do not invite the Divine Wrath on the community as a whole as long as they remain in check due to the society's collective will of moral uprightness and virtue and the community's state of affairs being generally sound. On the contrary, when the lapses spread from individuals to the nation and its religious sensitivity and moral conduct become so perverted that there is no check on vice and no incentive for virtue, then such a community and nation lose justification for the Lord's blessings and fall headlong from a status of respect to that of disgrace and indignity. The time eventually comes when the floodgates of the Divine Wrath are let loose to destroy the deviant communities altogether.

The Qur'an offers us a number of examples of the catastrophes that overtook the degenerate nations and communities of the past. The people of Prophet Noah (peace be upon him) were destroyed when the collective malaise of their faith and deeds reached the ultimate limits of incorrigibility. It was then that the Prophet of God begged the Almighty:

وَقَالَ نُوحٌ رَّبِّ لَا تَذَرْ عَلَى ٱلْأَرْضِ مِنَ ٱلْكَـٰفِرِينَ دَيَّارًا ﴿٢٦﴾ إِنَّكَ إِن تَذَرْهُمْ
يُضِلُّوا۟ عِبَادَكَ وَلَا يَلِدُوٓا۟ إِلَّا فَاجِرًا كَفَّارًا ﴿٢٧﴾

Noah said: 'My Lord, do not leave out of these unbelievers even a single dweller on earth, for certainly if You should leave them (alive) they will mislead Your servants, and will beget none but sinners and utter unbelievers.'

[*Nūh* 71: 26–27]

The People of 'Ād were similarly destroyed when socially they became so perverse that their most corrupt rose to positions of eminence and leadership and their noblest ones were treated like outlaws:

وَتِلْكَ عَادٌ ۖ جَحَدُوا۟ بِـَٔايَـٰتِ رَبِّهِمْ وَعَصَوْا۟ رُسُلَهُۥ وَٱتَّبَعُوٓا۟ أَمْرَ كُلِّ جَبَّارٍ عَنِيدٍ ۝٥٩ وَأُتْبِعُوا۟ فِى هَـٰذِهِ ٱلدُّنْيَا لَعْنَةً وَيَوْمَ ٱلْقِيَـٰمَةِ ۗ أَلَآ إِنَّ عَادًا كَفَرُوا۟ رَبَّهُمْ ۗ أَلَا بُعْدًا لِّعَادٍ قَوْمِ هُودٍ ۝٦٠

Such were 'Ād. They repudiated the Signs of their Lord, disobeyed His Messengers, and followed the bidding of every tyrannical enemy of the Truth. They were pursued by a curse in this world, and so will they be on the Day of Judgement. Lo, 'Ād disbelieved in the Lord. Lo, ruined are 'Ād, the people of Hūd.

[*Hūd* 11: 59–60]

The People of Lot were destroyed when they became morally so low and depraved that they lost entirely their sense of decency and their clubs and public places turned into places of debauchery and homosexuality:

وَلُوطًا إِذْ قَالَ لِقَوْمِهِۦٓ إِنَّكُمْ لَتَأْتُونَ ٱلْفَـٰحِشَةَ مَا سَبَقَكُم بِهَا مِنْ أَحَدٍ مِّنَ ٱلْعَـٰلَمِينَ ۝٢٨ أَئِنَّكُمْ لَتَأْتُونَ ٱلرِّجَالَ وَتَقْطَعُونَ ٱلسَّبِيلَ وَتَأْتُونَ فِى نَادِيكُمُ ٱلْمُنكَرَ ۖ فَمَا كَانَ جَوَابَ قَوْمِهِۦٓ إِلَّآ أَن قَالُوا۟ ٱئْتِنَا بِعَذَابِ ٱللَّهِ إِن كُنتَ مِنَ ٱلصَّـٰدِقِينَ ۝٢٩

> *We sent Lot and he said to his people: 'You commit the abomination that none in the world ever committed before you. What? Do you go to men (to satisfy your lust), engage in highway robbery, and commit evil deeds in your gatherings?'*
>
> [*al-'Ankabūt* 29: 28–29]

The punishment came to Midianites when the community became totally immersed in dishonesty, fraudulent handling of their trade and commerce and absence of faith. Manipulation of weights and measures was not just a common practice, any effort for reform was taken as interference in their personal matters and an affront to their integrity, which they knew they lacked so much:

وَيَٰقَوۡمِ أَوۡفُواْ ٱلۡمِكۡيَالَ وَٱلۡمِيزَانَ بِٱلۡقِسۡطِۖ وَلَا تَبۡخَسُواْ ٱلنَّاسَ أَشۡيَآءَهُمۡ وَلَا تَعۡثَوۡاْ
فِي ٱلۡأَرۡضِ مُفۡسِدِينَ ٨٥ ... قَالُواْ يَٰشُعَيۡبُ مَا نَفۡقَهُ كَثِيرٗا مِّمَّا تَقُولُ وَإِنَّا لَنَرَىٰكَ
فِينَا ضَعِيفٗاۖ وَلَوۡلَا رَهۡطُكَ لَرَجَمۡنَٰكَۖ وَمَآ أَنتَ عَلَيۡنَا بِعَزِيزٖ ٩١ قَالَ يَٰقَوۡمِ أَرَهۡطِيٓ
أَعَزُّ عَلَيۡكُم مِّنَ ٱللَّهِ وَٱتَّخَذۡتُمُوهُ وَرَآءَكُمۡ ظِهۡرِيًّاۖ إِنَّ رَبِّي بِمَا تَعۡمَلُونَ مُحِيطٞ ٩٢

> *My people! Give full measure and weight with justice, do not diminish the goods of others, and do not go about creating corruption in the land. … They said: 'O Shu'ayb! We do not understand much of what you say. Indeed we see you weak in our midst. Were it not for your kinsmen, we would surely have stoned you for you have no strength to overpower us.' Shu'ayb said: 'My people, are my kinsmen mightier with you than Allah that you (hold the kinsmen in awe while) you cast Allah behind your back? Surely my Lord encompasses all that you do.'*
>
> [*Hūd* 11: 85 and 91–92]

Orders came from the Lord to punish the Israelites and inflict upon them disgrace, dispersal and divine curse when they collectively became prone to vice, cruelty and violation of the Divine Law. Their leaders compromised on principles and there remained among them not a single group of well-meaning people who could stand up to the rampant vice and declare it wrong and call the people to the divine path of virtue:

وَتَرَىٰ كَثِيرًا مِّنْهُمْ يُسَٰرِعُونَ فِى ٱلْإِثْمِ وَٱلْعُدْوَٰنِ وَأَكْلِهِمُ ٱلسُّحْتَ ۚ
لَبِئْسَ مَا كَانُوا۟ يَعْمَلُونَ ﴿٦٢﴾ لَوْلَا يَنْهَىٰهُمُ ٱلرَّبَّٰنِيُّونَ وَٱلْأَحْبَارُ عَن قَوْلِهِمُ ٱلْإِثْمَ
وَأَكْلِهِمُ ٱلسُّحْتَ ۚ لَبِئْسَ مَا كَانُوا۟ يَصْنَعُونَ ﴿٦٣﴾

You will see many of them hastening towards sin and transgression and devouring unlawful earnings. Evil indeed is what they do. Why is it that their scholars and jurists do not forbid them from sinful utterances and devouring unlawful earnings? Indeed they have been contriving evil.

[*al-Mā'idah* 5: 62–63]

لُعِنَ ٱلَّذِينَ كَفَرُوا۟ مِنۢ بَنِىٓ إِسْرَٰٓءِيلَ عَلَىٰ لِسَانِ دَاوُۥدَ وَعِيسَى ٱبْنِ مَرْيَمَ ۚ ذَٰلِكَ
بِمَا عَصَوا۟ وَّكَانُوا۟ يَعْتَدُونَ ﴿٧٨﴾ كَانُوا۟ لَا يَتَنَاهَوْنَ عَن مُّنكَرٍ فَعَلُوهُ ۚ لَبِئْسَ
مَا كَانُوا۟ يَفْعَلُونَ ﴿٧٩﴾

Those of the Children of Israel who took to unbelief have been cursed by the tongue of David and Jesus, the son of Mary, for they rebelled and exceeded the bounds of right. They did not forbid each other from committing the abominable deeds they committed. Evil indeed was what they did.

[*al-Mā'idah* 5: 78–79]

Explaining the above *āyah*, *Sayyidunā* Rasūl Allah (peace be upon him) said:

'As vice started spreading among the Children of Isrā'il, a person on seeing his brother doing wrong checked him

> in the beginning and told him to be afraid of God. Subsequently, however, he socialized with the same person and in spite of seeing him indulge in vice did not dissociate with him or stop eating and drinking with him. When things came to pass, the diminishing number of their good people became influenced by the ever-growing number of bad and Allah turned all of them into one lot. They were then cursed through their Prophets David and Jesus son of Mary.'
>
> The narrator of the Hadith, Abū 'Ubaydah ibn 'Abd Allah ibn Mas'ūd, reported that after saying this the Messenger of Allah got up from his reclining posture and forewarned: 'By the One to Whom I owe my life, the same fate may befall you until you hold the wrongdoer by the hand and lead him to the right track.'[1]

The case of moral and social corruption is like that of an epidemic. The virus attacks in the beginning a few morally weak ones in society. If the overall environment is good, the hygienic conditions are sound, adequate arrangements are in place for the disposal and removal of pollutants and the infected persons are treated timely, the disease does not spread to become an epidemic and the people in general remain safe from its adverse effects. If, however, the physician is indifferent, the department of health and hygiene lax in its duty, and those in charge of cleanliness are tolerant to filth and dirt, then the harmful bacteria is bound to gradually affect the air and water making the whole environment injurious for health and conducive for disease. Eventually, when the whole population is left with nothing clean, from air, water and food to dress and home, it then becomes impossible even for the strongest among the people to save themselves from the epidemic's attack. The physicians and those responsible for public health and hygiene then also fall prey to the disease. When the situation

---

[1] *Jami' Al-Tirmidhī*, Nos 3047 and 3048; *Sunan Abū Dāwūd* (*Bāb al-Amr wal Nahy*) and *Sunan Ibn Mājah* (*Bāb al-Amr bil Ma'rūf wal-Nahy 'anil Munkar*).

becomes so grave, then even those individuals or groups who try to keep at least themselves safe by observing the prescribed measures of health and hygiene cannot remain immune to the killer virus because they have no cure for the poison in the air, filth in water, pollution of soil and degeneration of food.

The same example can be applied to the incidents of corruption of social conduct, moral degeneration and spiritual waywardness. The *'ulamā'* are like the physicians of the community, while rulers and those who wield positions of power and authority are like those responsible for the society's health and hygiene. The community's spiritual dynamism and collective moral uprightness are the vital elements essential for its healthy growth. The social environment occupies the same position as that of air, water, food, clothing and shelter, while from the point of view of spiritualism and morality, enjoining good and forbidding evil occupies the same place in a community's life as that held by timely measures for health and hygiene. When the *'ulamā'* and those at the helm of affairs give up their basic obligation of enjoining good and forbidding evil and instead are tolerant towards the forces of evil, the community's moral and spiritual health starts worsening. Moral waywardness and misconduct then spread among community members, their sense of spiritual integrity becomes weak and the whole social environment gets polluted and unfit for the healthy values of life and is better suited for the growth of the germs of corruption and vice. People become scared of everything good and are attracted to everything bad. There is then a reversal of moral values: the good becomes bad and the bad good. Depravity and misconduct then prosper by leaps and bounds and the soil, the air and water refuse to nurture the seedlings of goodness and virtue because the elements are then engaged entirely in the service and sustenance of vice. When a community reaches that level of perversion, it becomes most befitting for God's punishment. A massive doom thus strikes it, which spares none, not even those cloistered in a monastery worshipping God day in and day out. This is the mischief of which the Qur'an has forewarned the believers thus:

وَٱتَّقُواْ فِتْنَةً لَّا تُصِيبَنَّ ٱلَّذِينَ ظَلَمُواْ مِنكُمْ خَآصَّةً وَٱعْلَمُوٓاْ أَنَّ ٱللَّهَ شَدِيدُ ٱلْعِقَابِ ۝٢٥

And guard against the mischief that will bring punishment not only to the wrongdoers among you. Know well that Allah is severe in punishment.

[*al-Anfāl* 8: 25]

In his commentary on the *āyah*, 'Abd Allah ibn 'Abbas, the eminent Companion and Commentator of the Qur'an, said: 'What Allah *subḥānahū wa ta'ālā* is pleased to impress upon us here is that we should not let the vice stand in our way, because if we become lax and let it spread, we will then be liable as a community to His general chastisement, which will spare neither the good nor the bad amongst us.' This was explained further in the following Hadith: 'When the people see the wrongdoer [engaged in his oppressive acts] but do not rise to hold him by his hand, Allah is likely to spread the chastisement among them.'[2]

The best way to maintain moral and spiritual health of the community is to preserve its spiritual dynamism and sense of moral uprightness. For this the comprehensive term of *ḥayā'* or 'self-decorum' was used by *Sayyidunā* Rasūl Allah (peace be upon him). The oft-quoted Hadith tells us: الحَيَاءُ شُعبةٌ مِنَ الإيمَان ('Self-decorum is [an integral] part of faith'). When asked if this attribute was a 'part of religiosity', the Prophet (peace be upon him) stressed: 'No, it is the religiosity itself.'[3]

To further elaborate the Religion of Truth's noble social attribute of *ḥayā'*, we may say that it means 'natural aversion to vice and sin'. A person endowed with this quality will not just detest from the inner

---

[2] *Sunan Abū Dāwūd*, No. 122/4 (chapter on *Al-Amr wal-Nahy*); *Jami' Al-Tirmidhī* (chapters 12 and 17).

[3] *Ṣaḥīḥ Muslim*, chapter 1, Nos 13 and 15.

most core of his heart everything bad and sinful and refrain from indulging in such acts, he cannot even tolerate these in others. He can hardly compromise with tyranny and sin. On seeing vice being committed, his sense of spiritual uprightness will revolt and he will try to stop it either by the use of his individual or collective strength or through the word of his mouth, or he will at least become restless with a burning urge to rectify and reform the situation. The Prophetic Tradition impresses upon us in this respect:

مَنْ رَأَى مِنْكُمْ مُنْكَرًا فَلْيُغَيِّرْهُ بِيَدِهِ فَإِنْ لَمْ يَسْتَطِعْ فَبِلِسَانِهِ، فَإِنْ لَمْ يَسْتَطِعْ فَبِقَلْبِهِ وَذَلِكَ أَضْعَفُ الْإِيمَانِ

> Whoever amongst you sees any wrong being committed, he should use his hand [individual and collective strength] to rectify it; if he cannot, then use his tongue; and if unable to do even that, he should then condemn it at heart, and this is the weakest degree of faith.[4]

So long as individual members of the Muslim society are generally endowed with this quality, Islam as a way of life (*dīn*) is safe and its moral standards remain intact. The reason is that in such a society every individual is counsel for his fellow being. There is, thus, hardly any room for moral or social corruption to find inroads.

The Qur'an seeks to establish a model society in which each individual can perform his assigned role purely according to the dictates of his conscience. In a truly Muslim society each individual is inspired by his natural inclination of self-respect, decency and decorum. He remains a *divine disciplinarian* without being paid for it by the government or any outside source:

وَكَذَٰلِكَ جَعَلْنَٰكُمْ أُمَّةً وَسَطًا لِّتَكُونُوا۟ شُهَدَآءَ عَلَى ٱلنَّاسِ وَيَكُونَ ٱلرَّسُولُ عَلَيْكُمْ شَهِيدًا ... ﴿١٤٣﴾

4. *Ṣaḥīḥ Muslim*, chapter 20; *Jami' Al-Tirmidhī*, chapter 12; *Sunan Abū Dāwūd*, chapter 17.

And it is thus that We appointed you to be the community of the middle way[5] *so that you might be witnesses to all mankind and the Messenger might be a witness to you.*

[*al-Baqarah* 2: 143]

The Muslims as a community have therefore been reminded repeatedly that to enjoin the good and forbid the evil is their primary obligation and characteristic, which must be reflected in each and every male and female member of the Islamic society:

كُنتُمْ خَيْرَ أُمَّةٍ أُخْرِجَتْ لِلنَّاسِ تَأْمُرُونَ بِٱلْمَعْرُوفِ وَتَنْهَوْنَ عَنِ ٱلْمُنكَرِ
وَتُؤْمِنُونَ بِٱللَّهِ ۗ... ﴿١١٠﴾

You are now the best nation brought forth for mankind. You enjoin what is right and forbid what is wrong and believe in Allah.

[*Āl ʿImrān* 3: 110]

وَٱلْمُؤْمِنُونَ وَٱلْمُؤْمِنَٰتُ بَعْضُهُمْ أَوْلِيَآءُ بَعْضٍ ۚ يَأْمُرُونَ بِٱلْمَعْرُوفِ وَيَنْهَوْنَ
عَنِ ٱلْمُنكَرِ وَيُقِيمُونَ ٱلصَّلَوٰةَ وَيُؤْتُونَ ٱلزَّكَوٰةَ وَيُطِيعُونَ ٱللَّهَ وَرَسُولَهُۥٓ ۚ
أُو۟لَٰٓئِكَ سَيَرْحَمُهُمُ ٱللَّهُ ۗ إِنَّ ٱللَّهَ عَزِيزٌ حَكِيمٌ ﴿٧١﴾

---

5. 'The Arabic expression which we have translated as "the community of the middle way" is too rich in meaning to find an adequate equivalent in any other language. It signifies that distinguished group of people who follow the path of justice and equity, of balance and moderation, a group which occupies a central position among the nations of the world so that its relationship with all is based on righteousness and justice and none receives its support in wrong and injustice.... [According to the *āyah*], when the whole of mankind is called to account, the Prophet (peace be upon him) as God's representative will stand witness to the fact that he had communicated to the Muslims and had put into practice the teachings which expound sound belief, righteous conduct and a balanced system of life which he had received from on high. The Muslims, acting on behalf of the Prophet (peace be upon him), after the latter's return to God's mercy, will be asked to bear the same witness before the rest of mankind, confirming that they had spared no effort in either communicating to mankind what the Prophet (peace be upon him) had communicated to them, or in exemplifying in their own lives what the Prophet (peace be upon him) by his own conduct, had translated into actual practice.' (*Towards Understanding The Qur'ān*, abridged version of Sayyid Mawdūdī's *Tafhīm*, nos 44 and 45, p. 40).

The Believers, both men and women, are allies of one another. They enjoin good, forbid evil, establish Prayer, pay zakat, and obey Allah and His Messenger. Surely, Allah will show mercy to them. Allah is All-Mighty, All-Wise.

[*al-Tawbah* 9: 71]

... ٱلْـَٔامِرُونَ بِٱلْمَعْرُوفِ وَٱلنَّاهُونَ عَنِ ٱلْمُنكَرِ وَٱلْحَـٰفِظُونَ لِحُدُودِ ٱللَّهِ ۗ وَبَشِّرِ ٱلْمُؤْمِنِينَ ﴿١١٢﴾

who enjoin what is good and forbid what is evil, and who keep the limits set by Allah. Announce glad tidings to such .believers

[*al-Tawbah* 9: 112]

ٱلَّذِينَ إِن مَّكَّنَّـٰهُمْ فِى ٱلْأَرْضِ أَقَامُوا۟ ٱلصَّلَوٰةَ وَءَاتَوُا۟ ٱلزَّكَوٰةَ وَأَمَرُوا۟ بِٱلْمَعْرُوفِ وَنَهَوْا۟ عَنِ ٱلْمُنكَرِ ۗ ... ﴿٤١﴾

(Allah will certainly help) those who, were We to bestow authority on them in the land, will establish Prayers, render zakat, enjoin good, and forbid evil.

[*al-Ḥajj* 22: 41]

If the believers, individually and collectively, retain this characteristic, they will have nothing to worry about their social health and hygiene. They will not only keep themselves and their hearts and homes clean, but will remain equally mindful of the health and hygiene of their entire environment and ensure that it remains clean from everything unhealthy. A community of this character will obviously enjoy the best of health and happiness in an atmosphere free from all pollutants. As for some rare cases of sickness or sickly disposition, the affected person will be cured in a timely manner and such individual cases will have no danger of spreading as an epidemic to others in the community.

However, if the Muslim community does not rise up to the desired level, it is duty-bound by the dictates of its *dīn* to have within its ranks a cadre of people that performs this service and cleans the people's faith, manners and morals from all impurities and infections. This is essential to safeguard the spiritual and moral health of the society:

وَلْتَكُن مِّنكُمْ أُمَّةٌ يَدْعُونَ إِلَى ٱلْخَيْرِ وَيَأْمُرُونَ بِٱلْمَعْرُوفِ وَيَنْهَوْنَ عَنِ ٱلْمُنكَرِ ۚ وَأُو۟لَـٰٓئِكَ هُمُ ٱلْمُفْلِحُونَ ﴿١٠٤﴾

And from amongst you there must be a party who will call people to all that is good and will enjoin the doing of all that is right and will forbid the doing of all that is wrong. It is they who will attain true success.

[*Āl ʿImrān* 3: 104]

This is the *party* of the religious scholars and those holding positions of responsibility in the Muslim society. Their preoccupation with the task of enjoining good and forbidding evil is as essential as the effective involvement of the department of public health in its assigned task. In case they are negligent in the discharge of their duty, and no responsible group is left in society to invite the people to all that is good, enjoin them what is right and forbid what is wrong, its spiritual and moral demise then becomes certain; the way a population unmindful of its health and hygiene naturally faces decay. The nations of the past faced their eventual doom for the same reason. They were left with no men of such character who could prevent them from committing wrong and keep them on the right track:

فَلَوْلَا كَانَ مِنَ ٱلْقُرُونِ مِن قَبْلِكُمْ أُو۟لُوا۟ بَقِيَّةٍ يَنْهَوْنَ عَنِ ٱلْفَسَادِ فِى ٱلْأَرْضِ إِلَّا قَلِيلًا مِّمَّنْ أَنجَيْنَا مِنْهُمْ ۗ وَٱتَّبَعَ ٱلَّذِينَ ظَلَمُوا۟ مَآ أُتْرِفُوا۟ فِيهِ وَكَانُوا۟ مُجْرِمِينَ ﴿١١٦﴾

Why were there no righteous persons among the generations that passed away before you who would forbid others from causing corruption on earth? And if such were there, they were only a few whom We had saved from those generations, or else the wrongdoers kept pursuing the ease and comfort which had been conferred upon them, thus losing themselves in sinfulness.

[*Hūd* 11: 116]

لَوْلَا يَنْهَىٰهُمُ ٱلرَّبَّـٰنِيُّونَ وَٱلْأَحْبَارُ عَن قَوْلِهِمُ ٱلْإِثْمَ وَأَكْلِهِمُ ٱلسُّحْتَ ۚ لَبِئْسَ مَا كَانُوا۟ يَصْنَعُونَ ﴿٦٣﴾

Why is it that their scholars and jurists do not forbid them from sinful utterances and devouring unlawful earnings? Indeed they have been contriving evil.

[*al-Mā'idah* 5: 63]

The scholars of Islamic sciences and spiritualists (*'ulamā'* and *mashā'ikh*), and all those holding positions of responsibility in Muslim society, are accountable not just for their own actions as individuals. They are at the same time responsible for what their community does. One can thus imagine the 'reward' in store on the Day of Reckoning for the luxury-loving and pleasure-seeking oppressive rulers of the Muslim community and their coterie of sycophants, especially from amongst the *'ulamā* and *mashā'ikh*. As for those who are content to offer prayers and worship the Lord in their luxurious mansions and *khānqāh* (monasteries), they too cannot escape the brunt of accountability. At a time when corruption and misconduct are hitting the community hard like tidal waves, they are hardly expected to sit pretty in their cozy comfort. It is their religious duty to come forward and use whatever strength and authority Allah *subḥānahū wa ta'ālā* has bestowed upon them to meet the challenge. They may not be responsible to stop the storm, but are definitely accountable for failing to use the power at their command to check its adverse impact. If they do not rise up to discharge their responsibility, their individual act of worship and piety will not absolve them of the accountability of the Day of Judgement. You can never condone the official responsible for public health if he remains busy looking after himself and his family at a time when the whole city is faced with a deadly epidemic devouring thousands upon thousands of people. One may not object to an ordinary citizen if he shows sign of apathy, but an official of the department of health will be held accountable for his criminal negligence.

5 Idealism and Practical Wisdom in Islam*

[A learned reader of *Tarjumān al-Qur'an* misconstrued an earlier writing of Sayyid Mawdūdī that he was in favour of sacrificing even the fundamentals of Islam for the sake of striking a balance between an idealistic and a pragmatic approach, and that to him matters of immediate religious concern and interest enjoyed precedence over the fundamental principles of Islam. The reader's query may be summed up as follows – Editor.]

'In support of your premise you offered in your article an example from the Prophetic Tradition and said: "One of the basic principles of Islam was to do away with all ethnic and tribal distinctions and provide equal rights to every member of the Muslim society who had opted to join it." ... But when the question arose of governance of the Islamic State, the Messenger of Allah (*peace be upon him*) counseled: "الأَئِمَّةُ مِن قُرَيشٍ" ("The rulers are to be from among the Quraysh"). You justified this exception in favour of the Quraysh as follows: "The situation prevailing in Arabia then was such that a non-Arab, even a non-Quraysh, caliph could not have succeeded in properly exercising his authority after the Prophet. This is why the Prophet of God advised his worthy Companions against following in this matter the otherwise universally acclaimed Islamic principle of equality, because in the case of a setback to the Islamic order in Arabia itself following the Prophet's departure, who would have stood up to hold the banner of Religion aloft? This proves that to insist on such a strict observance of a certain principle even at the cost of greater Islamic objectives is contrary not only to the dictates of a pragmatic approach but also to those of religious idealism". Then, you added: "But the same stance

* *Tarjumān al-Qur'ān*, May 1958.

may not be correct in respect of each and every principle fundamental to Islam. We find no evidence from the life of the Prophet (peace be upon him) of any flexibility in respect of the fundamentals which form the basis of religion, like *tawḥīd* (Oneness and Uniqueness of God), *Risālah* (Prophethood of *Sayyidunā* Muhammad [peace be upon him] as the Last of God's Prophets), etc. No flexibility is ever possible in such matters under any circumstances."

Some people have drawn certain conclusions from your views as quoted above, on the basis of which they raise a number of objections. They say that according to your formulations, the Prophet (peace be upon him) launched the movement to establish the Islamic system for which he enunciated certain principles. Of these, some were concerned with the fundamentals of faith and those were inviolable and could never be compromised. But alongside these there were some which could be relaxed in exceptional cases, such as the principle of equality among Arabs and non-Arab Muslims in rights and obligations, the right of personal freedom, security of life and property, etc. According to you, this second category of principles could be relaxed in the event of their clash with the Islamic state's strategy for the supremacy of the Islamic order. Your detractors believe that you have, thus, opened the doors for the relaxation of Islamic principles that may appear to be in conflict with the objectives of the Islamic movement. There are similar other reservations about your views and writings on the Islamic system. We would be grateful for elucidation of your viewpoint to remove such misgivings.'

I am aware of such interpolations into my writings. Yet I have been patient with these as I have been earlier with the plethora of edicts, advertisements, articles and journals issued from time to time to malign me and distort my writings and views. Whatever little span of life and power of speech and pen, graciously granted to me by the Almighty, I would like them to be gainfully used in the service of Islam in this world and to be a reparation of my sins in the Hereafter. I am not willing to waste this little time and energy in futile arguments, which are of no avail except for bringing a bad name to the Religion and men of religion. In the paragraphs that follow I intend not to make those distortions the subject of my discourse but to clarify the misgivings that might have, thus, arisen in the minds of some sincere seekers of knowledge.

Let me begin with the following premise, which you have quoted from my article: '... to insist on such a strict observance of a certain principle even at the cost of greater Islamic objectives is contrary not only to the dictates of a pragmatic approach, but also to those of religious idealism.' Nobody who cares to reflect on the sentence, without bias or preconception, would fail to correctly understand my intent. What I mean to say is that in theory at least everything correct is to be observed and implemented and anything wrong has to be given up and eliminated. Practically, however, one is often faced during life's day-to-day tussle between the right and the wrong, with a situation where if one insists on a little goodness he loses the larger one, and if one gives up a smaller evil he may end up with a greater one. The reason, therefore, demands that a thing of more worth should not be bartered away for a thing of lesser worth. According to the Divine Law, a laudable strategy would be to tolerate the lesser evil in order to avoid the larger evil and that the ultimate good should not be sacrificed for the sake of the lesser good. I do not wish to make reason the sole criterion where someone may feel free to opt out of Islamic rules, regulations and injunctions on the pretext of practical requirements. It is, in fact, evident from the very sentence quoted above that I believe in an approach that determines in light of the standards set by the Shariah itself what has to be sacrificed, where, to what extent and for what sake.

5.1. Balance between pragmatism and idealism in light of the Qur'an and the Sunnah

Now, let us see if all this is a concoction on my part, or whether the Islamic Shariah itself has set such a precedent, i.e. is there a rule according to which a thing of lesser worth can be sacrificed for the sake of a thing of greater worth? Indeed, when we examine this, we find examples in the Qur'an, Ahadith, the conventions of *Sayyidunā* Rasūl Allah's illustrious Companions, the views of eminent jurists (*fuqahā'*) and *muḥaddithīn*. Let me quote in the paragraphs that follow just a few instances in this respect.

i. There is nothing as important in Islam as one's reaffirmation of faith in *tawḥīd*. This is the first requirement of faith in the Religion of Truth and the faith's prime demand from a believer. Theoretically speaking, there should be no room for any flexibility in this respect. The believer is expected to be firm and unwavering in his faith even at the cost of his life. But the Book of God permits a person, who is under duress and caught in a situation of life and death, to save his life by uttering words of apostasy, provided he remains firm in his faith at heart:

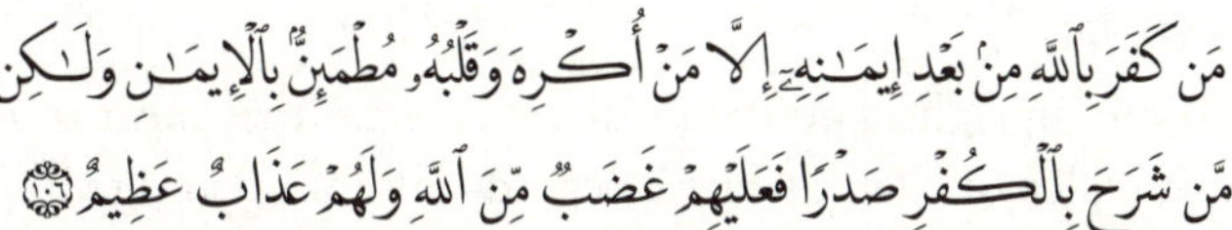

Except for those who were forced to engage in infidelity to Allah after believing the while their hearts remained firmly convinced of their belief, the ones whose hearts willingly embraced disbelief shall incur Allah's wrath and a mighty chastisement lies in store for them.

[*al-Naḥl* 16: 106]

It may not be a position of resolve but one of option. The fact, however, remains that this option has been given by no less an authority than the All-Merciful Lord Himself. Hence, it is confirmed in the eyes of the Shariah that a believer's life is costlier than his reaffirmation of faith and if one is faced with a situation where he has to decide between saving his life and the declaration of his faith, he is permitted to sacrifice the latter for the former. But is it also permissible for someone seeking to save his life to preach apostasy, kill a believer, or spy for those who are averse to an Islamic government? The reply is definitely in the negative, because such actions entail the sacrifice of things much more costly than one's life, which the Shariah can never allow under any circumstances.

ii. Islam prohibits wine, pork, carrion and the flesh of animals slaughtered in the name of idols. It similarly firmly prohibits fornication, burglary, robbery and murder. The Shariah opens up the door under compulsion for someone to save his life in case of the first category of prohibited items only. Under no circumstances, however, does it allow the violation of the sanctity of somebody else's life or property. One can drink wine or eat carrion, pork or flesh of animals slaughtered in the name of a deity other than God if he is left with no option but to do so to save his life. But he is not permitted, even at the cost of his life, to rape a woman, kill an innocent person, or rob someone of his property, because these evils are greater than the risk to one's own life.

iii. To be upright and truthful is among the most important principles of Islam, while it regards falsehood and telling lies as the greatest of evils. There are, nevertheless, some compulsions of practical life in which the telling of lies is not only permitted but in certain situations even obligatory. It is permitted, for example, as a strategy to discreetly suppress the truth and tell a lie in the interest of repairing strained relations, especially between a husband and wife. During war, if a Muslim warrior is caught by the enemy forces, he is not just permitted, but is rather duty-bound not to reveal the truth and, instead, provide wrong information to the enemy. Protection of the Islamic armed forces' strategic interests is obligatory and in this regard a Muslim warrior may have recourse to falsehood and untruth. Similarly, if a criminal or tyrant seeks to kill an innocent person and that person has taken refuge somewhere, it is not only a sin to disclose his whereabouts but is obligatory to save his life by giving wrong information.

The Shariah injunctions in respect of the cases mentioned above may be gleaned through the following Prophetic Traditions:

عَن اُمّ كُلثُوم بِنت عُقبة بِن مُعَيط قَالَت سَمِعتُ رَسُولَ الله صَلَّى اللهُ عَليهِ وَ سَلَّم يَقُول لَيسَ الكَذَّابُ الَّذِي يُصلِحُ بَينَ النَّاسِ فَينمِي خَيراً (متّفقٌ عَلَيهِ)

وَفِى رِوَايَة مُسلِم زِيَادَةَ: قَالَت وَلَم اَسمَعه ، يَرخَصُ فِي شَيء مِمَّا يَقُوله النَّاسُ الاَّ فِي ثلاثٍ : يَعنِى الحَربَ وَالإِصلَاحَ بَينَ النَّاسِ وَحديثَ المَرأة زَوجِهَا.

Umme Kulthūm, bint ‘Uqbah ibn Mu‘ayt, narrated from the Prophet of Allah the saying that ‘a liar is not the one who tries to conciliate between the people and for this he takes a good stance.’ Imam Muslim in his narration added the following: ‘Umme Kulthūm said that she heard the Prophet (peace be upon him) allowing no licence to the people in what they speak, except in three things: those concerning war, conciliation between the people and matters relating to a man and his wife.’[1]

عَن اَسمَآءَ بِنتِ يَزِيد عَنِ النَّبِي صَلّى اللهُ عَلَيهِ وَسَلَّم لَا يَحِلُّ الكَذِبُ اِلاَّ فِى ثَلَاثٍ تَحَدُّثِ الرَّجُلِ امرَاتَه لِيُرضِيَهَا، وَالكَذِبُ فِى الحَربِ، وَلِيُصلِحَ بَينَ النَّاس.

Asmā’ bint Yazīd narrated from the Prophet (peace be upon him) that: ‘speaking a lie is not permissible except in three things: a man speaking to his [estranged] wife to please her; making an incorrect statement in war; and to tell a lie for conciliation between people.’[2]

According to the famous Hadith, which Imam Bukhārī narrated from Muhammad ibn Maslamah, when ibn Muslamah was assigned to kill the Jewish Conspirator, Ka‘ab ibn Ashraf [for his virulent conspiracies against the Prophet and the Islamic

[1] *Mishkāt al-Masabih*, Nos 4809/5, vol. 2; *Ṣaḥīḥ Bukhāri* and *Ṣaḥīḥ Muslim*.
[2] *Mishkāt*, Nos 4810/6, vol. 2; *Masnad* Imam Aḥmad and *Jami‘ al-Tirmidhī*.

State of Madinah], he sought the Prophet's permission to use a deceitful tactic if the situation so demanded, and he was granted permission.

According to another Tradition, narrated by Imam Aḥmad, Nasā'ī, Ḥākim and Ibn Ḥibbān, Hajjāj ibn 'Allāt sought permission to discretely use some pretext for retrieving his wealth from the clutches of the Makkans during the Khaybar expedition and the Prophet allowed him to do so.

The *fuqahā'* and *muḥaddithīn* have deduced from these precedents the following points:

- According to Ibn Ḥajar, Muslim scholars agree about the permissibility of telling a lie in certain emergencies. For instance, if a tyrant wants to kill someone who is hiding at somebody else's place, the latter can deny that person's presence there to save his life. For this, he may even swear by God and will not be a sinner.
- While narrating the incident of Hajjāj ibn 'Allāt, '*Allāmah* Ibn Qayyim drew the following conclusion: 'This confirms that if a person lies about himself or someone else, it is permissible so long as his lie does not adversely affect a third person, and he rightly gets what is due to him through that lie.'
- Imam al-Nawawī, drawing conclusions from the Prophetic Traditions on the subject, said in *Riyāḍ al-Ṣāliḥīn*: 'If a good objective can be achieved without lying, it is forbidden to use a lie for that. If it cannot be attained except through a lie, then using a lie becomes permissible. If the achievement of a particular objective is *mubāḥ* (permitted), the lie too as a means is permitted. But in case the achievement of a particular objective is obligatory then the use of a lie also becomes obligatory.'

Thus the guiding principle that emerges is as follows: Universally, the truth is a great value and the lie a confirmed evil. From an ethical point of view, the former must be the hallmark of our social existence as Muslims and the latter must be discarded and absolutely avoided. Yet in situations where one is compelled to choose between something of higher worth morally and another of relatively less, one has to opt for the former and leave the latter even though the latter may be based absolutely on truth.

iv. Islam has disallowed probing into someone else's private life. It does not permit backbiting, slander and calumny and a person guilty of such social evils is castigated as one who eats the flesh of his own dead brother. However, we know that our learned scholars of Prophetic Traditions developed a unique science[3] called أَسمَاءُ الرِّجَال (Profiles of the Narrators of Hadith), wherein they ripped open everything concerning the private and personal sides of the lives of each and every *rāvī* (Narrator of Hadith). Accordingly, they categorized them into various classes to establish the level of authenticity of their narration. Under normal circumstances, such a sifting of somebody else's personal life would have been unlawful under the definition of backbiting and slander (*ghībah*). The reason for permitting this in the context of Prophetic Traditions was to ensure the authenticity of the most valuable material being transmitted and to make the veracity of transmission as foolproof as humanly possible. A research work of this magnitude would not have been possible

---

[3] As a science, *Fann Asmā' al-Rijāl* (the science of the Profiles of Narrators of Prophetic Traditions) is yet another gift of the Muslim intellectuals and scholars to humanity. It is also a miracle of the person of *Sayyidnā* Rasūl Allah (peace be upon him). In a world where the lives of great men of religion, including the much hallowed founders of Christianity, Judaism, Buddhism, and Brahmanism, are all shrouded in mystery, it goes to the credit of Islam and Islamic scholars that everything concerning the Messenger of Allah (peace be upon him) is available to mankind even today and till eternity in a completely recorded and scientifically documented form. This record does not concern only those associated with the Prophet, including his illustrious caliphs and family members, but the galaxy of Ṣaḥābah, Tābi'ūn and Tabi'ū al-Tābi'īn, covering a period extending to over two centuries. The science of *Asmā' al-Rijāl* profiles over 140,000 individuals in the chain of narration of the Prophetic Traditions. The data has been compiled and printed in volumes that serve as a treasure-house of knowledge and part of the great Islamic legacy to mankind – Editor.

without such an immaculate process and consequently the Ummah in particular and the world in general would have been deprived access to the pearls of wisdom and the golden treasury of knowledge, now available to humanity in such abundance. Such a probing, otherwise absolutely forbidden, was therefore not only desirable but obligatory in respect of *ruwāt* or narrators of ahadith due only to the nobility of the objective.

Similarly, in our day-to-day trade deals, marriage contracts, etc., it is not a sin but obligatory to disclose the wrong side of the merchandise or of a person or family whom we thoroughly know and about whom we are consulted. This is obligatory because of the nobility of the objective that is to save a person or parents of a girl from falling into a trap and ruining his or her career or even life.

v. It is totally forbidden, according to clear Islamic injunctions, to bare any part of a woman's body by a *ghayr mahram* or a person not bound in the marriage bond. Yet the female spy arrested by Hadrat 'Ali was threatened that unless she produced the letter she was carrying from Ḥātib ibn Abī Balta'ah to inform the Makkans about the Prophet's planned expedition to the city she would be subjected to that process (see *Zād al-Ma'ād*, vol. 2, p. 239). Ibn Qayyim deduced from this incident that a woman can be subjected to a body search if the supreme interest of the Islamic State so demands.

vi. The significance of *ṣalāh* in the Islamic system of worship hardly needs to be over-emphasized. Yet it is also historically correct that when the Prophet was with Banī 'Amr ibn 'Awf to resolve a dispute and conciliate among them, Prayer time was due and sensing a delay Hadrat Abū Bakr went ahead to lead it. The Prophet joined the congregation later.

vii. To reject the wrong is among the most important duties of the believer and the injunctions of the Qur'an and the Sunnah in this regard are explicit. But when to right a wrong means to fall into greater wrong, no hasty action is recommended. This is why the Prophet did not approve staging a revolt against a ruler, though profligate and morally depraved they may be. Imam Bukhārī narrated the following Hadīth in this context:

عَن اِبنِ عَبَّاسٍ رَضِيَ اَللهُ عَنهُمَا، عَنِ النَّبِيّ صَلَّى اَللهُ عَلَيهِ وَسَلَّم قَالَ: مَن كَرِه مِن أمِيرِه شَيأً فَليَصبِر، فَإنَّهُ مَن خَرَجَ مِنَ السُّلطَانِ شِبرًا مَاتَ مِيتَةً جَاهِلِيَّةً. وَ عَنه فِى رواية أخرى قَالَ : مَن رأى مِن أمِيرِه شَيأً يَكرَهُهُ فَليَصبِر عَلَيهِ فَإنَّه مَن فَارَقَ الجَمَاعة شِبرًا فَمَاتَ، اِلَّا مَاتَ مِيتَةً جَاهِلِيَّةً.

Ibn 'Abbas narrated that the Prophet (peace be upon him) said: 'Whoever disapproves of something done by his ruler, he should be patient, for whoever disobeys the ruler even a little will die as did those who died during the Days of Ignorance [i.e. as rebellious sinners].' Ibn 'Abbas further narrated: 'Whoever notices something of his ruler which he dislikes, then he should be patient, for whoever dissociates from the Muslims' collective order even a little and dies, he will die as those who died during the Days of Ignorance.'[4]

viii. Similarly, there are clear-cut injunctions for the enforcement of *ḥudūd* (the ultimate penal laws according to the Qur'an and the Sunnah). *Sayyidunā* Rasūl Allah (peace be upon him), however, stopped enactment of the *ḥadd* of chopping a burglar's hand off from the wrist in times of war. (Abū Dāwūd) The second caliph, Hadrat 'Umar, issued a decree ordering suspension of *ḥudūd* punishments when Islamic forces were engaged in battle in enemy territory. The reason was to prevent the possibility of a culprit joining the enemy ranks in retaliation and thus destablizing the Islamic State's strategic position. The provision is applicable even in times of peace. The Prophet (peace be upon him) carried out the *ḥadd* for *qadhaf* (libel, defamation) against the three sincere and dedicated Muslims, but let go

[4] *Ṣaḥīḥ* Bukhārī; *Kitāb al-Fitān* (chapter on Trials and Disorders), No. 9, pp. 177–178.

> scot-free 'Abd Allah ibn Ubayy, the Islamic State's *Ra'īs al-Munāfiqīn* (Chief of the hypocrites of Madinah). According to Imam Ibn Qayyim, the reason for this extraordinary exemption was that the Prophet knew that the enforcement of *ḥadd* would adversely affect the State's internal security. He also desired to win that unfortunate man's heart and through him the hearts of his influential tribe. Consequently, we see Ibn Ubayy dying a lonely and frustrated man's death, with even his own son serving the Messenger of Allah as a true believer and eminent Companion.[5]

It is evident from the examples quoted above that the rules and regulations of the Islamic Shariah are not monotonous in their weight and worth and there is always room for flexibility and an order of precedence. The fundamental principle in this respect is that: *If a little goodness leads to a bigger evil, it is better to leave that goodness. Similarly, one can opt for a lesser evil if this leads to a greater religious benefit.* This precept is based on the popular Arabic adage, often mistaken as a hadith:

مَنِ ابتُلِيَ بِبَلِيَّتَيْنِ فَلْيَختَرْ أَسهَلَهُمَا.

> Whoever is caught between two evils [one lesser and the other greater], – [with no option left but to choose between either of the two] – one should opt for the lesser evil.

It can further be deduced from these examples that there are certain values that carry a higher position in the Islamic legal order, which can never be sacrificed. Similarly, there are values of lesser importance, which under normal circumstances can never be sacrificed, but which in exceptional situations, as already mentioned may take a back seat. That is the import of my statements, which a section of our religious zealots have unfortunately misconstrued. What is important is how to maintain a balanced approach between pragmatism and idealism under all circumstances.

---

[5] *Zād al-Ma'ād*, vol. 2, p. 161.

As for my arguments with regard to the Prophet's observation: اَلأَ ئِمَّةُ مِنْ قُرَيْش (The rulers are to be from among the Quraysh), this has been dealt in depth in *Tarjumān al-Qur'ān's* issue of April, 1946 and needs no further elaboration. It is an established fact of Islamic history that based on the Prophet's observation and the precedents of his Companions and those who followed them, the Muslim jurists and scholars had for centuries considered the precondition of *Qarashiyat* essential for a caliph. There is, therefore, no justification in raising unwarranted questions on what I have stated in this context.

In the same context, it may be of interest also to add that during the 1950–1951 elections *Jamā'at-e-Islāmī* issued a statement declaring its policy aginst contesting elections or casting a vote in favour of any candidate because Islam did not permit candidacy for a position of profit. Subsequent experience, however, showed that the policy was counter-productive and the *Jamā'at* damaged even its sublime cause and the arduous struggle for the establishment of the Islamic social order in the country. A balanced approach between pragmatism and idealism demanded that instead of causing damage to a much nobler objective, we should not keep ourselves out of the election arena. The *Jamā'at*, therefore, decided to amend its erstwhile policy and while no person from the *Jamā'at* was allowed to offer his own candidacy for any office, it, nonetheless, agreed to lend support to the morally upright candidates who were in favour of the Islamic system and those closer to it ideologically. Our detractors, who are trying to misrepresent this policy as having been motivated by the *Jamā'at*'s 'lust for power', are better advised to seek forgiveness from Allah *subḥānahū wa ta'ālā* and review their stance.

6 The Mischief of Schism and Religious Intolerance[*]

Among the most dangerous tumults and turmoils that have surfaced during the days of the Muslims' socio-economic and political decline is the scourge of intolerance and schismatic divide – to dismiss one another as apostate, infidel, godless and accursed. The universal and easy to understand articles of Islamic faith were subjected to hair-splitting and unnecessary debates. Through misinterpretations and wrong inferences so many extraneous and peripheral issues were coined, which were self-contradictory, irrelevant and in most cases having no relevance to the teachings of the Qur'an and the Sunnah. May Allah forgive those involved in such misplaced 'scholarships', who attached so much importance to extraneous matters of their own invention that they assumed almost the status of the articles of faith. The first casualty of this sad development was the unity of the Muslim Ummah. The religion that helped unify the human race and dismantled the differences of castes, creeds, colour, ethnic and cultural barriers, was split into dozens of sects, with each sect labelling the other as kafir (unbeliever), *fāsiq* (disobedient to the Lord), misguided, sinner, etc. It was something Islam had never approved. Allah *subḥānahū wa ta'ālā* has drawn a clear line of distinction in His Book to distinguish between Islam and *kufr*. He gave nobody the right to declare on his own that this was Islam and that was *kufr*. Whatever be the motive behind this ugly phenomenon, whether narrow-mindedness, absence of the sincerity of purpose or prevalence of spitefulness and personal approach to things, it has caused inexplicable damage to the Muslims as a community.

---

[*] *Tarjumān al-Qur'ān*, May 1935.

So far as the question of someone being a believer or unbeliever is concerned, nobody has the right to pass judgment. The matter concerns God directly and He will decide that on the Day of Reckoning. As for the servants of Allah, they can only decide: who is within the borderlines drawn for Islam by the Lord and His Apostle and who has transgressed the well-defined limits. *Sayyidunā* Rasūl Allah (Allah's peace and mercy be upon him) explicitly conveyed to the Ummah the following to define the parameters of the Religion of Truth once and for all:

بُنِيَ الإِسلَامُ عَلٰى خَمسٍ: شَهَادَةُ أَن لَا اِلٰهَ اِلاَّ اللهُ، وَ أَنَّ مُحَمَّدًا رَسُولُ اللهِ، وَإِقَامِ الصَّلوٰةِ، وَإِيتَاءِ الزَّكوةِ، وَصَومِ رَمَضَانَ، وَحَجِّ البَيتِ.

Islam is based on five [pillars]: to bear witness that there is no god but Allah and that Muhammad is Allah's [Final] Messenger; to establish Prayer [*ṣalāh*]; give obligatory due [zakat]; keep the Fast of Ramadan [*ṣawm*]; and perform pilgrimage to the House of God [Hajj].[1]

The matter concerning Islam was not left in any way ambiguous and vague. The Prophet (may Allah's peace and blessings be upon him) explained its various aspects in crystal clear terms in so many ahadith:

اُمِرتُ أَن اُقَاتِلَ النَّاسَ حَتّٰى يَشهَدُوا أَن لَا اِلٰهَ اِلاَّ اللهُ وَأَنَّ مُحَمَّداً رَسُولُ اللهِ، وَيُقِيمُوا الصَّلوٰةَ، وَيُؤتُوا الزَّكوةَ، فَإِذَا فَعَلُوا ذٰلِكَ عَصَمُوا مِنِّي دِمَاءَهُم اِلَّا بِحَقِّ الإِسلَامِ، وَحِسَابُهُم عَلَى اللهِ عَزَّ وَجَلَّ.

I have been ordered to fight the people [who are enemies of Islam and the Muslims] till they bear witness that there is no god but Allah and that Muhammad is Allah's Messenger; establish *ṣalāh*; and give zakat. When they do that they can feel secure from me about their lives except

[1] *Jāmi' Al-Tirmidhī*, No. 2609, Book 38.

> that they have something against themselves concerning the rights of Islam. Eventually, they are accountable before the Lord.[2]

These are the parameters that govern the Islamic society. We have been ordered to deal with all those as Muslims who are within these well-defined boundaries. Nobody has the right to expel anyone out of the Muslim *millah* (community). As for those who transgress these limits, they are to be dealt with according to the dictates of Islam itself. We are not entitled to evaluate and pass judgement on something that concerns someone's inner self. We are to go only by how one acts and behaves. What to speak of ordinary mortals like us, even the Prophet of God (peace be upon him) went by physical evidence in this respect. According to a Tradition, narrated jointly by Imam Bukhārī and Imam Muslim, once Hadrat 'Ali sent an amount of money from Yemen to the Prophet (peace be upon him). The Prophet distributed it in equal proportion to the four persons present. On this, one of them interjected: 'O Prophet of God, be afraid of God!' On this the Mssenger of Allah said: 'Woe unto you! Am I not the best qualified among those on earth to fear God?' Hadrat Khalid ibn al-Walīd, an eminent Companion, who was also present on the occasion, sought permission to kill that man for his audacity. *Sayyidunā* Rasūl Allah did not approve of this and said: 'No, he may perhaps be performing his regular Prayers.' Khalid submitted: 'There are many who perform their Prayers, but what they utter from their tongue is not corroborated by their heart.' The Prophet's response to that was extremely significant:

> إنّي لَمْ أُومَرْ أن أُنقِّبَ عن قلوبِ النَّاسِ وَلاَ أَشُقَّ بُطُونَهُم.
>
> 'I have not been ordered to rip open the people's hearts or tear apart their belly.'[3]

---

[2] *Al-Jāmi' Al-Sahīh* of Imam Bukhārī, narrated by Ibn 'Umar, No. 24, Book 26; and *Jāmi' Al-Tirmidhī*, narrated by Abū Hurayrah, No. 2606, Book 38.

[3] *Ṣaḥīḥ* Bukhārī and *Ṣaḥīḥ* Muslim.

Imam Mālik, Imam Shāfi'ī and Imam Aḥmad in their compilation narrated that once a man from Anṣār (Companions from Madinah who welcomed the emigrants), tried to confide about someone to him. The Prophet interjected in a louder voice: 'Doesn't he bear witness that there is no god but Allah?' The man from Anṣār replied: 'Yes, O Prophet of God, but his witness cannot be trusted.' The Prophet asked: 'Doesn't he bear witness that Muhammad is Allah's Messenger?' The Anṣāri replied in the affirmative but doubted the other man's faith. The Prophet then asked: 'Doesn't he offer regular Prayers?' The reply was again in the affirmative with continued expression of doubt about the man's integrity as Muslim. The Prophet on this catagorically observed:

أُولٰئِكَ الَّذِينَ نَهَانِيَ اللهُ عَنْ قَتلِهِم.

'These are the people I have been forbidden by God to kill.'[4]

There cannot be a greater injustice, therefore, than declaring a Muslim 'unbeliever' and an outcast from the community although he reaffirms his faith in Islam and is well within the boundaries of his religion as determined by God and his Messenger (peace be upon him). This is an outrage more against God than His loyal subject. It will, in fact, be like challenging the divine law that confirms him as a believer. This is why the Prophet has strictly forbidden to pronounce anybody kafir or *fāsiq*:

اَيُّمَا رَجُلٍ قَالَ لِاَخِيه يَا كَافِر فَقَد بَاءَ بِها اَحَدُهُمَا.

'Whoever calls his [Muslim] brother '*O kafir*', this pronouncement is bound to revert to either of the two.'[5]

لاَ يَرمِى رَجُلٌ رَجُلاً بِالفُسُوقِ وَلاَ يَرمِيهُ بِالكُفرِ اِلَّا ارتَدَت عَلَيهِ اِن لَّم يَكُن صَاحِبُهُ كَذٰلِك.

[4] *Musnad* of Imam Shāfi'ī and Imam Aḥmad and *Muwaṭṭa* of Imam Mālik.

[5] *Ṣaḥīḥ* Bukhārī.

> 'When a person accuses another of disobedience to the Lord or unbelief, while actually he is neither disobedient nor infidel, the accusation then reverts to the accuser.'[6]
>
> مَن لَّعَنَ مُؤمِنًا فَهُوَ كَقَتلِهِ وَمَن قَذَفَ مُؤمِناً بِكُفرٍ فَهُوَ كَقَتله .
>
> 'If a person curses a believer, it is as though he killed him, and if he falsely accuses him of being infidel that too is like killing him.'[7]
>
> مَن دَعَا رَجُلاً بِالكُفرِ اَو قَالَ عَدوَّ الله وَلَيسَ كَذٰلِكَ اِلاَّ حَارَ عَلَيهِ .
>
> 'If a person calls someone infidel or an enemy of God, and he is factually incorrect, his statement would fall back to himself.'[8]

Such schisms and calumny impinge not only on the rights of an individual, but it is a public offence as well. It is an offence against the entire Muslim community causing it great damage, and with a little introspection we can understand why!

The fundamental difference between an Islamic social order and an un-Islamic one is that the non-Muslim societies are based on relationships of colour, ethnicity, language, and nationhood. As against this, the Muslim societies are built on the foundations of faith. In non-Muslim societies, the difference of faith and creed matters little, because such divergence has no effect on relationships based on ties of common nationhood, race, language or colour. They may be at total variance inwardly, but their social fabric remains intact. In Islam, however, it is the unity of faith and creed that welds together into a single nation peoples of different races, castes, colour and language. Hence, anyone who tries to sever the bonds of faith actually uses his scissors against the divine ties which bind together into a well-knit community those who believe in the One and Only God, the Last of His Prophets and His Book. To call an individual or a group of

---

[6] *Ṣaḥīḥ* Bukhārī.
[7] *Ṣaḥīḥ* Bukhārī.
[8] *Ṣaḥīḥ* Muslim.

Muslims kafir does not simply mean an attack on their faith and belief, it also means disrupting the relationship of brotherhood, love, social contract and cooperation between the society and the individual – or group of individuals – and that they are no more part of the Muslim Ummah's organic whole.

When an action like this has the sanction of the Book of God and Tradition of the Prophet, only then it is definitely correct. In such cases, to sever the rotten limb will mean to save the health of the whole body. If, however, in light of the divine guidance the limb is not rotten and has been chopped off arbitrarily, that would be absolutely cruel, not just for the affected part but for the whole body from which it has been severed. This is the reason why Allah *subḥānahū wa taʿālā* and His Messenger (peace be upon him) have especially stressed respect for religious ties:

...وَلَا تَقُولُوا۟ لِمَنْ أَلْقَىٰٓ إِلَيْكُمُ ٱلسَّلَـٰمَ لَسْتَ مُؤْمِنًا... ﴿٩٤﴾

'and do not say to him who offers you the greeting of peace: 'you are not a believer'.

[*al-Nisā'* 4: 94]

According to a famous Hadith, once a member of the Islamic military expedition killed someone who on encountering the Muslims saluted them with the greeting of Islam and then also recited the first article of faith: *There is no god but Allah and Muhammad is His Messenger*. The soldier who killed him was, however, motivated by the war discipline and took it as a tactic of deception by the enemy fighter just to save his life. When the incident was reported to the Prophet (peace be upon him), he became very angry and chastised him. The fellow members of the expedition then pleaded that he did that on security considerations, but the Messenger of Allah's response was very clear: هَلَّا شَقَقْتَ عَنْ قَلْبِهِ؟ 'Did you rip open his heart?'

The ahadith quoted above leads us to the conclusion that the believers' strength as individuals and community lies only in strengthening their religious bond. If they have no regard for this bond and start disrupting it on one pretext or the other, the Muslim

Ummah's unity is liable to be weakened. In the absence of this strong social bond, there will remain no cohesive force to keep the banner of Allah's Supremacy aloft and to continue the Muslims' mission of goodness and godliness.[9]

I do not mean to say that none can be declared kafir or *fāsiq*, not even when he is proved guilty of apostasy and openly flouts the Islamic norms and acts, speaks or writes in flagrant violation of the Islamic tenets. This is neither the connotation of the injunctions of the Qur'an and the Sunnah, nor of what has been stated so far. The expulsion of a believer from the Islamic fraternity is as harmful as to include or retain an unbeliever within its fold. What needs to be kept in view is that extreme care must be exercised in issuing a decree against any believer the way it is imperative to be extremely careful in issuing the decree of capital punishment against a criminal. If a Muslim is found uttering outrageous things against Islam, we should not at once jump to a conclusion but let him have the benefit of the doubt. Instead of an instant decision, we should adopt a more compassionate attitude and try to remove the misgivings or wrong notions he has nurtured due to his ignorance about Islam and Islamic teachings. If he persists in his anti-Islamic posture, we should revert to the Book of God and the Sunnah of the Prophet for a clear-cut stand against his transgressions. When his words or deeds do not precisely contravene the prescribed norms and there is a room for reinterpretation and elaboration of what he says, he cannot be declared kafir. He can at best be called misguided and having gone astray, and that too in context of that particular case and not for his conduct in general. In the case, however, that his conduct directly

[9] The mannerism taught by *Sayyidnā* Rasūl Allah (peace be upon him) lends so much strength to the Islamic bond that as Muslims we must be proud of it and always keen to preserve the sanctity of this bond. The Messenger of Allah (Allah's peace and blessings be upon him) said: سِبابُ المُسلِمِ فُسُوقٌ وَقِتَالُهُ كُفرٌ. 'Verbally abusing a Muslim is disobedience of the Lord and fighting him is unbelief.' (No. 2635, narrated by Imām Tirmidhī from 'Abd Allah ibn Mas'ūd — also narrated by Imām Bukhārī and Muslim)

In another hadith, the Prophet (peace be upon him) said: وَمَن قَذَفَ مُؤمِناً بِكُفرٍ فَهُوَ كَقِتَالِه. '... whoever accuses a believer of unbelief is like he has killed him.' (No. 2636, Imam Tirmidhī from Thābit ibn al-Dahhāk) – Editor.

contravenes the Islamic injunctions, and knowing this fully well he openly sticks to his anti-Qur'an and anti-Sunnah posture and there is no room either for any explanation or reinterpretation, only then can an edict be issued declaring him disobedient to the Lord (*fāsiq*) or an apostate and infidel (kafir) as the case may be. There can be no uniformity in crimes or among criminals. Justice, therefore, demands that difference in the level and category of crime and criminals must be kept in view while deciding the punishment. Uniform treatment in such cases cannot be but injustice.

As stated in the beginning, there is an internal side of Islam and *kufr* and an external one. The internal and hidden side concerns one's conviction (firmness of one's faith) and intentions (one's *nīyah*), while the external one concerns his words and actions. We can assess one's emotions and feelings by what one says or does. We can to some extent guess about a person's inner self from the words he utters and the way he acts. But this is just guesswork, on the basis of which no ultimate judgment can be passed about his faith. More appropriately, therefore, the matter concerning one's faith will have to be left to the All-Knowing Lord, who alone knows with certainty the exact level and degree of *īmān* within a person's heart:

... إِنَّ رَبَّكَ هُوَ أَعْلَمُ بِمَن ضَلَّ عَن سَبِيلِهِۦ وَهُوَ أَعْلَمُ بِمَنِ ٱهْتَدَىٰ ﴿٣٠﴾

> *Surely your Lord fully knows those who have strayed away from His Path and He also fully knows those who are rightly guided.*
>
> [*al-Najm* 53: 30]

We can form an opinion about who is a Muslim and who is not on the basis of what one says or does. It is quite possible that a person, who out of sheer ignorance is indulging in idle talk and even blasphemy, may be a true and faithful believer and in his heart of hearts deeply in love with God and His Prophet. In the same way, it is equally possible that a person forcefully displaying his faith in God and observing the injunctions of the Shariah in letter and spirit may in fact be a hypocrite involved only in a façade of piety. It is, therefore, imperative that while passing judgment about someone's faith or faithlessness on the basis of apparent features, one must be extremely careful and afraid of God's displeasure.

Human beings differ from one another on the basis of their temperaments, physical contours and intellectual prowess. Some are extremely simple and accept plain facts at their face value. They have neither the ability nor do they bother to learn the details and intricacies of things they have accepted. On the other hand, there are those who are more reflective and are never satisfied by a general purview of things. They are on the lookout for details and if none are available they use their imagination to create some. Then those with the reflective frame of mind also differ from one another in their intellectual capabilities and approach to life. Some of them have a skeptical frame of mind, while others are firm in their conviction. Some people are fond of material and more perceptible things and some of intellectual and rational ones; some are pragmatists and some given to the realm of idealism and imagination. In short, there are so many ways of thinking and perception that the human mind adopts according to its temperament and disposition. No ordinary mortal is capable of changing another person's disposition, tendencies and frame of mind, and similarly no one has the right to demand others to mould their disposition, tendencies, and mind-set according to one's own as though one was a perfect model for others.

Who else other than the Lord Himself, Who sent Islam for the guidance of mankind, is capable of knowing best the differences of human nature and temperaments? Who else can be the most caring for humans? This is the reason why Allah *subḥānahū wa ta'ālā* has laid down the foundations of the Religion of Truth on such simple and universal teachings and injunctions, so that everyone – ranging from the rural folk with a low IQ to a highly sophisticated intellectual and seeker of truth of the modern urban society – can comprehend and follow them. The simplicity, comprehensiveness and universality of these teachings are the hallmark of Islam as the global and eternal faith. For a man with a simple frame of mind it is sufficient to understand and believe that God is One and Muhammad (Allah's peace be upon him) is His Messenger; the Qur'an is the Book of the Lord; and we are all accountable to Him on the Day of Judgment for all that we do in this life. To a person of greater intellectual calibre, this brief Article of the Islamic Faith has so much depth and profundity of meaning that he can go as deep as he can in his earnest quest for truth. He can spend his life-time exploring the vast vistas of knowledge and wisdom without ever feeling as if he has reached the end of the road and can go no further.

Then, a thinking mind is free to follow for his intellectual pursuits a path of his choice, provided he moves within the well-defined parameters drawn by the Qur'an and the Sunnah between Islam and *kufr*. So long as he does not transgress those limits, everything that he says or does will be treated as lawful, even if we differ from him on peripheral matters. For example, the principal point regarding faith in Allah is to firmly believe that the Creator of the universe and its Sustainer is the One and Only God and He alone is worthy of being worshipped. This is a simple and self-evident truth, easy even for a man of common intelligence to comprehend and follow, while a more reflective and intellectual type may like to go deeper and explore new vistas and dimensions of this universal truth. It may, however, be quite difficult that someone with a certain frame of mind and temperament may follow the same course in his quest to know more about the Lord as taken by another person of a different disposition and intellectual background. There is no harm in this divergence so long as every seeker of truth firmly believes in the fundamentals of faith. Each one of them is then Muslim, in spite of their divergence of intellectual approach in minor details and lapses, if any.

Similarly, there are facts of a fundamental nature concerning Islam, like revelation, Prophethood, angels and the Day of Reckoning. Some details regarding these may be available in the Qur'an and the Sunnah. An inquisitive mind may feel tempted to go even further to discover facts through his imagination, or intellectual forays into the realm of the unknown. Thus he is likely to lose sight of the parameters drawn by the Lord. In such intellectual pursuits, he may be correct so long as he does not transgress the borderlines set by the Book of God and Ahadith. We cannot dismiss him as a deviant if he follows the right approach, in spite of the lapses of his thoughts and ideas, which may even call for our condemnation and on which we may take him to task for his ideological waywardness.

If we ponder a while here, we can easily understand what led to the rise of different sects in Islam. The plain and simple facts concerning the essentials of religion were mentioned succinctly in the Qur'an and the Sunnah, with brilliant indicators here and there concerning relevant details. Different scholars then followed different ways, according to their own frame of mind and intellectual capabilities, to grasp the meaning of these fundamentals, and through deduction and induction arrived at different conclusions regarding peripheral issues. No harm would have been done and no wrong committed had a certain group considered its own interpretation as correct and tried to logically convince its counterpart to follow the same course. Unfortunately, however, a section of zealots of that particular group took to extremism and went to the extent of declaring their own interpretation as the ultimate truth and those who ventured to differ as being guilty of *kufr*. This is how the schismatic divide started. This also marked the beginning of factional feuds. It is also a fact that the positions taken up in cases of minor details through the deductive and inductive process were generally faulty. Yet, every fault cannot necessarily be *kufr*. There is nothing wrong from a religious point of view to call a mistake a mistake and the one who commits that as erring and also to correct him if he is willing to respond positively. But Islam does not allow anybody to label someone infidel and apostate as long as he does not openly renounce his faith or refuses to believe in the fundamentals essentially needed to be a Muslim.

Unfortunately, most of our religious scholars appear reluctant to give up their time-worn practice. Their basic mistake is that they have overlooked the difference between the fundamental and the peripheral, the inviolable text and its interpretation. They insist on treating as essentials of religion the details gathered by themselves or their worthy predecessors through induction and deduction. They are thus prone to declare kafir anyone who differs from them even in minor details or refuses to accept their interpretation. This intemperance and atmosphere of conflict led at first to sectarian differences and divisions and then to the spreading of misunderstandings among

Muslims against their religious leaders and at times even about Islam. The people gradually lost their confidence in *'ulamā'* and instead of feeling attracted towards Islam began losing interest in everything religious. One should only pray that our religious scholars of different schools of thought would realize their mistake and do justice not only to Islam and Muslims but also to themselves and their stature as torch-bearers of a great religion.

7 Major Sins: Legal and Social Implications*

[Some members of an extremist Muslim group in India addressed a query to Sayyid Mawdūdī, seeking his views on the group's approach in certain matters. The query was:

> The group to which we belong believes that a Muslim who commits a major sin becomes kafir. They see no difference between *kufr* (rejection of faith) and *fisq* (disobedience of the Lord). (In certain matters) our group places common believers in the same category as those categorized by the Qur'an as the 'People of the Book'. Our men may take in marriage girls from outside the group but they do not give their daughters in marriage to other Muslims. What is your opinion about this line of thought and action? Is this correct? If not, then please explain to us convincingly, where did we go wrong?

After making a detailed investigation and gathering the necessary information about that group, Sayyid Mawdūdī responded to the above query in the article that follows. – Editor]

On careful scrutiny and investigation I have come to know that the group to which you belong has no men of learning, imbued with true knowledge of Islam and adequately qualified in juristic matters. This is further confirmed by the kind of issues you have raised, which appear to have cropped up due to lack of insight into the teachings of the Qur'an and the Sunnah. *Sayyidunā* Rasūl Allah (peace be upon him)

* *Tarjuman al-Qur'an*, November–December 1945.

said: الدِّيــنُ النَّصِـيحَـه ('Islam is to mean well and be sincere').[1] It should therefore taken as sincere advice if I stress that it is contrary to the very spirit of religion to hold rigid views in religious matters that govern the lives of Muslim individuals and society, and that too without adequate knowledge of the Qur'an and the Sunnah. To be a Muslim we have no option but to have firm faith and observe in letter and spirit the injunctions of the Book of God and the Sunnah of *Sayyidunā* Rasūl Allah (peace be upon him). In case, however, a person or group of persons, who are without necessary academic training or juristic insight into these injunctions, lend to their views the status of a religious decree, they are then following not Islam but their personal whims. There can possibly be no sin greater than this.

It may be of interest to add that the basic knowledge necessary for understanding the teachings of the Qur'an and the Sunnah, as also the general awareness about Islamic injunctions, are hardly enough to make somebody a religious scholar capable of juristic interpretations and issuing edicts. Such knowledge and awareness do not entitle him to formulate his personal views on matters of religious significance for the 'guidance' of others.

With this brief introductory note, let me now respond to the points raised by you in your letter.

First of all, let us ask what the term *kufr* actually means? It means the attitude of insolence and rejection that a person may display when Islam is offered to him as a distinct way of life and in spite of fully understanding its message his refusal to accept it or submit to its

---

[1] Full text of the Hadith narrated by Jarīr ibn 'Abd Allah and included by Imam Bukhārī in his *Ṣaḥīḥ* under the same title, is as follows;

> بَابُ قَولِ النبّي صَلي اللهُ عَلَيهِ وَ سَلَم : الدّينُ النَّصيحَه ـ عَن جَرير رض بِن عَبدَالله البَجَعي قَالَ: بَا يَعتُ رَسُولَ الله صَلى اللهُ عَلَيهِ وَ سَلَم عَلى اِقَامَ الصَّلوٰةِ، وَ اِيتَآء الزَّكوٰةِ ، وَالنُّصح لِكُلّ مُسلِم.
>
> 'Chapter on the statement of the Messenger of Allah (peace be upon him): "Religion is to be well meaning and sincere"; Jarīr ibn 'Abd Allah al-Baja'ī said: "I gave pledge (*bay'ah*) to Allah's Messenger for the following: (i) to offer and establish the order of *ṣalāh*; (ii) to pay zakat; and (iii) to be well-meaning and sincere to every Muslim."' (No. 52, *Al-Jāmi' Al-Ṣaḥīḥ*, Book of Faith, chapter 38) – Editor.

dictates and injunctions. A state of ignorance due to which a person may be leading unknowingly a life contrary to the teachings of Islam is not *kufr*, but *jāhilīyah*. Pagan Arabs were afflicted with *jāhilīyah* before the advent of the Prophet of Islam. They were declared kafir only when they rejected the Religion of Truth offered to them by *Sayyidunā* Rasūl Allah (peace be upon him).

It may not be amiss to also point out here that there are two aspects of *kufr*: (i) The state of rejection and rebellion which in essence is an exit from faith. (ii) The second aspect of *kufr* is the state of mind on the basis of which a person can be declared to have transgressed the boundaries of Islam and severed all his links with the Islamic social order.

The first category of *kufr* should not be confused with *sin*. A sin is no doubt contrary to faith, but a sin, however great, does not necessarily lead to a permanent loss of faith. Like an unbeliever, a *mu'min* too can be guilty of committing major sins. What differentiates between the sin of an unbeliever and that of the believer is that while committing sin, a believer leaves the state of *īmān*, but as he recovers from the stupor of his impulsive behaviour and the curtain that has fallen over his senses is lifted, he feels disturbed over his plight and in penitence reverts back to his Lord, repents and solemnly vows never again to repeat that mistake. Such a sinful act, howsoever abominable, does not render its perpetrator a kafir but only a sinner. Repentance brings him back into the fold of *īmān*. As against this, the sin committed by a kafir has permanence. It often becomes a part of his lifestyle and frame of mind. He may take it as a norm and even relish it. He cares not the least about the parameters laid down by the Lord and His Apostle for the lawful and the forbidden. He insists on committing sinful acts, and this he does with vehemence and without a sense of remorse. This kind of sinning causes loss of faith, though the sin committed may be of a minor nature. It will, therefore, be wrong to treat both these categories of sinners on an equal footing and label them both as kafir. It is correct that in principle wilful negation of the injunctions of the Qur'an and the Sunnah makes a person kafir. Nobody has, however, the right to pronounce him so and expel him from the Islamic fold until and unless he actually renounces his faith.

The Lord alone knows if a believer committing sin is left with any tinge of *īmān* in his heart or not.

Now, let us consider the second category of *kufr* that renders a person kafir and because of which all his ties with the Muslim community are severed once and for all. As it is something very serious that concerns not an individual alone but the society as a whole, the Islamic Shariah has left it to no one's personal discretion to pronounce somebody kafir. As in the case of capital punishment, it has to be approved and enforced only through a necessary judicial process. As nobody is authorized to issue a verdict condemning someone to death because in his opinion he was guilty of murder, similarly nobody is authorized by the Shariah to unilaterally pronounce someone kafir. To label a person kafir is like condemning him to spiritual death. A Shariah judge alone is authorized to thoroughly probe into the charge of *kufr* against somebody. He will have to record the statement of the accused, examine his words and deeds, verify the witnesses and then decide whether the accused is really guilty and ought to be thrown out of the Muslim community and beyond the fold of Islam. Where no such system of justice and its prerequisites are available a random decision on one's faith is liable to be wrong. Furthermore, it is beyond the lawful jurisdiction of individuals and non-entitled groups to arbitrarily issue edicts in matters of faith, which is as disastrous in its consequences as the uncalled for tolerance allowing the unbelievers to remain part of the Muslim society.

Well-meaning believers, honestly keen to religiously reform the common man, should first take into account the differences prevalent among various sections of people in a Muslim society. With the people immersed in ignorance, the society has those given to sin. Then, there are those actually involved in acts bordering *kufr*. Yet another category consists of people who rightly deserve to be declared social outcasts. It will be wrong to treat these various groups of people in one and the same way. We may try to religiously educate the un-informed till they start taking pride in being Muslims. There is no reason for us to unnecessarily let them believe otherwise. We should instead impress upon them to remain firm in their faith and try to learn more about Islam and follow its teachings properly. As for those given to a sinful way of life, we must encourage them too to give up their present lifestyle and earnestly and sincerely try to instil fear of God within their hearts and rekindle the light of *īmān*.

As for those who are apparently guilty of *kufr*, it is hardly advisable for us to insist on calling them kafir or declaring them unbeliever. On the contrary, sincere efforts need to be made to bring them back into the benign fold of Islam through sage counsel and selfless endeavours to inject faith within their hearts. As sincere Muslims, our instance should be like that of a physician who diagnoses cancer in his patient and is sure about his diagnosis, but then proceeds in all earnestness to treat the affected person. Conversely, it would be foolish for a physician to bluntly tell his patient that he was incurable without realizing that the very shock may kill him.

Regarding the last category of people, who may be a threat to the Muslim society and about whom the need is strongly felt to sever all ties with them, the correct approach would be to present their case to the Shariah Court. In the absence of the Islamic judicial system, however, the best course would be to avoid a public trial of such persons and pronouncements declaring them kafir. Members of the Muslim society would be better advised in such cases to stop making them friends and close associates and entering into friendly deals with them. While avoiding a relationship of intimacy, the doors should, however, be left open for some sort of interaction with such persons to discreetly preach to them the divine guidance.

Regarding your query about marriage contracts with other Muslim groups, it is rooted in the same rigid approach that cannot be called Islamic. To explain it further, I may add that this is unfair and un-Islamic to deal with the whole society strictly in a uniform manner. The Muslim society today is a combination of peoples of all kinds – those who are true to their faith and are upright and good, those who suffer from ignorance, and those who are knowingly involved in sinful acts. Then, there are people who are on the borderline of *kufr*, and also those who should have been expelled from the Muslim society but for the absence of the Islamic social order and legal system. It will be wrong to treat the people of all these catagories uniformly. The aversion to enter into a marriage contract with fellow Muslims simply because they do not belong to a particular group is nothing but an act of unwarranted bias. The Islamic Shariah has given you no licence for such schisms. As for those ignorant of their religion and those committed to profligacy, immorality and disregard for Shariah, it is definitely better not to enter into a marriage contract with such people, not because they are all kafir, but because of the injunctions requiring us to first look into the religious and moral side of the person with whom we are to enter into such solemn social contracts.

Perhaps the reason behind your group's aversion to give your daughters' hands in marriage to even a righteous Muslim outside your own group is your misinterpretation of the following Haditīh:[2] مَن شَذَّ شَذَّ اِلَى النَّار ('He who deviates from *Jamā'ah* [the Islamic social order], drifts towards the fire [of Hell]'). This is, however, an absolutely wrong deduction. The 'party' (or group) from which Muslims have been warned not to dissociate themselves is *Al-Jamā'ah al-Islāmiyah*, the 'Party of Islam' or the Islamic social order. We have been ordered to strictly observe the discipline of the Muslim community but not that of a particular group formed by few individuals. The term 'Party of Islam' or *Al-Jamā'ah* is applicable only to that group which has the following characteristics:

i. It has been formed with the sole purpose of introducing the Islamic way of life or, in other words, to establish the supremacy of Islam in all walks of our existence.
ii. It covers the mainstream of believers.
iii. It is committed to the mission for the supremacy of which Allah *subḥānahū wa ta'ālā* has raised the Muslim Ummah and is earnestly engaged in an all-round struggle (jihad) for the success of that mission.

[2] According to the complete text of the Haditih narrated by Imam Tirmidhī from 'Abd Allah ibn 'Umar, the Messenger of Allah said:

اِنَّ الله لَا يَجمَعُ اُمَّتِي عَلٰى ضَلَالَةٍ، وَ يَدُالله على الجَماعةِ، وَ مَن شَذَّ شَذَّ اِلَى النَّار.

'Indeed, Allah will never join together my Ummah on deviation; and Allah's hand [of Blessing] is over the *Jamā'ah* [the Islamic social order]; and whoever deviates, deviates to the Fire.' (*Jāmi' Al-Tirmidhī*, No. 2167, chapter on *Al-Fitan* [31]) – Editor.

If such a 'Party' or *Al-Jamā'ah* is physically there, then any wilful dissociation and segregation will mean dissociation from Islam itself. Anybody severing his ties with the 'Party of Islam' will be guilty then of severing his bonds with the Islamic community as a whole. The groups and parties which emerged to look after the Muslims' interests, individually and collectively, following the disintegration of the 'Party of Islam' and fragmentation of the Muslim Ummah or the Nation of Islam into splinter groups based on narrow communal, racial, linguistic and other considerations, can, however, be no substitute legally or practically to the Islamic social order until a particular broad-based and Islamically oriented group achieves the status of the original Party of Islam (*Al-Jamā'ah al-Islāmiyah*). As sincere Musims, howsoever noble and well-meaning we may be in our mission, the Islamic Shariah does not give us the licence to form an exclusive party of a few individuals and declare overnight that Muslims the world over, who are outside its fold, are non-Muslims or that anyone who dies without proclaiming allegiance to that party would die the death of *jāhilīyah*. Such an attitude means transgression from the legal jurisdiction of the Islamic social order. This can also hardly be conducive to the furtherance of the objectives for which that party or group has been formed. Instead of reforming the Muslim society, such an approach is bound to cause more disruption.

Let us coolly ponder for a while over the following aspects: What, after all, is the fault of a true and firmly-believing and practicing Muslim to be declared kafir? Is it because he has not joined a particular group, not due to any ill-will but because of either his unawareness or dissatisfaction? Then, what is the rationale for someone's exclusive prerogative over and above all other members of the Muslim community to organize such a group in the service of Islam?

During a period of political instability and ideological confusion, no single group or party can claim to have the desired capacity to successfully cope with the formidable demands of the Muslim Ummah's reform. It is, therefore, but natural for more than one party or group to emerge for sincerely and correctly discharging their duty in this respect. It is also quite natural that on the emergence of such groups or parties the people may take some time in deciding which reformist party or group to join. It will be Islamically wrong, therefore, for any particular person, party, or group to claim for himself or his group the exclusive right of the Muslim Ummah's leadership, or discard others as the misled ones. Instead of making such unwarranted claims, it will be more appropriate for each person or group to sincerely and devotedly work in their respective spheres for the community's moral uplift and social rejuvenation. They should all be imbued at the same time with a sincere passion for the eventual emergence of *Al-Jamāʿah* that was there during the glorious age of *Al-Khulafā' Al-Rāshidūn* (the four Rightly-Guided Caliphs). Meanwhile, every one of us will have to be extremely cautious against the likelihood of any group or party giving rise to factionalism and thereby causing division within the Ummah instead of safeguarding its unity and cohesion.

8 The Social Dimension of Dress*

Dress has been part of human civilization's cultural trappings for thousands of years. Naturally speaking, however, it can be viewed that the adoption of forms of dress were an outcome of man's instinctive urge to cover himself; a device evolved to cover certain parts of the body under the instinctive demands of shame as much as to protect one's body against the exigencies of weather. In its simplest form, dress should fulfil these two basic human needs and be easy to wear and cover. Due, however, to the difference in weather conditions, the style and shape of dress has varied from place to place. In places where the climate is hot, the dress may be light and cover fewer parts of the body, and where the climate is cold, it may be heavy and spread over a larger portion of the body.

According to our knowledge of the earliest humans and their society, we have come to the same conclusion. When dress was meant only to meet basic human needs and the simple requirements of nature, there was little variety in its form. Any noticeable differences were due mainly to variation in climatic conditions. Slowly and gradually, however, as human beings progressed intellectually and moved forward on the road of civilization, industries developed and fresh resources were discovered as human tastes became more mature and their initial needs expanded and became diversified. Future trends in dress were influenced by innumerable factors, and it was then that a

---

* The article was originally contributed by the author in 1929 for the monthly *Ma'ārif* of A'zamgarh (India). It was subsequently published in *Tarjumān al-Qur'ān* of January 1940. It was written at a time when the rulers of certain Muslim countries were busy forcing their people to change their traditional dress pattern on the assumption of elevating them through the western dress style from a state of ignorance and backwardness to that of enlightenment and progress – Editor.

variety of changes emerged in its original shape and form according to differences in taste and the environments of different communities.

It may not be possible for me here to discuss in depth every factor, large and small, which has been instrumental in determining the sartorial habits of humankind and the growth and development of various dress designs among different communities and nations. The community life of nations, as well as the personal life of individuals, become influenced during the course of millennia by so many external and internal factors which are difficult to record. Some of these are so subtle they may even escape detection. Leaving aside minor details, if we try to pinpoint only the major factors which have generally been responsible to determine the fashioning of dress and the sartorial habits of different communities, we can sum them up under the following eight broad categories:

i. Geographic conditions that make inhabitants of a certain country or region adopt a particular form of dress and lifestyle;
ii. ethical and religious teachings, which lead to different forms of dress for men and women in various communities;
iii. aesthetic tastes that naturally grow and develop differently among different peoples under their specific conditions;
iv. a community's lifestyle evolved according to its peculiar cultural, economic, intellectual, and moral conditions;
v. a community's economic status, which includes its source of income, vocations, arts and crafts and level of affluence or poverty;
vi. standards of decency and decorum peculiar to every people that lead to shaping their national dress;
vii. national values and traditions, according to which one generation inherits a particular lifestyle and fashion from its elders and leaves it behind for posterity with minor changes from time to time; and
viii. external factors, which cast their impact on the thoughts, ideas, and lifestyle of a community as a result of its

interaction with other communities. How far a community becomes influenced by others depends largely, however, on its political, intellectual and moral circumstances.

These eight major factors govern not only the dress code of a community, but also the entire spectrum of its social existence. Through the interplay of these factors emerges the style of its dress. In light of this broad overview, when we look at the issue of national dress, we arrive at the following conclusion:

1. Dress is not just a means to cover the body and protect it externally. It is also deeply rooted in a nation's psyche, civilization and culture, values, traditions and social milieu. It is, in fact, a manifestation and means to demonstrate the spirit that runs like life blood through a nation's corporeal frame. The dress of a nation is actually the medium through which it expresses its nationhood and introduces to the world its distinct personality.
2. Every factor behind sartorial habits, other than geographic, changes imperceptibly in every community. There is nothing static and constant about dress, it is naturally variable and vibrant. This phenomenon of change and evolution slowly and gradually casts its spell not just on dress but on all walks of life. When arts and sciences spread in a community, enlightenment grows, advancements are made in fields of business, commerce and industry. Economically the people become affluent, their interaction grows with others and the community draws lessons of different kinds from such interactions. Then there is naturally and automatically an evolutionary upsurge in a particular community's social existence and a corresponding change in its emotional behaviour, improvement in taste and temperament and refinement in lifestyle. New ways and means are adopted to meet new requirements, and respect for national values and traditions manifests itself in a more refined manner. As in other fields of national life, there is gradual improvement

> in the style, quality and decency of national dress. During this entire process of evolution, no need is felt to introduce a resolution in the national legislature for prescribing a particular form of dress for the community, or introducing it at one go. It is through the interplay of various social factors that improvements automatically emerge in old types of dress and designs and fresh forms and fashions gradually evolve according to a particular community's taste, temperament and collective vision.

This is the natural way for a national dress to take shape, for its modification, growth and development. Conversely, the unnatural way is to painstakingly and artificially introduce change in a nation's dress code by imposing a fashion and style imported from another community or nation. There is a great difference between these two phenomena. The natural process of change through evolution is like that of a tree's growth. The more it grows, the more normal is the process of its development, with its entire contours, leaves and foliage, fruit and flowers benefitting from this process. The tree's 'self' thus remains intact. If it is a tamarind tree it will be the same up to the last phase of its growth, and if it is a mango tree it will remain so throughout the entire process of its growth and development. It will gather all that it needs for its development from the soil, air, water, sunshine and rain, without losing its intrinsic goodness. On the contrary, forced change is like transplanting the bark and branches of a mango tree on a sapling that was originally meant to be tamarind tree, making it difficult for anybody to differentiate whether it is a tamarind or mango tree. No positive and meaningful change is possible, in fact, through such artificial and unnatural transplantations. Actually, such forcible transplants impede the natural process of evolution and growth. Those who lack insight into social issues and look at matters governing daily life superficially think with child-like simplicity that a nation can actually change by changing the external features of its dress and lifestyle.

Arguments generally advanced in favour of a state imposing a dress code on a nation are that a backward community can change mentally and its stagnation may give way to dynamism. It is generally presumed that weaknesses and flaws of the period of decline and backwardness may vanish into thin air the moment an old style of dress peculiar to that period is banned and replaced by a new style of dress, specially one borrowed from the West. According to a general misconception, by discarding centuries' old styles of dress and putting on the modern garb of Western origin one automatically becomes more decent, dynamic and cultured; like those from whom one has borrowed this new style. It is presumed that a person thus rises in the esteem of the developed nations and none can label him backward and regressive. These and similar other arguments are advanced to support the latest move by the rulers of certain Muslim countries.

We need to take up the matter in greater detail to help remove these deep-rooted misconceptions. Let us dispassionately sum up the case in light of the views expressed so far:

- As already established, the styles of dress and design are in themselves nothing but the outcome of the interplay of various physical and social factors. To agree to this fact would also mean to accept that the popularity of a particular style of dress among certain people is a natural phenomenon and to force them to adopt different dress styles which may not have evolved through the interplay of physical and social factors is contrary to this natural process.
- The dress of a nation is closely related to its lifestyle, and its lifestyle is interconnected with its civilization and culture. This interconnection remains intact during the natural process of change of dress and lifestyle, because life, with all its diverse facets, is in motion as a whole. Conversely, however, if dress and lifestyle are arbitrarily changed through unnatural means, the entire social structure is disturbed because other facets of life are not in harmony with that change.
- For dress to be sophisticated, beautiful and conforming to latest trends depends on how far a community is advanced,

cultured, enlightened and dynamic as a whole. The more it advances on the road of progress, the more refinement may take place in its dress styles in the same proportion. The internal dynamics of its social psyche will automatically continue to amend, improve and discard old trends and adopt and devise fresh styles better suited to its changed environment and needs. To leave this natural process and switch over from one dress to another in one go is like attempting a high jump from one state of affairs to another. Such freak actions produce no real change in community life.

- Attempts to raise standards of dress and lifestyle before improving a community's socio-economic conditions are just like an attempt to unnaturally recondition a boy, still in his adolescence, in order to let him achieve adulthood, by keeping him in an explosive environment and administering him hot and spicy food and potent drugs. On the analogy of the great disruption that is bound to take place in the poor child's physical, mental, and emotional state of health due to a transformation of such an extraordinary nature, one can very well imagine the extent of disruption and deterioration likely to occur in a nation's social, intellectual and moral health due to attempts to forcefully make it 'cultured and refined'.
- To superimpose on a nation a fashion and lifestyle which are beyond its economic capacity is tantamount to practically destroying it economically. How disastrous it would be for a nation, not able even to afford the basic amenities of life, to be moved to ape the more affluent nations not just in the sphere of dress and design, but in all walks of life?
- Dress, language and script are the three prime factors that establish a nation's identity and individuality. If these sheet-anchors of a community's existence are dismantled, it slowly and gradually loses its distinct identity and eventually gets absorbed into the nations it has sought to

follow. Ancient communities, whom we describe today as extinct races, gradually went into oblivion due to this. The meaning of their becoming extinct is not that each and every member of a particular community expired, leaving no generation behind, but that they became irrelevant because they lost their distinct individuality and identity as a nation. They themselves were guilty of demolishing the sheet-anchors of their nationhood or letting them be demolished. Individual members of their society went on adopting other nations' dress, language, script, manners and morals. With their nationhood getting weaker and weaker, they eventually became dead and nobody cared to remember what they stood for and how they looked like. The same fate awaits the nations who have willingly accepted as means of progress the imprudent policies of their self-seeking rulers.

- To adopt another nation's dress and lifestyle is in fact the result and declaration of a nation's inferiority complex. A nation thus declares that in its own estimation it is so backward and inferior that it has nothing to be proud of. Nor could its ancestors leave behind for posterity anything that it might have preserved without a sense of shame. Its national ego is so low and lacks even the level of creativity essential to evolve a better living for itself. It borrows from others to pass on as civilized. In a way, such people unabashedly declare that what is known as culture, civilization, sophistication and beauty is found only in the lives of other nations, who are to them the real touchstone of everything worthwhile in life. As for them, the hundreds and thousands of years that they have lived, they have actually lived like animals and not as a civilized nation. Obviously, no nation with even a grain of self-respect would ever tolerate becoming a manifestation of its own disgrace and indignity. History is a witness to the fact, as also the recent events of the contemporary world, that a nation tolerates ignominy and humiliation only (i) when it loses its morale and abjectly surrenders after suffering defeat after defeat at the hands of other nations, or (ii) when it has no lofty traditions, no distinct culture and civilization and no worthwhile creative faculties left intact to survive independently in the comity of nations.

- Should a nation borrow from another anything which is really worth taking, it is the output of its scientific research, the fruit of its creative and innovative capabilities and the means through which it has won laurels in the comity of nations. Useful lessons, if any, must also be taken from a nation's history, organizations, manners and morals. Factors responsible for its progress and success ought to be carefully examined and analyzed and whatever found useful and effective adapted. Such achievements are the common legacy of mankind and to disregard them and refuse to benefit from them due to narrow national bias is actually an act of ignorance. Can anybody with even a little common sense imagine for a moment that the progress made by Europe is due entirely to its outfit of jackets, jeans, neck-ties, hats and boots, etc.? Or because of its womenfolk adorning themselves with beauty-aids and cosmetics? If that is not so, and definitely it is not, then why do the so-called champions of progress and reform leave aside the phenomenon of Europe's centuries old ceaseless struggle for material and technological advancement and go all out for extremely superficial things as already discussed?

It is firmly established now by the facts stated above that to adopt a certain dress and lifestyle does not make a nation great. It is, in fact, unnatural and unreasonable to even think of giving up the lifestyle popular in one's own community in favour of an alien style of living. Such notions emerge only under abnormal conditions, the way we find some women eating less or excessively during pregnancy, or a squint-eyed person looking differently.

8.1. The Shariah perspective

Thus far, the matter concerning dress code was discussed from a purely social perspective. Now, let us examine it from the Shariah point of view.

Islam is *dīn al-fitrah*, or the natural way of life of humankind. In everything it adopts, that way corresponds exactly to common sense and the dictates of reason and sanity. Once a person removes from his eyes the tinted glasses of his personal biases, likes and dislikes, and starts looking at things with a clear vision and in their natural and real perspectives, then what he observes is exactly the same as viewed by Islam. Islam prescribes no particular form of dress or uniform for human beings. It approves, with certain conditions, any type of dress and style of living which may develop among peoples through civilization's natural processes. It lays down certain principles from a purely ethical and social standpoint and would like every Muslim community to observe these in its national dress code and lifestyle.

Let us now have a brief overview of the principles and guidelines that the Shariah lays down for the dress code of its followers:

i. The first basic principle enjoined by the Shariah to promote the element of decency in sartorial habits of the Muslims is observance of the parameters of *satr*, which is the ethical side of the Islamic dress code. According to this principle, it is imperative for every Muslim man, native of any country and member of any nation, that he must cover his body from navel to his knees, and for a Muslim woman to keep her entire body covered, except her face, hands and feet.[1] If a nation's style of dress falls short of fulfilling the requirement

[1] These are the essentials of *satr* for women's dress. The requirements of her hijab are slightly more. For a Muslim woman *satr* includes those parts of the body which must compulsorily be kept covered to everyone including her father and son, except her husband. Hijab is over and above *satr*, which disallows her free mixing with men other than her close relatives. The Islamic code of dress and decency does not permit society to make its females a 'showpiece' for others. It forbids Muslim women from moving out of their family limits, freely showing off their fineries and fashion to all and sundry. This is what is meant by hijab – Editor.

of *satr*, Islam would seek its followers to improve it according to the laid down parameters. Once this is done, any make or shape of dress would become lawful.

ii. The second hallmark of the Islamic dress code is its simplicity, sobriety, and aesthetic value. Wearing clothes made of silk is forbidden for men. Men have also been forbidden to wear jewellery of gold or silver (with the exception of silver rings). Both men and women have been asked to avoid wearing a dress that is pompous, luxurious and exudes pride and extravagance. Overflowing robes[2] that trail behind as a mark of vanity and arrogance have been strongly condemned by Islam. Islam does not approve of a dress worn as a mark of pride or to show off to impress on others one's affluence or status. Similarly, Islam does not like gorgeous clothes that reflect the personal ego and luxurious lifestyle of those wearing them.

iii. The third aspect of the Islamic dress code is that it must be free from the signs of polytheism and idol worship peculiar to some religious groups or sects. For example, it must not carry the sign of the cross or a religious symbol.

iv. In addition to these ethical and cultural reforms that Islam introduced in the dress code of the Age of Ignorance, the Muslims are also advised to wear dress that may distinguish them from non-Muslims. Their dress should be the hallmark of their identity as a distinct community. Islam has, however, prescribed no particular sign or symbol for this purpose and has left it to the popularly accepted norms and traditions of the Muslim society. At the outset of the Islamic Movement in Arabia, the Prophet (peace be upon him)

[2] The most prominent example of such dress is that worn by kings, the Pope, priests, the judges of superior courts and brides in the West. These robes drag along the ground, with their trails held in the hands of an equally pompously clad train of men or women. This is the dress of vanity about which the Prophet (peace be upon him) said: 'He who drags along his dress as a mark of arrogance Allah will not even look at him on the Day of Judgment' – Author.

and other Muslims used to wear clothes which were the conventional dress of Arabs as a community. He had, then, recommended to Muslims to wear an *'imāmah* (turban) in order to distinguish them from the pagans of Arabia.[3] The use of turbans over caps thus gradually became a mark of distinction for Muslims. This was initially considered necessary to distinguish Muslim Arabs from their non-Muslim compatriots. But when all of Arabia became Muslim, this mark of identification was no more needed as the Arab dress became the Islamic dress and there remained no infidel to distinguish from the Arab Muslim. Similarly, when Islam started spreading to Iran and other countries, the need was initially felt that the new Muslims should either wear Arab dress or put on a turban or a gown of a certain type over their native dress to differentiate themselves from their non-Muslim compatriots and as a mark of solidarity with the fledgling Muslim community. When, however, the majority of the population became Muslim and the above-mentioned ethical and cultural reforms were introduced in the local dress code, the native dress itself became Islamic. In the contemporary world today the national dress of countries with majority Muslim populations is Islamic in spite of the diversity of its make and style. As for the countries with a mix of Muslim and non-Muslim population, every dress that makes a Muslim distinct from a non-Muslim is Islamic. For the countries where non-Muslims are in the majority, it is understandable that anyone embracing Islam should make himself distinct from the majority population by

[3] According to a Tradition, narrated by Imam Tirmidhī, Abū Dāwūd and *mustadrak*, the Prophet (peace be upon him) said: 'Turbans over caps are a mark of distinction between us and the Infidels'. This, however, does not mean that it is part of the permanent code of Islamic dress for Muslims all over the world. As evident from the historic background of the Tradition, the Prophet had prescribed this to impress upon the Muslims the need to always retain their social identity in a non-Muslim environment – Author.

adding some sign to his outfit that may be well known there as a symbol of Islamic identity.

8.2. The phenomenon of copying others

As for the problem of imitation, we ought to know how Islam tackles this phenomenon. The trend to imitate and copy others generally manifests itself in the following four forms:

i. **Imitation among sexes**: The phenomenon of men imitating women and vice-versa is a deviation from the natural course. This reflects a confused frame of mind. It has, therefore, been condemned in strong terms by Islam. The Messenger of Allah (peace be upon him) strongly discouraged such trends: The men who put on female costume and women who adorn male attire are accursed.[4] No sane person with a healthy mind-set can approve of such a craze. It is naturally repulsive for any civilized society to have within its fold effeminate males or men-like females.

[4] The Hadith narrated by Abū Hurayrah and reported by Imam Shawkānī in his *Nayl al-Awṭār* says:

> إنَّ النَّبِيَّ صَلَّى اللهُ عَلَيهِ وَآلِهِ وَ سَلَّم لَعَنَ الرَّجُلَ يَلبَسُ لِبسَ المَرأةِ وَالمَرأةِ تَلبَسُ لِبسَ الرَّجُلِ.
>
> 'The Prophet, (Allah's peace and blessings be upon him and his family) has condemned the man who puts on woman's dress and the woman who adorns man's attire.' Imam Bukhārī also narrated a similar Hadith by 'Abd Allah ibn 'Umar.

The Islamic social order disapproves everything that tends to damage the inner self of a person or his/her external appearance. It therefore does not approve the modern day craze for unisex dress as well. The dress is a candid expression of one's personality. It speaks before one opens one's lips. It is a medium through which is conveyed one's likes and dislikes, taste and distaste, personal traits of decency, modesty, elegance or lack of these. Hence, the popular Arabic adage: النَّاسُ بِا لِّلبَاس (*The man is known by the dress he wears*). Men and women have distinct identities not just physically but also intellectually and spiritually. Even common sense, therefore, demands that the dress requirements of each should differ from the other – Editor.

ii. **Copying other communities**: It is similarly against human nature and common sense that a community or nation as a whole should adopt the lifestyle of another community or nation. Islam, therefore, does not approve of this as well. That is why during the golden days of the Rightly-Guided Caliphs the natives of conquered territories were compelled neither to unnecessarily copy the Arab dress code nor to give up their own. This helped, on the one hand, in the preservation of the distinct Muslim identity, and on the other facilitated the natives to retain theirs and also reflected the true Islamic spirit of assimilation and internationalism.

iii. **Individual cases of imitation**: At the individual level, when some members of a community adopt the lifestyle of another community it actually reflects a lack of their own self-confidence. The act of imitation is a sign of an inferiority complex. From a civilizational point of view, those who follow the pattern of imitating others eventually lose their identity. They belong neither to this community nor to that: مُّذَبْذَبِينَ بَيْنَ ذَٰلِكَ لَآ إِلَىٰ هَـٰٓؤُلَآءِ وَلَآ إِلَىٰ هَـٰٓؤُلَآءِ ۚ (*They dangle between the one and the other and belong fully neither to these nor to those*).[5] It was because of this that Hadrat 'Umer and Hadrat 'Ali (may Allah be pleased with them), strongly rebuked and rebuffed those Arabs who, while living in foreign countries, became influenced by the glamour of the Roman and Persian civilizations and adopted their styles of dress.

iv. **Imitating unbelievers**: For a Muslim to follow a particular lifestyle of non-Muslims is something extremely harmful for the cause of Islamic solidarity. This leads to the concerned person's alienation from the rest of the population and prevents a flourishing of the spirit of cooperation and support that Islam seeks to promote in a Muslim society. This is also harmful from a social point of view, because such persons

---

[5] *al-Nisā'* 4: 143.

may be mistaken as non-Muslims. *Sayyidunā* Rasūl Allah (peace be upon him) has, therefore, repeatedly exhorted the Muslims not to imitate others: خَالِفُوا اليَهودَ وَالنَّصَارىٰ وَخَالِفُوا المَجُوس (*'Remain different and distinct from the Jews and Christians, and also from Fire-Worshippers'*). There is yet another famous Hadith in this context: مَن تَشَبَّهَ بِقَومٍ فَهُوَ مِنهُم ('He who imitates other people, is one of them').[6] This obviously means that those trying to copy others, who are different from them in religion and culture, deserve to be treated as being one of those whom they are copying.

[6] *Sunan Abū Dāwūd*, No. 632, Book on Dress.

9 The Concept of Crime and Punishment in Islam*

[Islam remains a source of strength for humanity in spite of Muslims being subdued since the last two centuries or so of their political and economic decline. Hostile forces from the West and their local protégés have left no stone unturned in their denigration of Islam and its benign teachings on one pretext or the other. Unwarranted controversies and misgivings were specially raised against the Shariah laws. Sayyid Mawdūdī contributed this article way back in 1939 to enlighten us on the very important subject of Islam's legal system. This brief but forceful esssay helps, on the one hand, in removing the cobwebs woven round the most-misunderstood Islamic penal law of *ḥudūd* and, on the other, in giving us an insight into the Islamic concept of crime and punishment – Editor.]

There are certain aspects which need to be kept in mind while discussing Islam's penal laws. Let me briefly discuss the subject from a wider perspective.

In context of the penal laws of Islam, it must be kept in mind that the order to amputate the hand and execute other *ḥudūd* laws can only be enforced in a state where the administration is run according to the Islamic Shariah and the society is organized on the pattern recommended by Islam. The fundamentals of Islam and its legal code are an integral whole. There can be no pick and choose among them and the Shariah needs to be introduced in totality and not selectively.

Let us consider, for example, the *ḥudūd* laws concerning *zinā* (fornication) and *qadhaf* (defamation). Being integral to the Islamic

* *Tarjumān al-Qur'ān*, March 1939.

laws and injunctions regarding marriage, divorce, hijab, and unlawful sex relations, the *ḥudūd* laws cannot be taken in isolation. Allah *subḥānahū wa taʿālā* has ordained severe punishments for those found guilty of fornication and defamation in a society where men are morally groomed and women maintain Islamic manners and a decent lifestyle. In such a society there is no place for harlots and sex shops, no room for pornography and sexploitative material. This is a society where it is easier to marry and hard to flirt, and justice is available to every citizen and the state has made easier the enforcement of the laws concerning marriage, divorce, *khulʿ* (divorce at the insistence of the wife), separation and reunification. It is inherent in the very nature of such a society to sincerely try to impose severe punishments for preserving and safeguarding the just and the well-balanced social order that it has established.

The *ḥudūd* punishments, though apparently harsh, fulfil the demands of justice, especially when it is easier to satisfy sexual needs through lawful means and the society is purged of all the undesirable means of moral depravity and debauchery. In such a sublime social atmosphere, those who venture to commit sex crimes are extremely perverse and hence deserve to be awarded exemplary punishments to save the society and its individual members from the adverse fallout of their mischief. Conversely, where the situation is just the opposite, where men and women are free to mix, where schools, offices, clubs and public parks provide venues for the fully made-up dandies and damsels to interact freely, where sexploitation abounds and moral standards are on the decline, in such a social environment it would in itself be a great injustice to introduce *ḥudūd* laws for *zinā* and *qadhaf*. This is because the whole atmosphere of such a perverse society is conducive only for perversities and moral and sexual corruption. It is difficult even for a morally normal and temperamentally balanced person there to save himself from sex-related offences, including fornication and adultery. If a person commits an offence in such a society, you cannot say that he is a criminal of an abnormal nature. Punishments of lashes and stoning to death have not been prescribed by the Almighty for a dirty social set-up where criminals are in command.

The punishment prescribed for burglary and theft may also be taken on the same analogy. The law is applicable in a society where the economic precepts and Shariah laws of Islam are fully in force. The *ḥadd* punishment of severing the hand from the wrist and the Islamic economic discipline are so interlinked with each other that they cannot be handled in isolation. The society where the Islamic economic discipline is in action, there the enforcement of the Shariah *ḥadd* for theft and burglary (*sariqah*) is very much in accordance with the demands of justice and social security. But where there is no such discipline in force, the implementation of the law would in fact be a double offence. The *ḥadd* for *sariqah* is not meant for a society where interest or usury and all forms of *ribā* are in practice and the mandatory system of zakat is out of fashion. How can the *ḥadd* be enforced in a social set-up where money can purchase even justice; the basic necessities of life are out of the common man's reach due to inflation and heavy taxation; where the nation's wealth is squandered to provide affluent classes with luxuries and make them more prosperous? In such an environment, even the imprisonment of a thief may be a bit too hard a punishment.

The difficulty generally faced by people in understanding the criminal laws of Islam is mainly due to the mistake they commonly make when they keep in mind the corrupt system prevalent in contemporary societies of the 'civilized' world. They try then to compare the *ḥudūd* laws with the commonplace crimes rampant in those societies, such as theft, rape, fornication, defamation, alcoholism, etc. Islamic punishments are, therefore, bound to appear to such people as harsh and horrible, because in their subconscious they feel that in the society where they live theft is a normal occurrence and fornication and adultery are something their men, women, young and old cannot escape. Unfortunately, today we live in a social environment where there is nothing extraordinary in the news of spicy scandals of unmarried couples, and nothing alarming in the incidence of the younger generation growing up in bad company and committing crimes ignored by their elders. That is why modern man is generally apprehensive that the penal laws of Islam under the prevalent conditions would perhaps spare none from getting lashed, and thousands of hands might be chopped off every day, and hundreds of men and women would be stoned to death on a daily basis.

These apprehensions are definitely not misplaced. We too are of the same view that there can be nothing crueller today than retaining the decadent system of a decadent society and then trying to introduce only the criminal laws out of Islam's comprehensive and broad-based legal framework that covers each and every aspect of our social existence. The mistake, which these people do not seem to realize, however, is that they take this unjust, exploitative and oppressive social order of theirs, which unfortunately they have become used to, as something normal and natural. The fact is that the prevailing situation is not at all normal. The devil's disciples have in fact thrust this unnatural state of affairs on human society and the longer it remains the worst would be the future scenario. The social order of Islam, being holistic, has to be accepted in its totality if we are sincere in changing the present day's abnormal situation. It would become evident then to us that fornication, defamation, burglary, and alcoholism are no normal pastimes for a self-respecting human being, nor are the people in general expected to get involved in such heinous activities. The social environment that Islam seeks to create does not leave the field open for criminals, and for the very small number of exceptionally wicked people alone that commit such evil acts, and their cure lies only in the exemplary punishments of *ḥudūd* laws.

The second thing to be kept in view regarding the Islamic concept of crime and punishment is the glorious aspect of sagacity and moderation of the Shariah law code. Without an awareness of these characteristics the Islamic injunctions concerning *ḥudūd* and penal laws cannot be understood in their proper perspective. The penal laws of Islam go all-out, on the one hand, to uproot the causes and factors responsible for crimes and then to eliminate them in a manner that no one is able to adopt a criminal means for satisfying his natural desires and needs. On the other hand, severe punishments are awarded to prevent a criminal from repeating the crime while serving as deterrent to discourage others and help them check their criminal tendencies. The Islamic penal code aims at saving the people, as far as possible, from the ultimate punishment of *ḥadd*.

The guiding principle of the philosophy of crime and punishment in Islam is to create an environment for a crime-free society. For this a foolproof system of investigation and examination of witnesses has been laid down. A certain period is fixed for investigation before carrying out *ḥadd* to facilitate thorough examination of witnesses and allow the suspect the advantage of any lacuna so discovered. The task before the judges is not to liberally award the ultimate punishment, but to keep every aspect in view before pronouncing a verdict. This is based on the guidelines provided by *Sayyidunā* Rasūl Allah (peace be upon him) himself in the following Hadith:[1]

اِدرَؤُا الحُدُودَ مَااستَطَعتُم فَاِنَّ الاِمَامَ اَن يُخطِيَ فِى العَفوِ خَيرٌ اَن يُخطِئَى فِى العُقُوبة.

> Avert *ḥudūd* as far as possible, because it is better for the judge to make a mistake in pardoning a suspect than in issuing verdict. (*Jāmi' Al-Tirmidhī*, Book on *Ḥudūd Laws*)

On the other hand, once the crime goes through the legal process and is proved, there is no laxity for the culprit or room for violating the boundaries fixed by the Law-Giver. The criminal when convicted loses all chances of a pardon. Not even the head of the Islamic state or government can offer him reprieve. The Shariah allows him no benefit of his social status, family background, etc. The Qur'an says:

... وَلَا تَأۡخُذۡكُم بِهِمَا رَأۡفَةٞ فِي دِينِ ٱللَّهِ إِن كُنتُمۡ تُؤۡمِنُونَ بِٱللَّهِ وَٱلۡيَوۡمِ ٱلۡأٓخِرِۖ ... ﴿٢﴾

---

[1] There is another famous Hadith which Abū Dāwūd narrated in his *Sunan* under the chapter بَابُ العَفوِ عَنِ الحُدُود مَا لَم تَبلُغِ السُّلطَانَ (Exemption from *ḥudūd* so long as the matter remains unreported to authorities):

عَن عَبدِ الله بِن عَمرو بِن العَاص اَنَّ رَسُولَ الله صَلَّى الله عَلَيه وَسَلَّم قَال: تَعَافَوُا الحُدُودَ بَينَكُم فَمَا بَلَغَنِي مِن حَدٍّ فَقَد وَجَبَ.

> Abd Allah ibn 'Amr ibn al-'Ās narrated that Rasūl Allah (peace be upon him) said: "Let *Ḥudūd* punishments be in abeyance among you, for when reported to me it would become effective." (No. 971) – Editor.

> *And let not tenderness for them deter you from what pertains to Allah's religion, if you do truly believe in Allah and the Last Day.*
>
> [*al-Nūr* 24: 2]

According to the famous incident, narrated in a hadith, a woman named Fātimah from Quraysh's sub-tribe, Banū Makhzūm, used to borrow ornaments and food items from different households and when approached for their return deny ever having taken them. Her case was submitted to the court of *Sayyidunā* Rasūl Allah (peace be upon him) and the crime was proved. The elders from Quraysh were disturbed lest the *ḥadd* for *sariqah* be enforced. Nobody dared to approach the Prophet (peace be upon him) for condoning the punishment. Finally, her tribesmen convinced Usāmah, whom the Prophet greatly loved as the son of his freed slave and respected Companion Zayd, to intercede in her favour. When Usāmah pleaded her case on behalf of the powerful tribe of Quraysh – incidentally the tribe of the Prophet himself – *Sayyidunā* Rasūl Allah (Allal's peace and blessings be upon him) was so angry that his face turned red. Usāmah, trembling with fear, sought his forgiveness. The Prophet then asked the people to assemble and delivered the following historic statement, preserved in books of ahadith:[2]

---

[2] The famous incident of how much *Sayyidnā* Rasūl Allah (peace be upon him) disliked intercession from any quarter in legal matters was reported by Imam Tirmidhī as follows:

> عَن عُروه، عَن عَا ئشه اَنَّ قُرَيشاً اَهمَّ هُم شَأنُ المَرءَةِ المَخزُومِيّهِ اَلَّتِى سَرَقَت. فَقَالُوا: مَن يُكَلِّمُ فِيهَا رَسُولَ اللهِ صَلَّى اللهُ عَلَيهِ وَسَلَّم؟ فَقَالُوا مَن يَجتَرِئُ إِلَيهِ اِلَّاأُسَامَه بِن زَيدٍ، حُبُّ رَسُولِ اللهِ صَلَّى صَلَّى اللهُ عَلَيهِ وَسَلَّم. فَقَالَ رَسُولِ اللهِ صَلَّى اللهُ عَلَيهِ وَسَلَّم: اَتَشفَع فِى حَدٍّ مِن حُدُود اَللهِ؟ ثُمَّ قَامَ فَاختطَبَ فقَالَ: اِنَّمَا اَهلَكَ الَّذِينَ مِن قَبلِكُم اَنّهُم كَانُوا اِذَا سَرَقَ فِيهِم الضَعِيفُ اَقَامُوا عَلَيهِ الحَدَّ، وَاَيمُ الله لَواَنَّ فَا طِمة بِنتَ مُحَّمدٍ سَرَقَت لَقَطَعتُ يَدَهَا.
>
> 'Urwah narrated from [his aunt] *Sayyidah* 'Ā'ishah that the Quraysh were disturbed about the woman from Makhzūm tribe who was guilty of theft. So they said: 'Who will speak about her to the Messenger of Allah?' They thought that nobody else other than Usāmah ibn Zayd can do that as he was very dear to Rasūl Allah (peace be upon him).

> The communities that perished before you were guilty of a similar offence. When a respected person from among them committed any crime they let him go scot-free and when a crime was committed by someone of lower status he was punished. As far as I am concerned, I swear by the Lord, Who holds sway over my life, that even if Fatimah, daughter of Muhammad, was found guilty of theft I would have chopped off her hand.

After having taken note of these two basic aspects of the Islamic penal code, it is equally important for us not to lose sight of the very spirit, which is the life-blood of the Shariah laws. The Islamic concept of crime and punishment is benevolent and not malevolent. No death penalty is awarded out of anger or frenzy. There is no aspect of enmity either and the governing element behind punishment is to 'cleanse' and 'purify'. The convict is punished to cleanse his self and soul from the impurity which he contracts by committing a crime. He is allowed through conviction to escape punishment on the Day of Reckoning. Islam also instils in the convict the faith that Allah *subḥānahū wa ta'ālā* is the Supreme Judge from Whom he can hide nothing, and the actual court is the accountability Court of the Day of Judgment that everyone has to invariably face. He knows that the punishment awarded there would be the most disgraceful and if he succeeds in hiding his crime in this world, he would definitely face the Superior Court of the Lord, where he would stand helpless with the dossier of his crime in his hand. Conversely, if he gets his case settled in the law court of this world, the punishment awarded to him would purify him

---

Usāmah thus spoke to him. The Messenger of Allah questioned him [with anger]: 'Do you intercede regarding a punishment from the legal punishments enjoined by Allah?' Then he rose and addressed the people saying: 'Those before you were destroyed because they used to spare someone from among the elite if he committed [crimes like] theft, and punished the weak if he committed a similar crime. I swear by Allah *subḥānahū wa ta'ālā* that even if Fatimah, daughter of Muhammad, was found guilty of theft, I would chop off her hand.' (*Jāmi' Al-Tirmidhī*, No. 1430, chapter on *strong dislike for intercession in legal punishments*) – Editor.

and he would meet the Lord as if he committed no crime.[3] The same subject has been discussed thus in a Tradition, narrated by Imam Bukhārī:

إِنَّ مَنْ اَصَابَ مِنْ هٰذِهِ الْمَعَاصِى شَيئاً فَعُوقِبَ به فِي الدُّنيَا فَهُوَ كَفَّارَةٌ لهُ وَمَنْ اَصَابَ مِنهَا شَيئاً فَسَتَرَهُ الله فَهُوَ اِلَى الله اِن شَاءَ عَفَاعَنهُ وَاِن شَآءَعَاقَبَهُ

> If someone is guilty of any sinful act and is punished in this world, his punishment would be a reparation for his sin. If, however, Allah lets his sin be concealed here, it is, then, entirely up to His Grace. He may pardon him if He so wills, or punish him if it so pleases Him.[4]

It is a blessing of the revolutionary concept of crime and punishment in Islam that the believer has been fortified by a remarkable sense of moral responsibility. Let us recall in this context a few glorious examples from our history. One may see in them extraordinary glimpses of the Islamic system of justice, nobility of character and the revolutionary spirit that raised man to an extraordinary level as a moral being.

Once, a person named 'Amr ibn Samrah came to the Prophet (peace be upon him) and said: 'O Prophet of God, I stole the camel of such and such tribe. Please purify me.' The Prophet dispatched an official to that tribe to enquire into the matter. When it was confirmed that the crime had actually been committed, his hand was chopped off. With a sense of relief 'Amr then said: 'Thanks to Allah Who purified me.' He then addressed his severed hand: 'You wanted me to go to Hell but Allah *subḥānahū wa ta'ālā* has saved me.'

---

[3] It may be pertinent to note that a person who on his own offers himself to the dictates of justice, that very act speaks of his sense of guilt and remorse. Such a person thus gets purified of his sin once the punishment has been carried out. He is then no more a criminal, neither in this world nor in the Hereafter. On the other hand, a culprit who did not offer himself to the law and was caught and brought to face justice, the Prophet (peace be upon him) used to exhort him for penitence after the execution of his punishment – Author.

[4] *Al-Jāmi' Al-Ṣaḥīḥ*, No. 17, the Book of Faith.

The famous incident of the woman from Banū Makhzūm was partially reported earlier. When the Prophet pronounced judgment, her tribesmen requested: 'O Prophet of God, we are ready to pay ransom. Please set her free.' The Prophet ordered the punishment to be executed. On this, they pleaded further: 'O Prophet of God, we can pay five hundred dinars for her hand.' The Prophet firmly declared: 'Let her hand be chopped off.' After the punishment was carried out, the woman came to the Prophet (peace be upon him) and asked: 'O Prophet of God, is there a way that I may be spared before God?' The Prophet replied: 'Yes! You are now as free of your sin as the day when you were born of your mother.'

There is yet another famous incident of Mā'iz Aslamī, who submitted to the Prophet: 'O Prophet of God, I have committed adultery. Please purify me.' The Prophet turned his face away and told him to go and seek forgiveness of the Lord. Mā'iz then came in front of him and repeated his plea. The Prophet again turned his face the other way and repeated his statement. When Mā'iz admitted of his crime four times in this manner, the Prophet finally asked him: 'Are you insane?' He replied: 'No.' The Prophet, then, asked: 'Are you drunk?' Mā'iz said: 'No.' He was then asked: 'Are you married.' His reply was in the affirmative. On this, the Prophet (peace be upon him) enquired: 'Perhaps you only hugged and kissed?' He said: 'No.' The Prophet's next question was: 'Did you go to bed with her?' Mā'iz said: 'Yes.' 'Were you actually guilty of sexual intercourse?' was the next query and the reply was in the affirmative. On this, the Prophet repeated his questions a number of times by rephrasing it differently to reaffirm that Mā'iz had actually committed adultery for which the punishment was so severe. He then asked if he knew what adultery was, to which Mā'iz replied: 'Yes! I have committed an illegal act that a husband does lawfully.' Finally, the Prophet asked him: 'What do you want from all that you have stated?' Mā'iz replied: 'I want to be cleansed.' On this the Prophet (peace be upon him) proclaimed his verdict and Mā'iz was sentenced to *rajm* (stoning to death), the ultimate *ḥadd* punishment for adultery. Two or three days later, the Prophet declared in the assembly of Companions: 'Pray for Mā'iz ibn al-Malik. The penance done by him for his sin was such that if spread over the entire community it would suffice to forgive them all.'

There is yet another extraordinary case of Ghāmediyāh – the woman from the Ghāmedī tribe. She visited the Prophet to admit her crime and seek purification. She said she had committed the sin of adultery. The Prophet (peace be upon him) asked her to go home and seek Allah's forgiveness. She replied: 'You want me like Mā'iz to go away. Let me, however, tell you that I am pregnant due to this sinful act.' The Prophet replied: 'Then, go and wait till the birth of the baby.' Strongly impelled by her sense of penance, like Mā'iz Aslamī, the woman from the Ghāmedī tribe came again to *Sayyidunā* Rasūl Allah (peace be upon him) after delivering the baby to seek purification for her crime. She was told by the Prophet to go and feed the baby till the prescribed time for weaning. When the weaning period was over, she came again, this time holding the baby in her lap with a piece of bread in his hand. She pleaded the Prophet to cleanse her as she had done her last duty towards the child. The *ḥadd* of *rajm* was thus carried out. An eminent Companion, Khālid ibn al-Walīd, then uttered a few not so welcome words about the woman and those were reported to the Prophet. The Prophet censured him for this and said: 'Beware, Khālid! By the Lord Who holds sway of my life, her penance was such that if done by one guilty of illegal collection of tax he too may be pardoned.' The Prophet himself then led the prayer on her dead body.

On the occasion of the War of Qādisiyyah, a soldier, Abū Mihjan Thaqafī, was under detention on the charge of drinking wine. When the war was at its peak, he became restless in his prison cell. He requested the wife of the Commander of the Islamic legions, Sa'd ibn Abī Waqqās, to let him go so he could take part in the battle. He pleaded: 'If I am killed in the encounter with the enemies of Islam, there will, then, be no need for punishment and if I remain alive, I will return and put fetters on my feet myself.' The word of honour given by a Muslim, though a convict, carried so much weight that the wife of the Commander saw no reason to doubt him. She not only released Abū Mihjan but also gave him the best horse available in Hadrat Sā'd's stable. The man, who was to receive eighty lashes on his back, fought the battle so valiantly that even the Commander, Sa'd ibn Abī Waqqās, was astonished. When the battle was over with a convincing victory for the Muslims, Abū Mihjan, true to his word, returned quietly, went to the lock-up and wore his shackles. As a reward for this remarkable demonstration of sincerity of purpose and gallantry in the way of the Almighty, Sa'd declared: 'I will not strike with lashes the back of such a faithful servant of Allah.' Abū Mihjan's response was: 'I too will never drink wine again, because my hope so far was that I will get purified through punishment, but now that hope is gone.'

These incidents need no comment, the concept of crime and punishment in Islam is explained so vividly. They brilliantly elucidate how Islam injects the highest sense of moral accountability even within criminals, while at the same time closing all avenues to crime. Those who tend to see or describe the *ḥudūd* laws as 'barbaric', in fact are themselves victims of either paranoia or a criminal mind-set. The highest pedestal of human dignity and self-respect to which the Shariah laws have elevated mankind has no precedent in human history.[5]

Lastly, we may say that the *ḥudūd* laws also take into consideration the personal circumstances of the culprit and also the circumstances in which the crime is committed. During times of war, *ḥadd* punishment is held in abeyance. In times of famine or drought the thief's hand is not chopped off. Relaxation is also given to the culprit if it is established that he committed burglary or theft in dire need compelled by his personal circumstances. For example, during the reign of the second caliph, Hadrat 'Umar, some attendants of Hātib

---

[5] Incidents like these from Islam's glorious history demonstrate so convincingly the following two unique aspects of the exemplary social order established during the Golden Era of *Sayyidnā* Rasūl Allah and his Rightly-Guided Caliphs that: (i) individually each and every member — both male and female — of that angelic community was strongly committed to the supremacy of Islam and its benign teachings; and (ii) collectively the enforcement of the Shariah Law practically made it a model society where social justice, harmony and balance ruled supreme. It further reaffirms that whenever and wherever the teachings of the Qur'an and the Sunnah will be enforced in letter and spirit, humanity is bound to reap there the golden harvest of the Islamic social order the way it did during the *Khayr ul-Qurūn* – Editor.

ibn Abī Balta'āh stole a camel of a person from the Muzaynah tribe. The crime was reported to Hadrat 'Umar and was established. He decreed that their hands be chopped off. However, by chance the caliph came to learn about the sad personal plight of the culprits. He called for Hātib and reprimanded him: 'You took work from them and then let them go hungry! They have reached a stage where even if they eat something forbidden it would be permissible for them.' Hadrat 'Umar then set them free and ordered Hātib to pay a penalty to the owner of the camel.

There are plenty of examples which tell us that Islam's penal code is not a code of 'blind' laws, nor is Islamic justice 'blind'. The Islamic laws differentiate between the person forced to commit a crime and the person who committed it by his own free will. This is the reason why there is such a big difference in the punishment prescribed for fornication committed by a person who is unmarried and for adultery by a married individual, and punishment for a burglar by choice and for the one compelled to steal in dire need.

10 Inter-faith Marriage and Islam*

A number of our Muslim friends were alarmed over the growing incidence of the community's educated male members bringing their brides from the West. They would like me to explain the Shariah viewpoint on the subject as they think that the sanction to marry *kitābiyah* or a women of the 'People of the Book' is being grossly misused.

The phenomenon has certainly assumed alarming proportions these days. Even in countries with relatively limited incidence, as in our part of the world, marriage with *ahl-e-kitābiyah*, due to the socio-political dominance of the Colonialists, in many cases, has impacted negatively on Muslim societies. Due to a compromising attitude, thus developed non-Islamic social customs and values are unconsciously adopted in a family. This inner factor has been one important reason for the overall decline and fall of several Muslim communities. It is, therefore, but natural that well-meaning Muslims should feel the need to check the incidence. We, however, do not approve of any amendment in a juridical matter by over-stressing just one aspect of the community's interest. The Lord Who revealed the Qur'an is All-Wise and All-Knowing of our interests and needs. To understand His injunctions and properly apply them in a given situation, it is necessary to review every minor and major stake involved in a broadest possible perspective and give it the same level of importance as given by the Law-Giver Himself.

The sanction to marry women from the People of the Book has been accorded in the following *āyah* of Surah *al-Mā'idah*:

---

* *Tarjumān al-Qur'ān*, December 1937.

ٱلْيَوْمَ أُحِلَّ لَكُمُ ٱلطَّيِّبَٰتُ ۖ وَطَعَامُ ٱلَّذِينَ أُوتُوا۟ ٱلْكِتَٰبَ حِلٌّ لَّكُمْ
وَطَعَامُكُمْ حِلٌّ لَّهُمْ ۖ وَٱلْمُحْصَنَٰتُ مِنَ ٱلْمُؤْمِنَٰتِ وَٱلْمُحْصَنَٰتُ مِنَ ٱلَّذِينَ
أُوتُوا۟ ٱلْكِتَٰبَ مِن قَبْلِكُمْ إِذَآ ءَاتَيْتُمُوهُنَّ أُجُورَهُنَّ مُحْصِنِينَ غَيْرَ
مُسَٰفِحِينَ وَلَا مُتَّخِذِىٓ أَخْدَانٍ ۗ ... ﴿٥﴾

This day all clean things have been made lawful unto you. The food of the People of the Book is permitted to you and your food is permitted to them. And permitted to you are chaste women, be they from among the believers, or from among those who have received the Book before you, provided you become their protectors in wedlock after paying them their bridal-due, rather than going around committing fornication and taking them as secret-companions.

[*al-Mā'idah* 5: 5]

10.1. Different legal interpretations

The above *āyah* has been variously interpreted from juristic points of view. The majority of Muslim jurists and scholars have favoured the general applicability of the injunctions according to the obvious connotation of its wording. Allah *subḥānahū wa ta'ālā* adds no condition to the marriage of Muslim men with 'chaste women' from among the People of the Book. There is apparently no reason, therefore, to invent conditions and exceptions in this respect. The Ṣaḥābah and their successors regarded the *āyah* as containing a general sanction for marriage with the women of the People of the Book (*kitābiyah*). Some of them also set a precedent by acting upon this sanction. The third caliph, 'Uthmān ibn 'Affān, married Nā'ilah Kalbia, a Christian lady, and Talha ibn 'Abdullah, another eminent Companion, married a Jewish woman from Syria.

10.1.1. *The viewpoint of Ibn 'Umar*

'Abd Allah ibn 'Umar was the only prominent jurist from among the Companions of the Prophet (peace be upon him) who regarded marriage with *kitābiyah* as absolutely unlawful. His argument was based on the following command of the Lord:

وَلَا تَنكِحُوا۟ ٱلْمُشْرِكَـٰتِ حَتَّىٰ يُؤْمِنَّ ۚ وَلَأَمَةٌ مُّؤْمِنَةٌ خَيْرٌ مِّن مُّشْرِكَةٍ وَلَوْ أَعْجَبَتْكُمْ ۗ ... ﴿٢٢١﴾

Marry not the women who associate others with Allah in His Divinity until they believe; for a believing slave-girl is better than a (free, respectable) woman who associates others with Allah in His Divinity.

[*al-Baqarah* 2: 221]

On the basis of the above *āyah*, Ibn 'Umar argued: 'I can't think of a greater idolatry than declaring Jesus son of Mary or any servant of Allah, as God!' He, therefore, considered all Christian and Jewish women on a par with their counterparts from among other unbelievers because their faith is adulterated with idolatry and apostasy. According to him, the injunction in *āyah* 5 of Surah *al-Mā'idah* (5) meant only those 'chaste women' among the People of the Book, who converted to Islam.

This individual opinion of Ibn 'Umar has been contested, however, on certain more cogent grounds. The Lord Himself has declared the fundamentals of the Jewish and Christian faith as being based on idolatry. For example, the following *āyāt*:

لَقَدْ كَفَرَ ٱلَّذِينَ قَالُوٓا۟ إِنَّ ٱللَّهَ هُوَ ٱلْمَسِيحُ ٱبْنُ مَرْيَمَ ۖ ... ﴿٧٢﴾

And surely they disbelieved when they said: 'Christ, the son of Mary, is indeed God.'

[*al-Mā'idah* 5: 72]

لَّقَدْ كَفَرَ ٱلَّذِينَ قَالُوٓا۟ إِنَّ ٱللَّهَ ثَالِثُ ثَلَـٰثَةٍ ... ﴿٧٣﴾

Those who said: 'Allah is one of the Three certainly they disbelieved.'

[*al-Mā'idah* 5: 73]

لَّقَدْ كَفَرَ ٱلَّذِينَ قَالُوٓا۟ إِنَّ ٱللَّهَ ثَالِثُ ثَلَـٰثَةٍ ... ﴿٧٣﴾

The Jews say: 'Ezra ('Uzayr) is Allah's son', and the Christians say: 'The Messiah is the son of Allah.'

[*al-Tawbah* 9: 30]

In spite of these clear statements regarding their faith, the Qur'an never used the term *mushrik* (idolator/polytheist) for the Jews and the Christians. They were invariably called *Ahl Al-Kitāb*, meaning the 'People of the Book'.

The Qur'an has classified the people under three distinct categories: (i) *Mushrikīn* and *Kuffār*, i.e: 'idolaters' and 'unbelievers', those who are left with no adulterated or unadulterated source of Divine Guidance; (ii) *Ahl al-Kitāb* (the People of the Book), those who believe, in spite of all their fundamental and empirical deviation from the path of faith, in an apostle of God and the Divine Guidance; and (iii) *M'uminīn* (believers) or the followers of the Last Prophet (peace be upon him). The Qur'an uses these three categories distinctly in different contexts. It can, therefore, be said with certainty that the injunctions in *āyah* 221 of Surah *al-Baqarah* exclusively prohibits a Muslim's marriage with the 'idolatress', whereas *āyah* 5 of Surah *al-Mā'idah* clearly declares as lawful for Muslims their marriage with the *chaste women* from the People of the Book.

Secondly, *āyah* 5 of Surah *al-Mā'idah* declares also the 'food of the People of the Book' as lawful for Muslims. The injunction does not make any distinction in this respect between those from among the People of the Book who may have retained their faith and those who embraced Islam. This simply means that one part of the *āyah* can't be interpreted differently from the other.

Thirdly, there is hardly any Jewish or Christian sect which may be considered totally free from idolatry or unbelief. It is next to impossible to find among them the true faith in One and Only God preached originally by Prophet Moses or Jesus, peace be upon them. The reason for this is obviously the fact that they have lost the actual teachings of Prophet Moses and Prophet Jesus (Allah's peace be upon them). Whatever is available in their present *scriptures* is full of modifications and it is too difficult to differentiate the original revealed text from additions, alterations, and revisions. It will be wrong, therefore, to presume that the injunction about *kitābiyah* means women from among a Jewish or Christian sect of the later period. The small group of good-natured and well-meaning Christians and Jews, referred to in the Qur'an, was of those who either embraced Islam at the hands of

Sayyidunā Rasūl Allah (peace be upon him), or were about to enter its fold following their conviction about the truthfulness of the Islamic message.

Those who support the stand taken by 'Abd Allah ibn 'Umar, (may Allah be pleased with him) also refer in support of their stand to *āyah* 10 of Surah *al-Mumtahinah* (60): وَلَاتُمۡسِكُوا۟ بِعِصَمِ ٱلۡكَوَافِرِ (*Do not hold on to your marriages with unbelieving women*). This *āyah*, however, concerns exclusively those men and women who migrated from *Dār al-Ḥarb* (the non-Muslim community at war with the community of Islam) to *Dār al-Islam* with their wives or husbands left behind as unbelievers. The *āyah* explains that the marriage of such men and women stands annulled once they move to *Dār al-Islam* and the migrants are free to enter into fresh marriage contracts. The above injunction is particular and cannot be taken as general.

10.1.2. *The viewpoint of Ibn 'Abbas*

'Abd Allah ibn 'Abbas, another eminent jurist among the Companions, also put some prerequisites on marriage with the *kitābiyah*. He was of the view that sanction of marriage is exclusive for *dhimmī* women [those residing as citizens of *Dār al-Islam* and whose dignity, honour and property are thus a sacred trust (*dhimma*) of the Islamic state]. As for those who live outside the boundaries of a Muslim country, their marriage with the believers is not permissible. Ibn 'Abbas inferred in support of his argument to the following *āyah* of Surah *al-Tawbah*:

قَـٰتِلُوا۟ ٱلَّذِينَ لَا يُؤۡمِنُونَ بِٱللَّهِ وَلَا بِٱلۡيَوۡمِ ٱلۡـَٔاخِرِ وَلَا يُحَرِّمُونَ مَا حَرَّمَ ٱللَّهُ
وَرَسُولُهُۥ وَلَا يَدِينُونَ دِينَ ٱلۡحَقِّ مِنَ ٱلَّذِينَ أُوتُوا۟ ٱلۡكِتَـٰبَ حَتَّىٰ يُعۡطُوا۟
ٱلۡجِزۡيَةَ عَن يَدٍ وَهُمۡ صَـٰغِرُونَ ﴿٢٩﴾

> *Those who do not believe in Allah and the Last Day – even though they were given the scriptures, and who do not hold as unlawful that which Allah and His Messenger have declared to be unlawful, and who do not follow the true religion – fight against them until they pay tribute out of their hand and are utterly subdued.*
>
> [*al-Tawbah* 9: 29]

Additionally, he quoted the following divine command in support of his viewpoint:

لَّا تَجِدُ قَوْمًا يُؤْمِنُونَ بِٱللَّهِ وَٱلْيَوْمِ ٱلْآخِرِ يُوَآدُّونَ مَنْ حَآدَّ ٱللَّهَ وَرَسُولَهُۥ وَلَوْ
كَانُوٓا۟ ءَابَآءَهُمْ أَوْ أَبْنَآءَهُمْ أَوْ إِخْوَٰنَهُمْ أَوْ عَشِيرَتَهُمْ ... ﴿٢٢﴾

> *You shall not find a people who believe in Allah and the Last Day befriending those who oppose Allah and His Messenger even though they be their fathers or their sons or their brothers or their kindred.*
>
> [*al-Mujādalah* 58: 22]

This, he believed, was a clear injunction forbidding Muslims from entering into any relationship of love and kinship with those 'who oppose Allah and His Messenger'. There can be no relationship of love stronger than the ties of marriage and, hence, Ibn 'Abbas observed that marriage with a Christian or Jewish woman was not permissible because they too belong to the category of people *who oppose Allah and His Messenger*.

10.2. The way forward

There is a general consensus of prominent jurists from among the Ṣaḥābah and the Tābi'ūn (may Allah be pleased with them all) that marriage with *kitābiyah* is lawful in light of the unconditional injunction of *āyah* 5 of Surah *al-Mā'idah* (5). There is also a consensus that marriage with a Christian or Jewish woman living in *Dār al-Harb* or *Dār al-Kufr* (a non-Muslim country), though lawful, is, nonetheless, undesirable (*Makrūh*).

It is also correct that the term *Ahl al-Kitāb* (People of the Book) means exclusively the Christians and the Jews (be they Israeli or non-Israeli). It does not include people of other religions, as evident from the following *āyāt*:

وَهَٰذَا كِتَٰبٌ أَنزَلْنَٰهُ مُبَارَكٌ فَٱتَّبِعُوهُ وَٱتَّقُوا۟ لَعَلَّكُمْ تُرْحَمُونَ ﴿١٥٥﴾
أَن تَقُولُوٓا۟ إِنَّمَآ أُنزِلَ ٱلْكِتَٰبُ عَلَىٰ طَآئِفَتَيْنِ مِن قَبْلِنَا وَإِن كُنَّا عَن
دِرَاسَتِهِمْ لَغَٰفِلِينَ ﴿١٥٦﴾

> *And likewise We revealed this Book – a blessed one. Follow it, then, and become God-fearing; you may be shown Mercy. (You may no longer) say now that the Book was revealed only to two groups of people before us and that we had indeed been unaware of what they read.*
>
> [*al-An'ām* 6: 155 and 156]

Since the followers of other religions mostly lost track of the teachings of their scriptures, and whatever of their books could remain intact was reduced to conundrums and mechanical rites and rituals, the term cannot, therefore, apply to Fire-Worshippers, Hindus, animists or pagans and the plethora of texts attributed to their religions. This is the reason why the Prophet (peace be upon him) wrote to the Fire-Worshippers or the *majūs* of Ḥijr:

> فَإِن اَسلَمتُم فَلَكُم مَا لَنَا وَ عَلَيكُم مَا عَلَينَا، وَ مَن اَبىٰ فَعَلَيهِ الجِزيهُ غَيرَ اَكلِ ذَبَائِحِهم وَلَا نِكَاحِ نِسَائِهِم.
>
> If you embrace Islam, you will have the same rights as due to us and the same obligations as binding on us. Those of you who reject (the call of Islam), *jizyah*[1] will be levied on them, but neither their slaughtered animal will be eaten, nor their women be taken into marriage.[2]

This statement should dispel any misgivings with regard to the possibility of including non-Jewish and non-Christian women in the category of *kitābiyah*. The permission to take in marriage the Christian or Jewish woman is also not restricted to their being from *Dār al-Ḥarb* or *dhimmīyah* (living under Islamic rule), free or slave.

---

[1] *Jizyah* is the security tax lavied on non-Muslims in return for the Islamic state's guarantee (*dhimmah*) of protection and safety for their life, property, and honour and exemption from taking part in defence of the country. It is nominal in terms of money and much less than the mandatory zakat for the Muslim subjects – Editor.

[2] Imam Bayhaqī, *Al-Sunan al-Kubra*.

10.3. Marriage, more than a 'social contract'

From its legal perspective, let us move now to the religious and social aspects of marriage in Islam. According to the Islamic Shariah, marriage is not just a 'social contract' as it is generally taken today. Marriage in Islam has the element of religious sanctity as well. This sanctity has nothing to do with the ceremonious 'sacrament', as in the case of Hindu and Christian marriages. It occupies the status of a sanctimonious act of worship. Islam seeks to gain social and civilizational advantages as well as religious and spiritual benefits from this important institution. Marriage is also intended to be an active factor for moral reform, purification of society, growth, development, maintenance and perpetuation of correct Islamic social order and the raising of generations of good Muslims who keep Allah's Pleasure supreme and hold high the banner of His Faith. Marriage has been given the status of an act of worship, as it helps in the achievement of these noble objectives. A section of Muslim jurists, therefore, regard marriage as 'superior in some respect to jihad', because they think that the objectives achieved through marriage are more than those achieved through jihad and victory over unbelievers. Through the marriage-contract, they say, a whole generation of Muslims is saved from moral deviance and a new generation is facilitated to adorn the world.

In order to fully understand the Islamic viewpoint regarding marriage, a quick review of the Prophetic Traditions[3] on the subject

[3] Islam teaches moderation in every aspect of life, including even the acts of worship. The Hadith narrated by Imam Bukhārī from Anas ibn Mālik is very significant in in this respect. It tells us how a group of three notables visited the houses of *Ummahāt al-Mu'minīn* to learn about *Sayyidnā* Rasūl Allah's life of worship. On obtaining the required information their immediate response was as follows: 'Where are we as compared to the Messenger of Allah, whose past and future lapses have all been pardoned.' Thus, one of them vowed to keep awake the whole night praying; the second to observe Fast round the year; and the third never to marry and remain celibate throughout his life. Meanwhile, the Prophet of Allah came and learned about that, on which he addressed them:

اَمَا واللهِ اِنیِّ لَاَخشَاكُم للهِ وَاَتقَاكُم لهُ، لٰكِنّی اَصُومُ وأُفطِرُ، وَ أُصَلِّی وَأَرقُدُ، وَأَتَزَوَّجُ النِّسَاءَ.فَمَن رَغِبَ عَن سُنَّتِي فَلَيسَ مِنِّي.

may be of immense help. Abū Y'alā, in his *Musnad*, narrated that the Prophet (peace be upon him) once asked 'Akkāf ibn Waddā'ah al-Hilāli: 'Did you marry?' He said; 'No.' The Prophet asked; 'Do you have a bondmaid?' 'Akkāf said: 'No.' He was then asked: 'Are you physically fit and financially well off?' He replied in the affirmative. On this, the Prophet said: 'Then, you are either one of the devil's cohorts, or from the Christian community. If you wish to join our society, you will have to do what we do and marriage is part of our way of life. The worst among you are those who remain single and the worst among those who die are the ones who die bachelor.'[4]

In another well known Tradition, *Sayyidunā* Rasūl Allah (peace be upon him) said:

> تَنَاكَحُوا وَتَنَاسَلُوا وَتَكَثَّرُوا، فَانِّي مُكَاثِرٌ بِكُمُ الاُمَمَ يَومَ القِيَامَةِ.
>
> Enter into marriage bond, propagate well your progeny, and increase your number, because I would like to be proud of your numerical strength amongst the nations of the world on the Day of Reckoning.[5]

The following Tradition is also very significant in this context:

> اَربَعٌ مَن اُعطِيَهُنَّ فَقَد اُعْطَي خَيرَ الدُّنيَا وَالآخِرة، قَلباً شَاكِراً وَلِسَاناً ذَاكِراً وَبَدَناً عَلَى البَلآءِ صَابِراً وَزَوجَةً لَاتَبغِهِ خَوفاً فِي نَفسِهَا وَمَالِهِ.
>
> He who is gifted with four things, is blessed with the best bounties of this world and the Hereafter: a heart thankful to Allah for all that He gave him, a tongue vibrant with His remembrance, a body steadfast on tribulations and a wife upright and given to no breach of trust in herself or in the property of her husband.[6]

'By Allah, I am more submissive to Allah and more fearing of Him than you can possibly be; yet I observe *ṣawm* and break Fast as well; I do offer *ṣalāh* and do also marry women. So, he who does not follow my Sunnah [Tradition] is not from among my followers.' (*Al-Jāmi' Al-Ṣaḥīḥ*, No. 1828, *The Book of Nikāh* (Wedlock), chapter 1) – Editor.

[4] *Musnad Abī Ya'lā.*

[5] Al-Nasā'ī, *Kitāb al-Nikāh.*

[6] Narrated by al-Tabrānī.

The message contained in the following two ahadith is also of immense value for the Muslim society:

> مَن اَرَادَ اَن يَلقَى الله طَاهِراً مُطَهَّراً فَلْيَتَزَوَّج الحَرائِر.
>
> He who desires to meet his Lord clean and pure must marry a noble woman.[7]
>
> لاَتَزَوَّجُوا النِّسَاءَ لِحُسنِهِنّ فَعَسَىٰ حُسنُهُنّ اَن يُّردِيَهُنَّ، وَلَا تَزَوَّجُوهُنَّ لِاَموَالِهِنِّ فَعَسَىٰ اَموَالُهُنَّ أن تُطغِيَهُنَّ، وَلٰكِن تَزَوَّجُوهُنّ عَلَى الدّينِ، فَلَاَمَةٌ خَرقَاءُ سَودَاءُ ذاتُ دِينٍ اَفضَلُ.
>
> Do not marry women for their beauty, maybe their beauty spoils them; and do not marry them for their wealth, maybe their wealth turns them rebellious. Yes, marry them for their religion. A simple and clumsy black bondmaid, if religiously oriented, is superior [to other women].[8]

There are a number of Traditions which tell us that the significance of marriage in Islam is more than its being the means to fulfil a civilizational need. Its principal objective, instead, is fortification of human self, purity of conduct, promotion of Islamic values, and propagation of a generation of righteous Muslims. For this purpose, it is not enough for believers to marry but also to marry women who are Muslims, religiously disciplined, of sound character and chaste. This is because a righteous Muslim society can flourish only through marriage bonds between Muslim men and women of sound character. Such a couple alone can bring up a morally upright new generation.

10.3.1. *Issues in heterogeneous marriages*

Keeping the religious aspect aside, even if seen purely from a sociological viewpoint heterogeneous marriages would generally appear extremely harmful for the society as well as family life. A husband and wife who differ entirely from each other in their manners and morals

---

[7] Narrated by Ibn Mājah.

[8] Ibid.

and approach to life and are born and brought up under two different value-systems and lifestyles, find it hard to have the peace of mind and real happiness in their personal lives by the simple act of coming closer through the marriage bond. It would not be easy for them to make their home a cohesive unit of the Islamic social order, or produce a generation that can properly adjust to Islam's civilizational norms. They may retain the spirit of their mutual love and comradeship till the last moments of their lives, but that love and comradeship would be restricted at best to their ownselves with no civilizational benefits accruing to the society to which they belong. The heterogeneity of religion and value systems leaves a big cleavage. Such marriages do not prove useful even for the success of family life and betterment of a social system because the two sides belong to two different domains of the same society. Even the difference of urban and rural background sometimes leads to such disharmony.

Homogeneity in as many aspects as possible between the husband and wife and their respective families is of basic importance for conjugal harmony. Not only that the husband and wife should be co-religionists, it is equally important that their lifestyle be similar; there is harmony in their views and approach to life and in their economic and social status; and their family traditions are also not that different from each other. It is this essential aspect of perfect harmony that the Islamic Shariah terms as *kafā'ah* or compatibility and match. Thus, Islam has attached great importance to the requirements of *kufū'* (perfect match), so that the husband and wife are similar to each other in as many aspects of life as possible. This quality of perfect compatibility leads not only to a relationship of mutual love and compassion between husband and wife, but is also beneficial for the society as a whole and on that depends the healthy growth of future generations. Without such harmony, marital ties are nothing more than a physical union, which may be totally or nearly barren from a civilizational point of view.

10.3.2. *Challenges of religious disharmony*

The absence of essential ingredients of compatability leads to lack of love, compassion and a fruitful partnership between husband and wife. Disharmony in spiritual values is the most harmful element in match-making and its disadvantages are obviously so many. The most obvious danger in a match like this is that the children brought up under the care of a non-practising mother are not expected to internalize the values of the Qur'an and the Sunnah. She may also promote un-Islamic manners and customs in a Muslim household. Homes having ties with such a family may also become affected by its un-Islamic impact. The husband may himself be the first to face the negative fall-out of such a relationship. His natural attachment to his non-practising wife may unconsciously cause dilution in his commitment to Islam. Conversely, his strong attachment to his *dīn* may create distance between the couple leading to the disruption of the family life.

The impact of heterogeneous marriages may sometimes be damaging from socio-political angles as well, as witnessed by a number of Muslim societies in the past. The Islamic social order was polluted in India by pagan culture and idolatrous customs and traditions through the induction of such influential women in the Mughal court. They joined the Muslim ruling class families either with their religious faith intact or becoming Muslims only formally. Mothers who reared their progeny on the milk of apostasy and pantheism became instrumental in inflicting enormous damage to the social conduct, manners and morals of younger generations. The Muslim governments faced their doom mostly due to the rulers' emotional attachment to their non-practising 'better-halves', a phenomenon that made these women de facto sovereigns of their states. The Western or Westernized ladies, are expected to bring no different results.

10.4. The uniqueness of Islam's matrimonial law

With this backdrop in mind, we may easily conclude that the Muslims' marriage with non-Muslim females of the People of the Book should have been discouraged. Then, why has Islam allowed it? To arrive at a correct answer, when we look at the other side of this issue, we discover the extreme balance and great wisdom behind the Divine Law.

The man-made laws tend to suffer from lack of balance, because human nature cannot escape taking sides nor can these be imbued with the same legal insight and all-embracing vision of the Divine Law. Sometimes these laws stress too much on collective interest, overlooking the interest of the individual. At times, personal interests dominate so much that the collective aspect stands ignored. For the Supreme Law-Giver, however, there are no favourites or biases in favour of or against any individual or group. He is All-Knowing and nothing escapes His notice. The All-Merciful Lord gives individuals and the society the care and attention that each deserves. The interest of Muslim individuals and society demanded that the Muslim men should marry practising Muslim women and for this too the principles of compability and harmony be given due consideration, as explained above. The principle of *kafā'ah* was therefore laid down for this purpose.

According to the famous hadith, narrated not by one but three eminent Companions: the Mother of the Faithful *Sayyidah* 'Ā'ishah Siddīqah, Hadrat 'Umar and Anas (may Allah be pleased with them all), *Sayyidunā* Rasūl Allah (peace be upon him) said:

> تَخَيَّرُوا لِنُطَفِكُم وَانكِحُوا الأكَفاءَ
>
> Look for better repositories for your human seed and marry those who make an appropriate match.[9]

The religious aspect stands out as the first and foremost consideration in the life of a Muslim and this occupies an important place in his match-making as well:

> وَٱلْمُؤْمِنُونَ وَٱلْمُؤْمِنَـٰتُ بَعْضُهُمْ أَوْلِيَآءُ بَعْضٍ ۚ يَأْمُرُونَ بِٱلْمَعْرُوفِ وَيَنْهَوْنَ عَنِ ٱلْمُنكَرِ وَيُقِيمُونَ ٱلصَّلَوٰةَ وَيُؤْتُونَ ٱلزَّكَوٰةَ وَيُطِيعُونَ ٱللَّهَ وَرَسُولَهُۥٓ ۚ أُو۟لَـٰٓئِكَ سَيَرْحَمُهُمُ ٱللَّهُ ۗ إِنَّ ٱللَّهَ عَزِيزٌ حَكِيمٌ ٧١
>
> *The believers, both men and women, are allies of one another. They enjoin good, forbid evil, establish Prayer, pay zakat, and obey Allah and His Messenger. Surely Allah will show mercy to them. Allah is All-Mighty, All-Wise.*
>
> [*al-Tawbah* 9: 71]

---

[9] Narrated by Ibn Mājah, Book on *Wedlock*.

يَـٰٓأَيُّهَا ٱلَّذِينَ ءَامَنُوا۟ قُوٓا۟ أَنفُسَكُمْ وَأَهْلِيكُمْ نَارًا وَقُودُهَا ٱلنَّاسُ وَٱلْحِجَارَةُ ... ﴿٦﴾

Believers, guard yourselves and your kindred against a Fire whose fuel is human beings and stones.

[*al-Taḥrīm* 66: 6]

وَمَن لَّمْ يَسْتَطِعْ مِنكُمْ طَوْلًا أَن يَنكِحَ ٱلْمُحْصَنَـٰتِ ٱلْمُؤْمِنَـٰتِ فَمِن مَّا مَلَكَتْ أَيْمَـٰنُكُم مِّن فَتَيَـٰتِكُمُ ٱلْمُؤْمِنَـٰتِ ۚ وَٱللَّهُ أَعْلَمُ بِإِيمَـٰنِكُم ۚ بَعْضُكُم مِّنۢ بَعْضٍ ۚ ... ﴿٢٥﴾

And those of you who cannot afford to marry free, believing women let them marry such believing women whom your right hands possess. Allah knows all about your faith. All of you belong to one another.

[*al-Nisā'* 4: 25]

According to the Tradition narrated by Ibn Mājah and also quoted earlier, the Prophet said: تَزَوَّجُوهُنّ عَلَى الدِّينِ فَلاَمَةٌ خَرقَاءُ سَودَاءُ ذاتُ دِينٍ اَفضَلُ ('Marry them [the women of your match] for their religion. A simple and clumsy black bondmaid, if religiously oriented, is superior to other women'). On the other hand, there is a personal side of the matter that demands not to absolutely shut down all avenues of marriage with members of other communities. Exceptional situations may arise, as in the case of a Muslim male badly in love with a non-Muslim female, though she is willing to embrace Islam on marriage. In the event of a total ban on such marriages, he was likely to slip onto the forbidden track. There may also be a person who does not find a suitable match among his relatives and acquaintances, while remaining a bachelor may lead him astray. The Supreme Law-Giver has kept the doors open, therefore, to meet such exigencies. It was, however, ensured at the same time that while taking personal interests into consideration, the common interest of the society must not be ignored either.

10.4.1. *Prohibition of Muslim female's marriage with non-Muslim male*

Due to the reason explained above, the Islamic Shariah has permitted Muslim men to marry Christian or Jewish woman in exceptional cases. No such permission, however, exists for Muslim women. Allah *Subḥānahū wa ta'ālā* proclaimed:

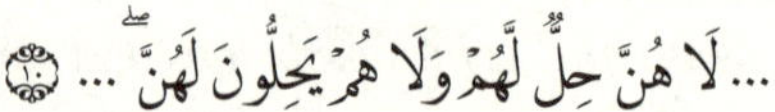

Those women are no longer lawful to the unbelievers, nor are those unbelievers lawful to the (believing) women.
[*al-Mumtahinah* 60: 10]

One apparent reason for this ban is to maintain harmony and mutuality in the family and to avoid an ongoing clash and conflict of values and practices which directly effect the upbringing of children. A Muslimah is required to cultivate Islamic values and practices in her children. While a non-muslim husband may demand otherwise. Such marriages may also have serious problems for a wife in practising her faith with any interference from a non-Muslim husband. Moreover, it also has a legal dimension. A child in Islamic law traces his lineage to his father. Islamic law does not allow a Muslim child to get any inheritance from a non-Muslim father, nor can a Muslim wife inherit from a non-Muslim husband. Due to these and other reasons in the interest of family welfare, Islamic Shariah does not allow a Muslimah to marry a non-Muslim.

10.4.2. *Preconditions for marriage of Muslim men with non-Muslim women*

The permission for Muslim men to marry *kitābiyah* is also not unconditional. The non-Muslims have been classified into the following two categories for marriage purposes: (i) those having nothing in common with the Muslims socially, culturally, in their faith, lifestyle, manners and morals; and (ii) those who are nearer to Islam at least to the extent of belief in Prophethood, Revelation, faith in God and the Day of Reckoning and whose moral principles and social laws emanate largely from their scriptures.

Of these two categories, no marriage relationship has been allowed with those of the first category:

وَلَا تَنكِحُوا الْمُشْرِكَاتِ حَتَّىٰ يُؤْمِنَّ ۚ وَلَأَمَةٌ مُّؤْمِنَةٌ خَيْرٌ مِّن مُّشْرِكَةٍ
وَلَوْ أَعْجَبَتْكُمْ ۗ وَلَا تُنكِحُوا الْمُشْرِكِينَ حَتَّىٰ يُؤْمِنُوا ۚ وَلَعَبْدٌ مُّؤْمِنٌ خَيْرٌ
مِّن مُّشْرِكٍ وَلَوْ أَعْجَبَكُمْ ۗ أُولَٰئِكَ يَدْعُونَ إِلَى النَّارِ ۖ وَاللَّهُ يَدْعُو إِلَى الْجَنَّةِ
وَالْمَغْفِرَةِ بِإِذْنِهِ ۖ ... ﴿٢٢١﴾

Marry not the women who associate others with Allah in His Divinity until they believe; for a believing slave-girl is better than a [free, respectable] woman who associates others with Allah in His Divinity, even though she might please you. Likewise, do not give your women in marriage to men who associate others with Allah in His Divinity until they believe; for a believing slave is better than a [free, respectable] man who associates others with Allah in His Divinity, even though he might please you. Such people call you towards the Fire, and Allah calls you, by His leave, towards Paradise and forgiveness.

[*al-Baqarah* 2: 221]

As for the second category, the believers are permitted to enter into marriage contract with the *kitābiyah*, but have at the same time been forewarned of the challenges inherent in such relationships. It has been impressed upon them that the permission given to them is only to let them avoid an illicit relationship:

... وَالْمُحْصَنَاتُ مِنَ الْمُؤْمِنَاتِ وَالْمُحْصَنَاتُ مِنَ الَّذِينَ أُوتُوا الْكِتَابَ
مِن قَبْلِكُمْ إِذَا آتَيْتُمُوهُنَّ أُجُورَهُنَّ مُحْصِنِينَ غَيْرَ مُسَافِحِينَ وَلَا مُتَّخِذِي
أَخْدَانٍ ۗ وَمَن يَكْفُرْ بِالْإِيمَانِ فَقَدْ حَبِطَ عَمَلُهُ وَهُوَ فِي الْآخِرَةِ مِنَ الْخَاسِرِينَ ﴿٥﴾

And permitted to you are chaste women, be they from among the believers, or from among those who have received the Book before you, provided you become their protectors in wedlock after paying them their bridal-due, rather than

> *going around committing fornication and taking them as secret-companions. The work of he who refuses to follow the Way of faith will go to waste, and he will be among the utter losers in the Hereafter.*
>
> [*al-Mā'idah* 5: 5]

The concluding portion of the *āyah* is noteworthy. It clearly warns of the danger to faith in the case of marriage with a *kitābiyah*. The permission that has been granted is obviously valid only under exceptional conditions and extraordinary circumstances.

In a letter to the eminent Companion of the Prophet (peace be upon him) Ḥudhayfah ibn al-Yamān, who held a position of responsibility in the conquered territory of Syria and was one of the best exponents of Shariah in his time, *Sayyidunā* 'Umar advised him against marrying a *kitābiyah*, lest his example might adversely affect the environment of Muslim households in a fledgling Islamic society.

It may be pertinent to note in this context that marriage with women of the People of the Book was viewed as least desirable when Islam was a dominant world power. Under circumstances when Muslims today are a subdued and suppressed lot, living under the political, economic and cultural domination of non-Muslims, the undesirability of marriage with a *kitābiyah* has become more obvious. It is thus under the category of items though lawful (*jā'iz*), yet *highly undesirable* (*mukrūh*). There is a consensus as well of Muslim jurists on this. From the precedent of Hadrat 'Umar's action it can further be deduced that on the analogy of his directive to Hadrat Hudhayfah against marrying a *kitābiyah*, those in authority in an Islamic state may issue orders discouraging something that was sanctioned under certain conditions by the Shariah but is likely to be against the public interest in certain situations. For this, however, those taking action must be duly qualified in the field of Islamic law.

11 The Qur'anic View of Permissible Food*

Those who travel abroad, to Europe or the USA, for education, trade or any other purpose, invariably have to face the problem of Islamically-permitted halal food. Some of them are totally oblivious to the requirements of halal and haram (lawful and forbidden) and as such nothing matters to them so long as something is available to eat or drink. Others, though aware of the parameters of halal and haram food, find it hard to avoid succumbing to the demands of physical needs and consume whatever comes their way. On the other hand, there are those who are genuinely careful in this respect and try strictly to observe the parameters of halal and haram. I often receive queries from them regarding the borderlines between the lawful and the forbidden and what they should eat and what must be avoided.

A number of such queries addressed to me in private have been responded to, albeit briefly, through *Tarjumān al-Qur'ān*. The matter, however, has now taken a new turn. When our educated youth abroad see Muslim expatriates, especially from some Arab countries, eating without inhibition the meat of animals mechanically slaughtered and express their reservations to them, those expatriates produce their religious scholars' fatwa declaring such meat halal. A Pakistani student from London has recently sought our views on a similar legal decree issued by some Iraqi religious scholars. I would like, therefore, to critically examine the matter in the following paragraphs.

In his letter, the London-based Pakistani student says:

> The issue concerning meat has become a bone of contention between me and some Muslim students from the Middle East. I tried to explain to them the points you

* *Tarjumān al-Qur'ān*, April 1959.

raised in your Q and As (*Rasā'il wa-Masā'il*) but to no avail. Now, two religiously-oriented friends have given me a copy of the decree they specially obtained from some religious scholars of Iraq. They would like me to seek your considered opinion on that. They are keenly awaiting your response. One thing which I would like to know is whether a particular way has been prescribed in the Qur'an and the Sunnah for slaughtering the animal, or is it enough to recite the name of Allah while slaughtering it mechanically? As there are different ways of slaughtering an animal in different European countries, it is difficult to consider every slaughtered piece as flesh of a dead animal and hence forbidden. I would like, therefore, to know more regarding the Qur'anic injunctions where it has been forbidden to slaughter the animal without invoking Allah's name and prohibition of the one slaughtered in the name of a deity, etc.

Contents of the two decrees, attached to this letter, are summed up below:

Decree No. 1

The reply to your query about the meat of animal slaughtered by the People of the Book is as follows. No injunction from the Almighty is without wisdom. While declaring the food of the People of the Book halal, the Almighty did not say that only the meat of the animal slaughtered by the People of the Book was halal for Muslims, but He said: 'The food of the People of the Book is halal for you.' This means that except for pork, whatever the People of the Book take as food is lawful for believers. No restriction was imposed either for saying the name of God or slaughtering the animal the way the Muslims do. *Āyah* 3 of *Surah al-Mā'idah* 5, proclaims: *This day I have perfected for you your religion, and have bestowed upon you My Bounty in full measure*. The *āyah* immediately precedes the verse in which the food of the People of the Book was declared halal for the believers. While perfecting the Religion for Muslims, the All-Merciful Lord knew that the time would come when the People of the Book would kill their animals for food by inserting nails in their heads. According to a Tradition, the Prophet was once offered for food the mutton of a poisoned goat at a banquet arranged by a Jewish woman. Without ascertaining whether the food was slaughtered in an Islamic way or not, he took a little from that mutton. Then, there is a clear injunction of the Qur'an that one should not unnecessarily probe whether a certain thing is halal or haram, unless clearly declared otherwise by the Qur'an and Sunnah. Imam Ibn al-'Arabī al-Ma'āferi quoted arguments to prove that if a Christian chops off a chicken's head with a sword, it will remain halal for a Muslim. The same is true about the tinned beef or mutton prepared for sale by Jews and Christians.

The animal slaughtered by a polytheist can never be halal, even though he may recite the name of God a hundred times while slaughtering. On the contrary, if a Muslim slaughters the animal and forgets to say the name of Allah, his slaughtered animal is halal. Once the Prophet was asked about the meat of animals brought to the city for sale by desert folk. He allowed its consumption after reciting Allah's name on it. On another occasion, when enquired about the Roman cheese and was informed that it was made of the fat that the Romans obtain from a swine's newborn, he [reportedly] said: 'I do not make halal things haram.' [*An unauthentic report for which no source has been quoted* – Author].

Decree No. 2

In *āyah* 5 of Surah *al-Mā'idah*, Allah *ta'ālā* says: *This day all clean things have been made lawful to you. The food of the People of the Book is permitted to you and your food is permitted to them.* This is a clear injunction making the food of the People of the Book, including slaughtered meat, etc. lawful for the believers.[1]

11.1. The case in perspective

There is nothing new in the decrees issued by the Iraqi *'ulamā*. They have in fact followed the line earlier taken by mufti Muhammad 'Abduhū and *'Allāmah* Rashīd Ridhā of Egypt. The arguments advanced by them are almost similar. Before I take these up, however, let us examine the issue in its correct perspective.

11.1.1. *Meat declared haram by the Qur'an*

The first and the foremost restriction imposed by the Book of God, and mentioned in clear terms at four different places, is that *dead meat, blood, the flesh of swine, and that on which has been invoked the name of other than Allah*'s are absolutely forbidden (haram). This injunction can be found among the Makkan surahs in *al-An'ām* (6: 145), *al-Naḥl* (16: 115), *al-Baqarah* (2: 173) and *al-Mā'idah* (5: 3). Of the Madinan surahs, *al-Mā'idah,* which is the last of the 'statute' surahs, adds two more to the forbidden items. The first includes, in addition to the meat of the animal that died a natural death, the one killed by strangling, by a violent blow, by a headlong fall, by being gored to death, and the animal killed by a wild beast. The second is the animal sacrificed on altars – an idolatrous practice included in the broad category of animals slaughtered in the name a deity other than God.

The Prophet included among the above forbidden meat items the meat of donkeys, wild beasts, birds of prey, those with claws, and carrion-eaters. For details, reference can be made to *Nayl al-Awtār* by Imam Shawkānī (chapter on *Food Items, Game and Slaughtered Animals*).

---

[1] For the sake of brevity the remaining part of the decree has been left out as it followed the same line of argument as the first one – Editor.

11.1.2. *The proviso of purification (tazkīyah)*

Describing the forbidden items of food, *āyah* 3 of surah *al-Mā'idah* says:

حُرِّمَتْ عَلَيْكُمُ ٱلْمَيْتَةُ وَٱلدَّمُ وَلَحْمُ ٱلْخِنزِيرِ وَمَآ أُهِلَّ لِغَيْرِ ٱللَّهِ بِهِۦ وَٱلْمُنْخَنِقَةُ وَٱلْمَوْقُوذَةُ وَٱلْمُتَرَدِّيَةُ وَٱلنَّطِيحَةُ وَمَآ أَكَلَ ٱلسَّبُعُ إِلَّا مَا ذَكَّيْتُمْ وَمَا ذُبِحَ عَلَى ٱلنُّصُبِ ... ﴿٣﴾

> *Forbidden to you are carrion, blood, the flesh of swine, the animal slaughtered in any name other than Allah's, the animal which has either been strangled, killed by blows, has died of a fall, or by goring or devoured by a beast of prey – unless it be that which you yourselves might have slaughtered while it was still alive – and forbidden to you also is that which was slaughtered at the altars.*[2]

According to the above injunction, it is absolutely clear that the only animal fit for food is one which has been duly purified by slaughtering in the prescribed manner, while animals and birds that may have died without 'purification' (*tazkīyah*) are included in the statute of حُرِّمَت, or *those forbidden by the Lord*. In order to determine the exact meaning of the Qur'anic term *tazkīyah* (purification) used here, we will have to revert to the Sunnah of the Prophet (peace be upon him). There, we learn about two forms of *tazkīyah*:

i. The first form of *tazkīyah* relates to birds and animals that are not domesticated but wild, and are running away from us or flying high in the skies, or are within our custody but somehow we don't have the means to properly slaughter them. In such a situation, *tazkiyāh* can be achieved by shedding the bird or animal's blood through some sharp-edged tool. If the animal thus purified dies by our action, it is then halal, but if it dies before we slaughter it is forbidden

[2] *Al-Mā'idah 5: 3.*

as 'dead meat'. The Prophet (peace be upon him) said: 'Shed the blood [of your game] by any [tool] available to you.'[3]

ii. The second form of *tazkīyah* relates to animals and birds in our custody. Proper *tazkīyah* is essential to make their meat halal. For this, *naḥr* has been prescribed for camel and *dhabh* for other animals including birds. *Naḥr* (نحر) is the age-old form of slaughtering camels among Arabs, in which a lancet-like sharp and pointed tool is pierced into the animal's throat releasing a fountain of blood. As the blood pours out, the animal falls onto its belly and dies. There is a reference to this form of slaughter in the Qur'an as well: فَصَلِّ لِرَبِّكَ وَانْحَرْ (*So offer Prayer and sacrifice* [*nahr*] *to your Lord alone*).[4]

As for *dhabh* (ذبح), we find the following injunctions in Ahadith:

i. Abū Hurayrah narrated that *Sayyidunā* Rasūl Allah (*peace be upon him*) dispatched (as his emissary) Budayl ibn Warqā' Khuzā'ī to Mina to announce to the pilgrims at the time of hajj that the right point of slaughter is the portion between the animal's throat and the gullet and that the animal must not get suffocated due to haste [or mishandling]. (Narrated by Dārqutnī)
ii. 'Abd Allah ibn 'Abbās said that the Prophet (peace be upon him) prohibited the animal to be torn apart [with his throat chopped off]. (Al-Tabrānī)
iii. Imam Muhammad al-Shaybānī narrated from Sa'īd ibn al-Musayyab: 'The Messenger of Allah (peace be upon him) forbade slaughtering of the goat in such a way as to slit even its spinal marrow.'

---

[3] Narrated by Abū Dāwūd and Al-Nasā'ī.

[4] *Al-Kawthar* 108: 2.

In light of these Traditions and on the authority of the practice during the time of *Sayyidunā* Rasūl Allah and his Companions, the followers of Imam Abū Ḥanīfah, Imam Shāfiʿī and Imam Aḥmad ibn Ḥanbal, consider the proper way of slaughtering an animal as to slit the place between its throat and gullet. Imam Mālik takes it to be close to its throat and jugular vein.

All these forms of the emergency and normal ways of the animal's *tazkīyah*, as ordained by the Qur'an and explained by the Sunnah, have the following points in common: (i) The animal's death is not sudden, and the link between its body and brain remains intact till it breathes its last. (ii) Through twitching and convulsive movements, blood gushes out until the last drop is thus squeezed out of its body. (iii) Shedding of blood alone should be the cause of an animal's death. If the animal is killed without fulfilling the proviso of purification, it is not halal.

In addition to the aforementioned ways of purification, the Qur'an mentions yet another form. According to this, the animal is halal if it is killed by a beast of prey, provided the beast is duly trained and keeps its prey intact for its master. The animal remains halal even if it dies by the hunting animal's stroke:

... وَمَا عَلَّمْتُم مِّنَ ٱلْجَوَارِحِ مُكَلِّبِينَ تُعَلِّمُونَهُنَّ مِمَّا عَلَّمَكُمُ ٱللَّهُ فَكُلُوا۟
مِمَّآ أَمْسَكْنَ عَلَيْكُمْ وَٱذْكُرُوا۟ ٱسْمَ ٱللَّهِ عَلَيْهِ ... ﴿٤﴾

... and such hunting animals as you teach, training them to hunt, teaching them the knowledge Allah has given you – you may eat what they catch for you – but invoke the name of Allah on it.[5]

Explaining the injunction, Allah's Messenger (peace be upon him) said:

فَإن امسك عَلَيكَ فأدركتهُ حَيًّا فاذبحه، وَإن ادركتهُ قد قُتِلَ وَلَم
يَاكُل مِنه فَكُلهُ وإن اُكِل فَلَا تَأكل فَإنَّما امسكَ عَلىٰ نَفسِهِ.

---

[5] *Al-Mā'idah* 5: 4.

> If the hunting animal [dog] catches the game for you and you get it alive, slaughter it. If you find the game killed but uneaten, even then it remains fit for eating. But if the hunting animal has also eaten from it, then do not eat from that game, because the animal then caught it for itself.[6]

In another Hadith, it is added: 'The hunting you did by your untrained dog and caught the game alive and slaughtered it, then the game is purified and halal for you to eat.' (Imam al-Bukhārī, Imam Muslim) The Prophet (peace be upon him) excluded from this category the game killed by the dog that is a pet but not trained for hunting. Thus, purification of the animal by shedding its blood through proper slaughtering remains the key condition for the animal meat being halal for consumption.

11.1.3. *The proviso of pronouncing Allah's name* (*tasmīyah*)

The third restriction imposed by the Book of God for making animal meat halal is *tasmiyāh*, or pronouncing Allah's name while slaughtering by reciting *Bismillāhi Allāhu Akbar* (In the name of Allah. Allah is the Greatest!). This injunction appears in the Qur'an at different places in different ways as mentioned below:

فَكُلُوا۟ مِمَّا ذُكِرَ ٱسْمُ ٱللَّهِ عَلَيْهِ إِن كُنتُم بِـَٔايَـٰتِهِۦ مُؤْمِنِينَ ﴿١١٨﴾

> *If you believe in the Signs of Allah, eat* [*the flesh*] *of that over which Allah's name has been pronounced.*[7]

وَلَا تَأْكُلُوا۟ مِمَّا لَمْ يُذْكَرِ ٱسْمُ ٱللَّهِ عَلَيْهِ وَإِنَّهُۥ لَفِسْقٌ ... ﴿١٢١﴾

> *Do not eat of* [*the animal*] *over which the name of Allah has not been pronounced* [*at the time of its slaughtering*], *for that is a transgression.*[8]

---

[6] Narrated by Imam Bukhārī, Imam Muslim and Imam Aḥmad.

[7] *Al-An'ām* 6: 118.

[8] *Al-An'ām* 6: 118.

Similar instructions have also been given in respect of the pets trained for hunting:

... وَمَا عَلَّمْتُم مِّنَ ٱلْجَوَارِحِ مُكَلِّبِينَ تُعَلِّمُونَهُنَّ مِمَّا عَلَّمَكُمُ ٱللَّهُ ۖ فَكُلُوا۟
مِمَّآ أَمْسَكْنَ عَلَيْكُمْ وَٱذْكُرُوا۟ ٱسْمَ ٱللَّهِ عَلَيْهِ ۖ ... ﴿٤﴾

... and such hunting animals as you teach them to hunt, teaching them according to the knowledge Allah has given you – you may eat what they catch for you – but invoke the name of Allah on it.[9]

لِّيَشْهَدُوا۟ مَنَٰفِعَ لَهُمْ وَيَذْكُرُوا۟ ٱسْمَ ٱللَّهِ فِىٓ أَيَّامٍ مَّعْلُومَٰتٍ عَلَىٰ مَا رَزَقَهُم
مِّنۢ بَهِيمَةِ ٱلْأَنْعَٰمِ ۖ فَكُلُوا۟ مِنْهَا وَأَطْعِمُوا۟ ٱلْبَآئِسَ ٱلْفَقِيرَ ﴿٢٨﴾

... to witness the benefits in store for them, and pronounce the name of Allah during the appointed days over the cattle that He has provided them. So eat of it and feed the distressed and the needy.[10]

وَلِكُلِّ أُمَّةٍ جَعَلْنَا مَنسَكًا لِّيَذْكُرُوا۟ ٱسْمَ ٱللَّهِ عَلَىٰ مَا رَزَقَهُم مِّنۢ
بَهِيمَةِ ٱلْأَنْعَٰمِ ۗ ... ﴿٣٤﴾

For every people We have laid down a ritual of sacrifice [although the purpose of the ritual is the same] that they pronounce the name of Allah over the cattle He has provided them.[11]

... فَٱذْكُرُوا۟ ٱسْمَ ٱللَّهِ عَلَيْهَا صَوَآفَّ ۖ فَإِذَا وَجَبَتْ جُنُوبُهَا فَكُلُوا۟ مِنْهَا
وَأَطْعِمُوا۟ ٱلْقَانِعَ وَٱلْمُعْتَرَّ ۚ ... ﴿٣٦﴾

---

[9] *Al-Mā'idah* 5: 4.
[10] *Al-Ḥajj* 22: 28.
[11] *Al-Ḥajj* 22: 34.

> *So make them stand [at the time of sacrifice] and pronounce the name of Allah over them, and when they fall down on their sides [after they are slaughtered] eat and also feed them who do not ask and those who ask.*[12]

The recurrent use of the term *tasmīyah* for *dhabh*, or the act of slaughter, is evidently a clear proof of *tasmīyah* and *dhabīhah* (halal meat) being synonymous with each other. Slaughtered animal's meat, therefore, becomes halal only with *tasmīyah*, while the *dhabīhah* is only that animal on which Allah's name has been pronounced while slaughtering.

Now, let us see with the help of the Prophetic Traditions what importance Shariah attaches to *tasmīyah*. 'Adī ibn Ḥātim, an eminent Companion of the Prophet and son of Arabia's legend in generosity, Ḥātim al-Tā'ī, often asked the Messenger of Allah questions concerning game and its rules. Following were the hunting rules the Prophet (peace be upon him) taught him:[13]

---

[12] *Al-Ḥajj* 22: 36.

[13] The following Traditions regarding the game and its purification (*tazkīyah*) quoted by Imām Bukhārī offer more details:

> عَن عَدىٍّ بِن حَاتِمٍ رَضِىَ الله عَنه قَال: سَأَلتُ النَبِيَّ صَلى اللهُ عَلَيهِ وسَلَّم عَن صَيدِالمِعراضِ، قال: مَا أصَابَ بِحَـدِّه فَكُلهُ ، وَمَا أصَابَ بِعَرضهِ فهوَ وَقِيذٌ. وَسَألتهُ عَن صَيدِ الكَلبِ، فقَال: مَا أَمسَكَ فكُل، فَإِنَّ أَخذَ الكَلبِ ذَكَاةٌ ، وَإن وَجَدتَ مع كَلبِكَ أَو كِلاَبِك كَلباًغيرَهُ ، فَخَشِيتَ اَن يَكُونَ اَخذَهُ مَعهُ وَقَد قَتلهُ فَلاَ تَاكُل، فَإِنَّمَا ذَكَرتَ الله عَلٰى كَلبِكَ وَلَم تَذكُرهُ عَلٰى غَيرَه.
>
> 'Adī ibn Ḥātim narrated: 'I asked the Messenger of Allah about the game killed through *mi'rād* [the sharp-edged piece of iron rod or wooden lancet used for hunting]. He said: "You may eat of the game killed by its sharp edge, but if it is killed by its blunt side [being hit by its shaft] then the game is unlawful to eat." When I asked him about hunting by a trained hound, his reply was: "If the hound catches the game for you, eat of it because killing that way is like the purified way of slaughter. But if you see with your hound or hounds another dog, and you think that he too might have joined them in hunting, you should not eat of it, because you mentioned Allah's Name on your hound and not on the other dog."' (*Al-Jāmi' Al-Ṣaḥīḥ*, No. 1915, *The Book of Slaughtering and Hunting*)
>
> عَن اَبِي ثَعلَبه الخُشَنِي رَضِيَ اللهُ عَنهُ قَالَ: قُلتُ يَا نَبِيَّ الله أَنا بِأَرضِ قَومٍ اَهلِ كِتَابٍ أَفَنَأْكُلُ فِى آنِيتهم؟ وَبأَرضِ صَيدٍ، أَصِيدُ بِقَوسِي، وَبِكَلبِي الَّذِي لَيسَ بِمُعَلَّم وَ بِكَلبِى المُعَلَّم، فَمَايَصلُح لِيَ؟ قَال: أَمَّا مَاذَكَرتَ مِن اَهلِ الكِتَابِ، فَإن وَجَدتُم غَيرَهَا فَلاَ تَاكُلُوا فِيها، وَ اِن لم تَجِدُوا غَيرَهَا

إِذَا اَرسَلتَ كَلبَكَ فَاذكُر اسمَ الله، فَإن اَمسَكَ عَلَيكَ فَادرَكتَهُ حَيّاً فَاذبَحه، وَإن ادرَكتَهُ قَد قُتِلَ وَلَّم يَاكُل مِنهُ فَكُله، وَإذَا رَمَيتَ سَهمَكَ فَاذكُرِ اسمَ الله.

When you release your hound [for hunting], pronounce the name of Allah. If the dog catches the game for you and you get it alive, slaughter it. If you find it killed but uneaten by him, you can use the meat. When you release your arrow [on a game], do pronounce the name of Allah. (Narrated by Imam Bukhārī and Muslim)

وَمَا صُدتَ بِقَوسِكَ فَذَكَرتَ اسمَ الله عَلَيه فَكُل، وَمَا صُدتَ بِكَلبِكَ المُعَلَّم فَذَكَرتَ اسمَ اللهِ عَلَيه فَكُل ... اَمرِرِ الدَّمَ بِمَ شِئتَ، وَاذكُرِ اسمَ الله.

The animal you hunt by bow and arrow and have also pronounced the name of Allah on it, you can eat of its meat. Also eat from the game hunted through your trained dog if Allah's name has been invoked over it. ... Shed blood through anything [sharp-edged] and pronounce Allah's name. (Abū Dāwūd and al-Nasā'ī)

مَا عَلَّمتَ مِن كَلبٍ اَو بَازٍ ثُمَّ أَرسَلْتَهُ وَذَكَرتَ اسمَ الله عَلَيه فَكُل مِمَّا اَمسَكَ عَلَيكَ.

فَاغسِلُوهَا وَكُلُوا فِيها. وَمَا صِدتَ بِقَوسِكَ فَذَكَرتَ اسَمَ الله فَكُل، وَمَا صِدتَ بِكَلبِكَ المُعَلَّم فَذَكَرتَ اسَم الله فَكُل، وَمَا صِدتَ بِكَلبِكَ غَيرِالمُعَلَّم فَادرَكتَ ذَكَاتَهُ فَكُل.

Abū Tha'labah al-Khushanī narrated that he asked: 'O Messenger of Allah, we are living in the land of the People of the Book. Can we take our meals in their utensils? There is plenty of game there as well and I hunt by my arrow and also with my hound that is untrained and with the trained one. What is good for me in this respect?' The Prophet said: 'As for what you mentioned about the People of the Book, if you can get other utensils, do not eat out of theirs, but if you cannot then wash their utensils before eating. When you hunt by your bow and arrow and also mention Allah's Name, eat of it. As for hunting by your trained hound after you have mentioned Allah's Name, eat of it; if you hunt by an untrained dog but are able to purify the game by proper slaughtering before it dies then it is permissible for you as well.' (Ibid. No. 1916) – Editor.

> Whether dog, or falcon, whichever you train [for hunting] and release [on game], pronounce Allah's name over it and then eat of what (the bird of prey or the dog) has caught for you. (Abū Dāwūd and Imam Aḥmad)

It is evident from these clear-cut injunctions that according to the Shariah, *tasmīyah* is a binding condition for the slaughtered animal to be halal and the meat of the hunted animal or bird killed without pronouncing Allah's name is totally haram.

11.2. Leading jurists' views on halal meat

According to Imam Abū Ḥanīfah, Imam Mālik and Imam Aḥmad, if *tasmīyah* has been intentionally avoided, the meat of that animal would be haram. If this happens by mistake, however, or while slaughtering the Muslim hunter forgets to pronounce Allah's name, there is no harm in eating from that animal. Hadrat 'Ali, 'Abdullah ibn 'Abbas, Sa'īd ibn al-Musayyib, Imam Zuhrī, Tā'ūs, Mujāhid, Imam Ḥasan al-Baṣrī, and others were also of the same view.

Imām al-Shāfi'ī, however, viewed differently. According to him, *tasmīyah* is not an essential condition and pronouncing the name of Allah on the animal is part of the Islamic tradition but not obligatory. The arguments advanced by this school are, however, too weak to sustain and when critically examined appear to carry no weight as compared to the arguments in favour of *tasmīyah* as a precondition for *dhabīhah* (the slaughtered animal) being halal.

In light of the injunctions of the Qur'an and Ahadith, the following are the three preconditions for the animal meat to be halal:

i. The meat must not be of the animals declared haram by the Qur'an and the Sunnah.
ii. Purification by properly shedding blood (*tazkīyah*) must have been performed.
iii. The precondition of *tasmīyah* (invoking Allah's Name) must have been observed.

11.3. Meat of the animal slaughtered by the People of the Book

Now, let us see how the Islamic Shariah deals with the meat of animals slaughtered by the People of the Book. Allah *subḥānahū wa taʿālā* says in Surah *al-Māʾidah*:

ٱلْيَوْمَ أُحِلَّ لَكُمُ ٱلطَّيِّبَٰتُ ۖ وَطَعَامُ ٱلَّذِينَ أُوتُوا۟ ٱلْكِتَٰبَ حِلٌّ لَّكُمْ وَطَعَامُكُمْ حِلٌّ لَّهُمْ ۖ ... ﴿٥﴾

> *This day are (all) things good and pure made lawful unto you. The food of the People of the Book is lawful unto you and yours is lawful unto them.*
>
> [*al-Māʾidah* 5: 5]

From the wordings of the *āyah* and its context, it is obvious that the food declared halal for Muslims from the dining table of the People of the Book must essentially be up to the approved standards of 'good and pure' [*tayyibāt*]. How can anyone construe from the *āyah* that those *impure and bad things* (*khabāʾith*), which the Qur'an and the Sunnah have declared haram for Muslims and which we can eat neither in our own home nor at the home of any other Muslim, are permitted for us to eat if served by a Christian or a Jew? Both Imam Abū Ḥanīfah and Imam Aḥmad were of the view that one must observe the rules and preconditions of *tazkīyah* and *tasmīyah* for food when taking it even from a Christian or a Jew.[14]

According to the Shāfiʿī school, the meat of the animal slaughtered by a Jew or a Christian is halal, even if Allah's sacred name has not been pronounced, as they do not view *tasmīyah* as obligatory. But the Shawāfiʿ too discard meat as haram if a name other than that of Allah *subhānaḥū wa taʿālā* is invoked.

The example of *Sayyidunā* Rasūl Allah (peace be upon him) accepting the meat offered by a Jewish woman during the Khaybar expedition has been completely misconstrued. How can that be taken to imply the permissibility of the meat of the animal slaughtered without *tasmīyah*? There is nothing in the precedent to suggest that the Jews during the days of the Prophet (peace be upon him) slaughtered their animals without invoking God's name. The Prophet of God

---

[14] ʿAbd al-Raḥmān al-Jazīrī, *Al-Fiqh ʿala al-Madhāhib al-Arbaʿah*, vol. 1, pp. 726–730.

was well aware that the Jews then followed the hallowed tradition of pronouncing God's name while slaughtering their animals and that is why he accepted the gift with no hesitation.[15]

'Abdullah ibn 'Abbas was the only eminent jurist from amongst the Companions of the Prophet to interpret that the injunction about the food of the People of the Book being halal for Muslims (*āyah* 5 of Surah *al-Mā'idah*) offered an exception from the applicability of the proviso of *tasmīyah* as laid down in *āyah* 121 of Surah *al-An'ām*: *Do not eat of* [*the animal*] *over which the name of Allah has not been pronounced* [*at the time of slaughtering*], *for that is a transgression.* Being an individual's opinion, it cannot, however, override the almost consensus of the Ṣaḥābah and Tābi'ūn about the obligatory nature of *tasmīyah* in light of the clear injunctions of the Qur'an and the Sunnah. If we follow such isolated opinions, this would naturally render halal everything that the Jews and Christians ate or drank. We know very well, however, that it is not the case and no jurist from any school of thought permitted forbidden items like pork and wine. There can be no exception, therefore, in the case of the injunction on *tasmīyah.*

I would, therefore, go by the stand taken by Ahnāf and Ḥanābilah, as it is logically closer to the import of the Qur'anic injunctions. This is the interpretation that has been almost universally accepted by the Muslims, whose vast majority abstains from the meat of animals slaughtered in an un-Islamic manner.

It may be worthwhile to add that sometimes the throats of birds and chickens get slit apart while slaughtering. Religious scholars and *'ulamā'* have condoned such acts of simple negligence because these are not intentional. That cannot obviously be applied, however, to the practice of mechanically chopping off animals' heads. Therefore, the injunctions of *tazkīyah* and *tasmīyah* remain binding except only under those extraordinary circumstances of compulsion where the Book of God allows a person to eat even carrion if nothing else is available for food and his life is at stake.

---

[15] In fact, according to the Jewish Law that remains the authentic way of slaughtering animals even today. Except for animals killed mechanically, those slaughtered normally by Jewish meat sellers go through the process that they call *kosher,* and in Hebrew *shechita.* This is almost the same as the Islamic system of *dhabīhahs* – Editor.

PART TWO

Islam and the State

12 Imam Abū Ḥanīfah on the Ethical and Legal Dimensions of Revolt in a Muslim State*

12.1. The institution of Caliphate

In any theory of statecraft, the first question of prime importance has always been to whom sovereignty belongs. In this context, the well known concept of statehood in Islam, as practically demonstrated in the institution of caliphate, may be summed up as follows:

> *Sovereignty belongs to Allah; the Prophet as His Representative is to be obeyed; and Shariah, revealed by the Lord is the supreme law of the land, which is to be followed in all walks of life and contrary to which no conduct is lawful.*

As the leading exponent of Islamic Law, Imam A'ẓam Abū Ḥanīfah explained the subject not as part of political science but in legal and juridical terms. He said:

> When I get a decree in the Book of God, I stick to it. But when I do not get it there, I seek guidance from the Sunnah of the Prophet and the Traditions transmitted through reliable sources and trusted by the trustworthy. In case, I get an injunction neither in the Book of God, nor from the Sunnah of the Prophet, I follow the consensus (*ijmā'*) of the Companions of the Prophet (peace be upon him). If they differ (in some details), I accept one version and leave the other, but never go beyond what they have transmitted. … Just as other jurists have the right of interpretation (*ijtihād*), I too have the same.[1]

---

* *Tarjumān al-Qur'ān*, August–September 1963.

[1] Al-Khatīb al-Baghdādī, *Tarīkh Baghdād*, vol. 13, p. 368.

Imam Abū Ḥanīfah attached great importance to Prophetic Traditions as well. Al-Dhahabī noted the following in this respect: 'All the disciples of Imam Abū Ḥanīfah are unanimous on the fact that the Imam's approach was to give preference to the Prophetic Tradition, though *dā'if*,[2] over his own deduction and induction or personal views.'[3]

It is evident from these statements that Imam Abū Ḥanīfah regarded the Qur'an and the Sunnah as the 'final authority' and that the 'legal sovereignty' of an Islamic state belonged to Allah and His Messenger. Responding to a letter from Khalīfah al-Manṣūr regarding his approach as an eminent jurist of Islam on the concept of legal sovereignty, the Imam said:

> What has been reported to you is not correct. My first preference is the Book of God, then the Tradition of Rasūl Allah (peace be upon him), then the judgment of Abū Bakr, 'Umar, 'Uthmān and 'Alī (may Allah be pleased with them all), and finally the stand taken by other Companions of the Prophet. Yes, in case of any difference of opinion among them, I follow the deductive and inductive method (*qiyās*).[4]

12.1.1. *Grabbing power by force*

It is not lawful for a caliph in Islam to first grab power by the use of force and then solemnize his rule by seeking the pledge of allegiance (*al-bay'ah*). According to Imam Abū Ḥanīfah, the correct form of caliphate is that which is established by *al-bay'ah al-'ammah* (the popular pledge of allegiance and support or popular vote), and in consultation with the *ahl al-ra'y*, or opinion leaders. The Imam publicly expressed this view at a time when even an insinuation to that effect meant putting one's head under the guillotine.

---

[2] *Dā'if* literally means 'weak'. As a term of the *Usūl 'Ilm al-Hadīth* (Principles of the Science of Prophetic Traditions), a hadith is called *dā'if* by *muḥaddithīn* when among its chain of narrators there is a person or two whose antecedents are not well-confirmed. The authenticity of the narrative itself may be beyond doubt, but the traditionists place it in the order of precedence second to the *Sahīh* and *Ḥasan Aḥādith*, or Traditions with unblemished chain of narrators – Editor.

[3] Al-Dhahabī, *Manāqib al-Imām Abī Ḥanīfah wa Ṣāhibayh*, p. 21.

[4] Al-Shā'rānī, *Kitāb Al-Mīzān* (Cairo, 1925), vol. 1, p. 62.

Caliph al-Manṣūr's Chamberlain, Rabīʿ ibn Yūnus, narrated that the caliph invited the three eminent jurists of the day, Imam Mālik, Ibn Abī Zi'b and Imam Abū Ḥanīfah and asked them: 'What do you think of the government authority that Allah *taʿālā* has bestowed on me among the Muslim Ummah? Am I fit for it?'

Imam Mālik's reply was: 'Had you not been fit for it, it would not have been granted to you by the Almighty.' Ibn Abī Ziʿb's response was, however, rather terse: 'The worldly kingdom is given by Allah *subḥānahū wa taʿālā* to whom He wills. But the kingdom of the Hereafter is granted only to him who is a seeker of that kingdom and whose efforts the Almighty crowns with success. Allah's help would be near at hand if you obey Him. Otherwise, if you disobey Him it will not be with you. Actually, the caliphate is established by the assembly of the God-fearing people. Anybody who himself usurps this (office), he has no love and fear of God (*taqwā*). You and your associates have deviated from the right course and hence are out of Allah's grace. Now, if you seek proximity to the Almighty and beg for salvation and guidance for good deeds, you may get it. Otherwise, you will remain your own captive.' Imam Abū Ḥanīfah subsequently observed on this statement: 'When Ibn Abī Zi'b was telling all this to al-Manṣūr, I and Mālik gathered our clothes around us fearing that soon his head would roll leaving all over a splash of blood.'

Al-Manṣūr finally turned to Imam Abū Ḥanīfah who responded in a more detailed way: 'The seeker of the right path for the sake of religion always refrains from rash behaviour. If you probe your own conscience, you will yourself know that you have invited us not for Allah's Pleasure, but because you would like us to utter words that might please you the most so that the people too could know of it. The fact remains that you assumed the office of caliph unendorsed even by a two-member assembly of those eligible to issue formal legal opinion (fatwa), whereas the caliphate needs endorsement through the Muslims' popular consent and consultations. See, how Abū Bakr al-Siddīq refrained for six months before deciding (to formally take over the office of the Caliph) until such time as he had obtained the verdict of allegiance from the people of Yemen [the farthest governorate of the Islamic caliphate of Arabia].'

After explaining their viewpoints freely to the all powerful ruler of the day, the three great personalities of Islamic learning and jurisprudence rose from al-Manṣūr's Court. The caliph dispatched his Chamberlain Rabī' to follow them with the gift of a sackful of dirhams for each one of them and ordered Rabī': 'If the gift is accepted by Imam Mālik, it should be given to him, but if Abū Ḥanīfah and Ibn Abī Zi'b agree to receive it, bring back their heads, chopped off.' Imam Mālik received the gift, but when Rabī' reached Ibn Abī Zi'b, his response was: 'How can I take the money that I do not consider halal even for al-Manṣūr.' The reply of Imām Abū Ḥanīfah to the Chamberlain was: 'I would not touch this money even at the risk of losing my head.' When this was reported back to Al-Manasūr, he heaved a sigh of relief and said: 'This show of indifference by them has saved them their lives.'[5]

12.1.2. *The Islamic concept of statecraft*

Until the time of Imam Abū Ḥanīfah, the terms and conditions for the office of the caliph in respect of the Islamic concept of statecraft were rather well established but not yet codified, and the Muslim jurists relied principally on the practical examples and opinions expressed by the the leaders of various schools of thought, as noted above. Later on, however, the subject was treated as an independent discipline by scholars like al-Māwardī and Ibn Khaldūn. The principal reason for this was the fact that these terms and conditions were almost an accepted reality then and needed no debate. For example, there was a consensus on the precondition of the caliph being *a Muslim male, a free citizen of the State, having the required level of knowledge* and being *intellectually and physically fit.*

The following two issues of the time, however, aroused debate and needed clarification: (i) whether a tyrant and profligate person can become a caliph? and (ii) if the proviso of his belonging to the House of Quraysh remained binding? Let us discuss these two important aspects of the matter in greater detail.

---

[5] Al-Kardarī, *Manāqib al-Imām al-A'ẓam*, vol. 2, pp. 15–16.

12.1.3. *Leadership of a despot and the morally wayward* (*fājir*)

Imam Abū Ḥanīfah was the pioneer jurist to offer detailed rulings on the Islamic concept of statecraft. We have, therefore, to naturally rely on his views to understand the subject in its proper perspective. The time when he gave his rulings was marked by an intense conflict between the two extremist views in Iraq, in particular, and the Muslim world in general. On the one side, there were those who held the leadership of an evildoer and the morally wayward (*fājir*) absolutely unlawful for the state and any social activity under his rule totally illegal. There were others who argued that it was unlawful to rebel even against a tyrant or the morally wayward who might have seized power by fair means or foul and established himself as the ruler, because this causes anarchy and bloodshed.

Imam Abū Ḥanīfah struck a balance between these two extremes. In his famous book *Al-Fiqh al-Akbar*, he said: 'The mandatory Prayer is lawful under the leadership of a believer, good or a bad.' Imam al-Ṭaḥāwī, explaining his approach wrote: 'Both hajj and jihad would continue until the Last Day under the leadership of those in authority in the Islamic state, whether those persons be good or bad. Nothing invalidates these obligations, nor can anything disrupt their continuity.'[6]

This is just one side of the issue. The other side, according to Imam Abū Ḥanīfah, is that justice (*'adālah*) and honourable personal conduct are the essential qualifications for a person holding a position of authority. A tyrant and usurper can neither be a legitimate *khalīfah*, *qāḍī* (judge/magistrate), hakim (ruler/governor), nor mufti (official expounder of Shariah injunctions). If such a person takes power himself, his leadership will be *ultra vires* and the people are not bound to give him allegiance and obey his orders. At the same time, however, it is lawful for the people to perform their duties as part of their social obligations following such a person's hoisting himself into a position of authority; and the verdicts issued by the judges appointed by him are also valid. In his renowned book *Aḥkām al-Qur'ān*, Abū Bakr

[6] Ibn Abil 'Izz Al-Ḥanafī, *Sharḥ al-Ṭaḥāwīyah*, p. 322.

al-Jaṣṣās, an eminent jurist of the Ḥanafi School, elaborated the Islamic concept of statecraft according to Imam Abū Ḥanīfah as follows:

> *Āyah* 124 of Surah *al-Baqarah* says: قَالَ إِنِّي جَاعِلُكَ لِلنَّاسِ إِمَامًا (*He [the Lord] said: 'Indeed I am going to appoint you a leader of all people.' When Abraham asked:* قَالَ وَمِن ذُرِّيَّتِي قَالَ لَا يَنَالُ عَهْدِى الظَّـٰلِمِينَ *'… is this covenant also for my descendants?' the Lord responded: 'My covenant does not embrace the wrongdoers.'* (*al-Baqarah* 2: 124) The *āyah* thus reaffirms that those occupying positions of leadership in matters concerning religion must also be just and righteous and not wrongdoers. It similarly invalidates a godless person's leadership of the state: he cannot become *al-khalīfah*. If such a person hoists himself to that position and he is known for his profligacy and disobedience to the Lord, it is not obligatory for the people to obey him. This has also been put so succinctly in the famous saying of the Messenger of Allah (peace be upon him): لَاطَاعَة لِمَخلُوقٍ فِى مَعصِيَّةِ الخَالِق ('There can be no obedience for any creature at the cost of disobedience to the Creator'). The above *āyah* of Surah *al-Baqarah* also indicates that no *fāsiq* (someone disobedient to the Lord) is eligible to hold an office of authority like that of a judge or magistrate. His rulings would be *ultra vires* and unfit for execution. Neither is he qualified to be a witness, nor a Narrator of Hadith, nor his decree as a mufti has legal validity.[7]

Al-Sarakhsī, in his book *Al-Mabsūṭ* (vol. 10, p. 130), dispelled the notion that Imam Abū Ḥanīfah approved of a *fāsiq* to hold a position of authority. Al-Jaṣṣās explained this in these words:

> Some people think that Imam Abū Ḥanīfah approved for a *fāsiq* to hold a position of leadership in the land and become *al-Khalīfah*. … If this view was attributed to him not as a calculated lie, it is then surely a case of misunderstanding

[7] Abū Bakr al-Jaṣṣās, *Aḥkām Al-Qur'ān*, vol. 1, p. 80.

> and the reason may have been the statement of Imam Abū Ḥanīfah, and not of Imam Abū Ḥanīfah alone but of all the eminent *fuqahā'* of Iraq, that if the *qāḍī* himself is an honest and just person (*'ādil*), his judgment would be valid even though he may have been appointed to that position by a ruler who is disobedient to the Lord (*fāsiq*) and morally wayward (*fājir*). *Ṣalāh* is also lawful behind the *imāmate* of such rulers.[8]

Al-Dhahabī and Al-Muwaffaq al-Makkī quoted the following statement on the subject from Imam A'ẓam: 'The ruler who misappropriates public funds *(fay)*, or recourses to injustice and tyranny (al-ẓulm), his holding of public office is unlawful and his rulings null and void.'[9]

As evident from these statements, Imam Abū Ḥanīfah differentiated between the *de facto* and the *de jure* positions. According to the extremist notions of Khawārij and Mu'tazilites, the absence of a *de jure* ruler who fulfilled the conditions of righteousness and justice meant the disruption of the entire administrative and social order of the state and the society. The courts could not function, nor were religious duties like pilgrimage to Makkah and establishment of the *Jumu'āh* and *Jamā'ah* possible, nor could any other social and political activity be considered lawful. Imam Abū Ḥanīfah rectified these schools' extremist approach by decreeing that if a *de jure* ruler is not available, the system of the state and the Muslim society should be allowed to run as an exceptional case under the *de facto* ruler, though he may not fulfil the preconditions laid down for that office.

12.1.4. *The precondition of Qarashiyat*

On the second precondition, Imam A'ẓam upheld the view that the caliph should come from the House of Quraysh.[10] This was in fact the

---

[8] Ibid. vol. 1, pp. 80–81.

[9] Al-Dhahabī, *Manāqib Al-Imām Abī Ḥanīfah wa Ṣāhibayh'*, p. 17 and Al-Muwaffaq al-Makkī, *Manāqib al-Imām al-A'ẓam Abī Ḥanīfah*, vol. 2, p. 100.

[10] Al-Mas'ūdi, vol. 2, p. 192.

consensus of the *Ahl al-Sunnah* as a whole at the time.[11] The reason was not that the constitutional right to rule belonged exclusively to the house of Quraysh alone. It was rather necessitated by the socio-political condition of the time, due to which it was considered essential for the caliph to be from the Quraysh so that the popular support and esteem of the Muslim citizens could be held together. Ibn Khaldūn explained this factor elaborately. According to him, Arabs at a point in time were the backbone of the Muslim society and its mainstay and their consensus for the leadership was possible only on a person belonging to their intellectually most outstanding and politically most powerful tribe, the Quraysh. Elevation of a person from other smaller social units would have led to dissentions and disunity endangering the very institution of the caliphate and the entire political fabric of the state. That was the wisdom behind the Prophet's ruling that: 'Let the leader be from the House of Quraysh,'[12]

The Islamic Shariah, however, does not forbid a non-Qarayshī from holding the office of leadership in an Islamic state. Had it not been so, *Amīr al-Mu'minīn* 'Umar would not have stated at the time of his death: 'Had Sālim (the freed slave of Huzayfah) been alive, I would have proposed him to be my successor.'[13] While proposing to retain *al-Khilāfah* among the Quraysh, the Prophet (peace be upon him) had himself made it conditional on certain pre-qualifications, making it quite clear that the position of caliph was not a birthright of a person belonging to the Quraysh tribe and would remain with them so long as they fulfilled those conditions and prequalifications.[14]

The Mu'tazilites and Khawārij were at the other end of the spectrum, and true to their extremist views believed in the 'democratic' right of every Muslim citizen to stand for the office of the caliph, even at the cost of the Islamic state's political and administrative stability and the people's unity and cohesion.

---

[11] Al-Shahristānī, *Kitāb Al-Milal wal Niḥal*, vol. 1, p. 106.

[12] *Musnad Aḥmad*, Nos 926 and 2133, vol. 2, pp. 129, 83 and vol. 4, p. 421; *Sunan Abū Dāwūd*.

[13] Ibn Jarīr, *Tarīkh al-Ṭabarī*, vol. 3, p. 192.

[14] Ibn Ḥajar al-'Asqalānī, *Fatḥ al-Bārī*, vol. 13, p. 95.

12.1.5. *The sacrosanct position of the public exchequer* (*Bayt al-Māl*)

One of the dominant trends among the rulers of later years was their tendency to abuse government funds and encroach on public property. Imam Abū Ḥanīfah strongly criticized this trend. In his view, unfairness of personal conduct, tyranny in judgment, and dishonesty in public account rendered the official status of a ruler unlawful (al-Dhahabī). The Imam also did not approve of the ruler taking for his personal use the gifts and offerings presented to him by foreign countries and their dignitaries. According to him, those were part of the public account and must be retained in the national treasury, and the caliph and his family had no claim over them. His argument was that the precious gifts were offered to the caliph not in his personal capacity, but as head of an Islamic state and as a mark of its collective resolve and image abroad.[15]

Imam Abū Ḥanīfah similarly did not approve of the caliph using public funds for his personal use. He disallowed him to indulge in lavish and uncalled for expenditure and awarding gifts and presents from the national treasury. That was the reason why he never accepted any gift himself from the caliphs of his day. Once, a major conflict arose between him and al-Manṣūr, who had to ask him why he didn't accept his gifts. The Imam responded thus:

> The gifts were given to me by the *Amīr al-Mu'minīn* not from his own purse. Had it been so, I would have never rejected it. I refused to accept it because it was offered to me from the public exchequer belonging to the Muslim citizens. Moreover, you knew full well that I was neither a soldier fighting for public defence, nor one of their dependents to justify a share of public money. Nor do I deserve public support as a destitute.[16]

When al-Manṣūr sentenced the Imam to thirty lashes because of his refusal to accept the position of Chief Justice and his whole body was soaked in blood, the caliph's uncle, Abd al-Samad ibn 'Alī,

---

[15] Al-Sarakhsī, *Sharḥ al-Siyar al-Kabīr*, vol. 1, p. 98.

[16] Al-Muwaffaq al-Makkī, *Manāqib al-Imām al-A'ẓam Abī Ḥanīfah*, vol. 1, p. 215.

admonished him for such an act of brutality toward 'the Imam of Iraq and celebrated Jurist of the Orient'. With a sense of guilt and shame in the face of Imam A'ẓam's exemplary firmness, al-Manṣūr sent to him a gift of 30,000 dirhams, 1,000 dirham for each lashing; but the Imam declined the offer. He was then told to accept it and donate the money in charity. His reply was: 'Does he (al-Manṣūr) have any amount of halal money with him?'[17] About the same time, when politically the Imam waas experiencing very hard trials and tribulations and nearing his glorious end, he expressed in his will the desire not to be buried in that part of Baghdad which al-Manṣūr had developed by usurping public property. When the caliph came to know of his will, he cried in anguish: 'O Imam, who can save me from your chastisement in life as well as in death!'[18]

12.1.6. *Independence of the judiciary and the executive*

According to the Islamic concept of Statecraft, the judiciary must always be independent of the pressure and interference of the executive so as to facilitate its unhindered deliverence of justice. According to Imam Abū Ḥanīfah, the *qāḍī* must be in a position to enforce his judgment even on the caliph should he be guilty of the infringement of the people's rights. During the last days of his life, when the Imam was sure that the government would no longer let him live in peace, he assembled his students and disciples and, in addition to so many pearls of wisdom bequeathed to them, he stated: 'If the Caliph is found guilty of a crime that concerns human rights, *Qāḍī'l-quḍāt*, who is next to him in status, should enforce his judgment on him.'[19]

The main reason for Imam A'ẓam's refusal, both under the Umayyads and the Abbasids, to accept any position of eminence in the government, especially in the judiciary, was his conviction that the judiciary did not enjoy the freedom that was its due. The Imam was afraid not of his inability to bring the caliph to the dock, nor of any difficulty in establishing the writ of law and justice, but more of his own self being used as a tool of oppression and being forced to issue

[17] Ibid. vol. 1, p. 216.

[18] Ibid. vol. 2, p. 180.

[19] Ibid. vol. 2, p. 100.

wrong judgments. He was equally apprehensive of interference in the free discharge of an onerous responsibility, not only by the Caliph but from everyone associated with his court.

Yazīd ibn 'Umar ibn Hubayrah, the Governor of Iraq during the Umayyads, was the first to force the Imam to accept an official position. In the year 130 Hijrah, Iraq was in the grip of a rising storm against the Umayyad rule, which eventually swept them out of power during the next two years. It was Ibn Hubayrah's passion then to associate eminent personalities like the Imam with the government and use their position and influence among the people in favour of the rulers. Thus, he succeeded in elevating to senior positions some noted scholars of the day, like Ibn Abī Layla, Dāwūd Ibn Abī Hind and Ibn Shubramah. Finally, he invited Imam Abū Ḥanīfah and said: 'I place in your hand my seal of authority. No directive would be issued unless you put your stamp of approval and no funds would be disbursed from the treasury till you ratify the expenditure.' The Imam declined to accept the offer for which he was apprehended and was sent to jail. Ibn Hubayrah also warned him of the punishment of flogging unless he agreed to the offer. Other jurists and scholars of the day tried to convince the Imam to have pity on himself, citing their own examples that they had to accept the official positions under duress just to save themselves from the dire consequences of the refusal. The Imam's resolute response was: 'Even if he (the governor) wished me to count the gates of Wāsit's Grand Mosque, I would not do so for him, let alone assist him in discharge of such dreadful acts as endorsing his decree to execute someone. By the Merciful Lord, I will never join hands with him in a position of responsibility.'

Ibn Hubayrah then offered him many other offices of eminence but he continued declining until he decided to appoint him the *Qāḍī* of Kūfah and threatened to sentence him to whipping if he declined. Swearing by the Almighty the Imam said: 'It is easier for me to face his whips in this world than to suffer the ignominy of the Hereafter. By Lord the Merciful, I refuse to accept his offer even if he kills me.' Ultimately, Ibn Hubayrah sentenced him to striking his head with twenty to thirty whips for ten days. When Ibn Hubayrah was told that the Imam might die due to this, he helplessly said: 'Is there no wise counsel to help him make up his mind?' When this was conveyed to the Imam, he said: 'Allow me to consult my friends.' On this he was released and then left Kūfah for Makkah al-Mukarramah, where he remained until the end of the Umayyad's rule.[20]

The Imam was then pressured during the 'Abbasid era by Caliph Abū Ja'far al-Manṣūr (136 Hijrah/754 CE–158/779) to accept the highest position of the state's judiciary, but he declined. When al-Nafs al-Zakīyyah and his brother Ibrāhīm launched their anti-Manṣūr movement, Imam A'ẓam did not wait to openly lend his support to them.[21] According to al-Dhahabī, al-Manṣūr was almost burning with rage against the Imam, but felt handicapped in taking any drastic action to eliminate him. He had seen what had happened to the Umayyads after the hatred ignited against them among the people at the tragedy of Karbalā and the brutal murder of Imam Ḥusayn. Al-Manṣūr, therefore, planned to bind Imam A'ẓam in chains of gold and silver instead of killing him and thereby inviting popular wrath against himself and his family. The Imam was eventually offered charge of the Supreme Judge of the Abbasid Empire. When al-Manṣūr insisted, the Imam politely explained to him the reason for his refusal: 'Only such a person is eligible for a position in the judiciary who is strong enough to enforce the rule of law and his judgment on yourself, your princes and commanders of your legions. I do not find myself

---

[20] Al-Makkī, vol. 2, pp. 21–24; Ibn Khallikān, *Wafayāt al-A'yān*, vol. 5, p. 41; Ibn 'Abd al-Barr, *Al-Intiqā'*, p. 171.

[21] Muhammad *Al-Nafs al-Zakīyyah* (Pure Soul) was the great-grandson of Imām Ḥasan. He was held in high esteem for his piety and sagacity. He was based at Al-Madinah al-Munawwarah and refused to give oath of allegiance to Abul 'Abbas Al-Saffāḥ, al-Manṣūr's brother and founder of the Abbasid dynastic rule (132/750–136/754). Together with his brother Ibrāhīm, Al-Nafs al-Zakīyyah revolted against al-Manṣūr. Following al-Manṣūr's failure to capture them, as they went into hiding and decided to secretly carry on their movement, the caliph had their father, 'Abd Allah, imprisoned. At this, Al-Nafs al-Zakīyyah came into open and denounced al-Manṣūr for his disrespect of the Islamic Shariah. The revolt was crushed by al-Manṣūr's troops and Al-Nafs al-Zakīyyah was martyred in Ramadan (145/December 762). Muhammad Al-Nafs al-Zakīyyah's brother Ibrāhīm, also a popular rebel fighting against al-Manṣūr, was the next to be overpowered and killed. For related details, see *The Cambridge History of Islam*, vol. 1, p. 110 (1970) – Editor.

capable of doing that. In fact, whenever you call me I feel at ease only when I am out of your sight.'[22]

On another occasion, during the course of a heated conversation the Imam told al-Manṣūr in rather more direct terms:

> I swear by the Almighty that even if I agree to accept your offer, you will not find me worthy of your trust. ... In case of anything going against you in my verdict and your coercion to change it in your favour or else face being thrown into the Euphrates, I would prefer to be drowned instead of inserting a wilful change in the judgment. Then, you have so many courtiers ... and need a judge who may be able to take care of them too for your sake.'[23]

When al-Manṣūr finally realized that he would never win favour with the Imam, he went out openly to avenge his moral defeat and had the Imam whipped and thrown into prison, where he was denied even a proper diet. Following prolonged physical and mental torture he subjected him to house arrest, where the Imam breathed his last, most probably due to slow poisoning.[24]

12.1.7. *Freedom of speech*

The right to express one's views freely may at times be very negative and harmful for the society and the state, because there are views which are also unlawful, unethical, and anti-social. Views may also be subversive and detrimental to law and order. No state can tolerate such freedom or allow it to disturb public peace or the state's security. The Qur'an and the Sunnah, therefore, use the term *al-amr bi'l ma'rūf wal-nahy 'anil-munkar* (enjoining good and forbidding evil) for man's right of freedom of expression, because the most correct and best way

---

[22] Al-Muwaffaq al-Makkī, *Manāqib al-Imām al-A'ẓam Abī Ḥanīfah*, vol. 1, p. 215.

[23] Al-Makkī, vol. 2, p. 100; Al-Khatīb al-Baghdādī, *Tarīkh Baghdād*, vol. 13, p. 328.

[24] Al-Makkī, vol. 2, pp. 173, 174 and 182; Ibn Khallikān, *Wafayāt*, vol. 5, p. 46; al-Yāfi'ī, *Mir'āt al-Jinān*, p. 310.

to express one's views is to be in the service of everything good and against everything bad. Through this Qur'anic term, Islam not only determines the best course for the expression of views and makes it one of the fundamental rights of the people, it makes its proper use their duty as well and obligatory for every Muslim in the supreme interest of the state and the society. The Islamic system of statecraft ensures this fundamental right to every member of the community, and on the collective level, one of the binding duties of the state.

The way Imam Abū Ḥanīfah believed in the freedom of the judiciary, he similarly attached great importance to the right of the citizen to express his views unchecked in the cause of good and for eradicating evil. This basic right was taken away from the people by the political system of the day. The Muslim populace too was not quite sure about the mandatory nature of this duty. There were, on the one hand, the liberals called *murhabites*, who openly incited the people through their anti-Islamic views to promiscuous behaviour and profligacy, and on the other hand were the pro-government *hashwiyites*, who described the injunctions of *al-amr bi'l ma'rūf wal-nahy 'anil-munkar* as a threat to the state. On the political front, the despotic governments of the Umayyads and the Abbasids did what they could to crush the popular spirit of anger against state tyranny and oppression. The state machinery was used ruthlessly to suppress every voice of dissent and disapproval. Against such a backdrop, Imam A'ẓam tried through his words and deeds to revive this spirit of freedom and also draw a line of demarcation for it.

As reported by al-Jaṣṣās, responding to a query from the well known jurist of Khurāsān Ibrāhīm al-Sā'igh, the Imam said: '*Al-amr bi'l ma'rūf wal-nahy 'anil-munkar* is a mandatory duty.' In this context, he narrated on the authority of 'Ikramah from 'Abd Allah ibn 'Abbas that the Prophet (peace be upon him) said: 'The most exalted among the martyrs is Ḥamzah ibn 'Abdul Muṭṭalib and then a person who stands up to a despotic ruler to enjoin him with good and forbid him from evil and is then killed for this 'crime' of his.' Al-Jaṣṣās added: 'Al-Sā'igh was so much inspired by this Hadith that on his return to Khurāsān, he started openly criticizing Abū Muslim Khurāsanī (the powerful 'Abbasid prefect of Khurāsān) for his oppression and tyranny. He repeatedly tried to check him till he was killed a martyr to the cause of truth.'[25]

In 148 Hijrah (768 CE), the people of Mūsal rebelled against al-Manṣūr. According to the pledge he took from them after quashing their earlier revolt, it was impressed upon them that their life and property would be halal for him if they rebelled again and he would be under no obligation to protect them as their caliph. On their second uprising, al-Manṣūr invited all the senior *'ulamā'* and jurists, including Imam A'ẓam, to seek their views on what he viewed as a violation of their pledge by the people of Mūsal and whether he would be justified in shedding their blood and crushing the rebellion. According to the majority of scholars and jurists, the caliph had the option either to grant the people of Mūsal pardon after quashing their uprising, or to teach them a lesson for breaking their pledge. The Imam kept silent. When al-Manṣūr insisted on his views, he said:

> The people of Mūsal had allowed as permissible (*mubāh*) for you something which was not theirs (their life) and you let them agree to a condition which you had no right to do. Tell me, if a woman makes herself halal for somebody without marriage, can she be halal for him? If somebody tells someone to kill him, would it be halal for that man to shed that person's blood?

Al-Manṣūr's answer was: 'No.' The Imam then concluded: 'So, do not let your hands be soiled with the blood of the people of Mūsal as it is not halal for you.' At this, the caliph angrily adjourned the meeting. In an aside then he told the Imam: 'What you are saying is correct. But don't issue edicts that implicate your leader (caliph) and encourage the rebels.'[26]

The Imam frequently exercised this right of the freedom of expression in respect of the judiciary as well. Whenever he felt that a certain judgment was wrong, or it had some lacuna from the legal

---

[25] Al-Jaṣṣās, *Aḥkām Al-Qur'ān*, vol. 1, p. 81.

[26] Ibn al-Athīr, *Usudul-Ghābh fi Ma'rift al-Ṣaḥābah*, vol. 5, p. 25; al-Kardarī, *Manāqib al-Imām al-A'ẓam*, vol. 2, p. 17; al-Sarakhsī, *Kitāb Al-Mabsūt*, vol. 10, p. 129.

point of view, he at once expressed his views to correct the wrong. To him, respect for the judiciary did not mean overlooking its mistakes and allowing it to issue wrong verdicts. As a consequence, the Imam was once prevented from issuing *fatāwa* for a fairly long time.

The right to freedom of expression is so sacrosanct in the Islamic system of governance that Imam A'ẓam considered it unlawful to punish or apprehend a person who opened his lips even against a just ruler and his lawful government. The Imam also ruled out conviction of those who used abusive language, including threats of murder, against the head of government, so long as they were not involved in an open conspiracy, armed uprising, or disruption of law and order. He based his opinion on the precedent of the fourth Caliph Hadrat 'Alī's observation in a similar situation. During the days of his caliphate, five people were arrested in Kūfah on the charge of abusing the the fourth caliph, with one of them threatening to kill him. When the accused were brought to his presence, he ordered their release. He was told that one of them was guilty of openly threatening to kill the *Amīr al-Mu'minīn*. Hadrat 'Ali (may Allah elevate him to greater glory) observed: 'Should I kill him just because he expressed his intention?' He was informed that the culprits were publicly abusing him. His reply was: 'If you so desire, you may abuse them too.' Imam Abū Ḥanīfah similarly quoted in support of his stand the statement of Imam 'Ali regarding *Khawārij*: 'We will not prevent you from attending the mosques. We will not also deny to you the share from the revenue of the conquered lands so long as you do not indulge in armed activities against us.'[27]

12.2. Revolt against a Muslim ruler

The most important issue that has always faced an Islamic State has been whether the Muslim population can rise in revolt against an oppressive and tyrant ruler? There has been a sharp difference of opinion on this crucial issue even among the *'ulamā'* of *Ahl al-Sunnah*. The majority of the Salafī School (*Ahl al-Hadith)* has been of the view that to raise one's voice against oppressive rule and speak truth before

[27] Al-Sarakhsī, *Kitāb al-Mabsūt*, vol. 10, p. 125.

a tyrant was a lawful course but not to revolt, even if the ruler is guilty of shedding innocent people's blood, violation of human rights, or public display of promiscuous behaviour.

Imam Abū Ḥanīfah was of the view that the leadership of a tyrant and profligate was not only illegal, but it was also lawful to rise in revolt against him, provided it resulted in a successful and positive outcome. An uprising is lawful to him only if it can lead the people to a righteous and justice-loving ruler and not merely anarchy and loss of precious lives and the state's resources. According to Abū Bakr al-Jaṣṣās, Imam A'ẓam 'believed that it is obligatory to initially use word of mouth for enjoining good and forbidding evil. But when the words fail to produce results, then the (use of) the sword becomes a must.'[28]

To further illustrate Imam A'ẓam's standpoint on the issue of revolt, let us note in the following paragraphs the line of action the Imam himself took during some important uprisings of his time.

12.2.1. *Revolt by Zayd ibn 'Alī*

The first major uprising during the lifetime of Imam A'ẓam was the one led by Imam Zayd ibn 'Alī Zayn al-'Ābidīn, from whom the *Zaydīyyah* faction of the Shia sect draws its origin. He was the grandson of Imam Ḥusayn and brother of Imam Muhammad al-Bāqir. Zayd ibn 'Alī was a great religious scholar, jurist, and an outstanding personality known for his piety and virtue. Imam Abū Ḥanīfah had himself benefitted from his scholarship. In 738 CE (120 Hijrah), when the ruler Hishām ibn 'Abd al-Malik dismissed his Governor of Iraq, Khālid ibn 'Abdallāh al-Qasrī on charges of corruption, he invited Zayd from Madinah al-Munawwarah to Kūfah as a witness in the investigations. It was the first occasion after a very long interval that an eminent person from the House of Imam 'Alī had visited Kūfah, which had traditionally been the stronghold of the Shia Muslims. The visit of Zayd provided a new lease of life to the 'Alavite movement and the local people started gathering around him. The Iraqis were also fed up with the oppressive Umayyad rule and were on the lookout for support to rise against it. In the figure of an eminent personality from the House of Imam 'Alī, they at once discovered someone round whom they could rally the

[28] Al-Jaṣṣās *Aḥkām al-Qur'ān*, vol. 1, p. 81.

people of Iraq against the Umayyads. They convinced Imam Zayd ibn 'Alī of the popular support he enjoyed from around 100,000 people of Kūfah. The Imam was assured that 15,000 of them had already registered as volunteers following their oath of allegiance to him. While preparations were secretly under way for revolt, the news was leaked to the governor. On this, Imam Zayd prematurely launched his movement in 740 CE/122 Hijrah. But true to their tradition, the Shias of Kūfah once again betrayed Imam Zayd during his armed encounter with the Umayyad forces and he was left with only 218 volunteers to face the state's armed might. During the fight he was hit by an arrow which caused his death.[29]

Imam A'ẓam's moral support in that revolt was entirely with Imam Zayd ibn 'Alī. He also provided him with financial support and exhorted the people as well to side with him. He described his revolt as being similar to the Prophet's move at al-Badr.[30] The Imam thereby meant that just as the Prophet (peace be upon him) was beyond any doubt correct in his rise against the idolatrous Quraysh at al-Badr, similarly Imam Zayd was right to challenge the repressive rule of the Umayyads. In spite of his moral support, when Imam A'ẓam received Imam Zayd's message to lend him physical support, he told the courier:

> Had I known that the people of Kūfah were sincerely with him and would rally round him till the last, I would have joined him and engaged myself in jihad because he is definitely the right leader. But I am afraid these people would betray him the way they did his grandfather (Imam Ḥusayn). Yes, I would definitely lend him financial support.[31]

The position taken by the Imam was exactly in line with his principled stand explained earlier regarding the question of revolt against a repressive rule. He was aware of the past history of the Shiites of

[29] Ibid.

[30] Al-Muwaffaq al-Makkī, *Manāqib al-Imām al-A'ẓam Abī Ḥanīfah*, vol. 1, p. 260.

[31] Ibid. vol. 1, p. 260.

Kūfah and their psyche. Their social conduct and the way they had behaved since the days of Imam 'Alī was known to everyone. That was why Dāwūd ibn 'Alī, Ibn 'Abbas's grandson, had also forewarned Imam Zayd and advised him against the revolt.[32]

Imam Abū Ḥanīfah also knew that the anti-Umayyad movement was limited to the governorate of Kūfah alone. There was no likelihood of any organizational or moral support coming from any other part of the empire and in Kūfah too it was a 6-month-old half-baked pie. He did not expect that the revolt would succeed or produce the desired result. There was yet another reason for the Imam not to physically join the movement. At that time he was not publicly prominent enough to wield any influence over the populace and make up for the weakness of the movement through his participation. Until 120 Hijrah, the *imāmate* of Iraq's *Madrasah Ahl al-Rā'i* (School of the Leaders of Public Opinion) was in the hands of its dean, Imam Hammād, and Imam A'ẓam was then one of his eminent students. At the time of the revolt, he had just taken over as the Dean of the School, but was yet to attain the status and influence of *Faqīh Ahl al-Sharq* (the Legist of the Orient).

12.2.2. *Revolt by Al-Nafs al-Zakīyyah*

The second very important uprising of Imam A'ẓam's time was the revolt of the two brothers from the family of *Sayyidunā* Imam 'Alī, Muhammad ibn 'Abdallāh (Al-Nafs al-Zakīyyah) and Ibrāhīm ibn 'Abdallāh. That was the time when Imam Abū Ḥanīfah had reached the peak of his popularity as a great scholar and leader of a prominent school of jurisprudence. As mentioned earlier, the two brothers' movement had started during the Umayyad rule. Even al-Manṣūr had taken oath of allegiance then to Al-Nafs al-Zakīyyah against the Umayyads. After the establishment of the Abbasid rule, the members of this movement went into hiding and began working secretly for their cause. Their missionaries were spread all over Khurāsān, al-Jazīrah, Ray', Tabaristān, Yemen, and North Africa. Al-Nafs al-Zakīyyah had set up his headquarters in Hijāz, while his brother Ibrāhīm was

[32] Ibn Jarīr al-Ṭabarī, *Tarīkh al-Rusul wa'l-Mulūk*, vol. 5, pp. 487–491.

based in Basra. According to Ibn al-Athīr, hundreds of thousands of armed volunteers were ready in Kūfah as well. Al-Manṣūr was already aware of their secret plans and was very afraid of the two brothers' movement, as it was running parallel to the Abbasid campaign for power. That is why he was busy conspiring from the beginning of his rule to break their movement with whatever force was available to him. When Al-Nafs al-Zakīyyah physically moved from al-Madinah al-Munawwarah in Rajab 145 Hijrah, al-Manṣūr hurriedly left his construction plans in Baghdad and landed in Kūfah. He was so afraid of the campaign that he often felt desperate and doubted that he would ever be in a position to establish his rule. He received the news of the uprising from different places, including Basra, Fāras, Ahwāz, Wāsit, and al-Madā'in. For two months he remained dressed in the same clothes, did not sleep in bed and spent the night on a prayer mat. He kept ready his fastest stallions so that he could escape from Kūfah in the event of the revolt's success. Had luck not been on his side, the movement would have succeeded in toppling the Abbasid rule at its very outset.[33]

Imam Abū Ḥanīfah's line of action was entirely different then from what it was during the earlier abortive coup of Imam Zayd ibn 'Ali. Even though the Abbasid ruler was present in Kūfah and the city remained under dusk to dawn curfew, the Imam openly supported the revolt to the extent that his disciples and students became afraid of facing the government's wrath. They openly encouraged the people to make an oath of allegiance to Ibrāhīm and told them that their support to the anti-Abbasid movement was 50–70 times greater in reward from the Lord than the supererogatory pilgrimage to Makkah al-Makarramah.[34] From the accounts of the Imam's role during those trying times, as narrated by Al-Muwaffaq al-Makkī, al-Kardarī and Abū Bakr al-Jaṣṣās, it is evident that the Imam considered the efforts to rid the Muslim society of the shackles of a corrupt dynastic rule much nobler than to fight against the infidels outside.

[33] *Tarīkh Al-Ṭabarī*, vol. 6, pp. 155–263; al-Yāfi'ī, *Mir'at al-Jinān*, vol. 1, p. 299.

[34] Al-Kardarī, *Manāqib al-Imām al-A'ẓam*, vol. 2, pp. 71–72; al-Makkī, *Manāqib al-Imām al-A'ẓam Abī Ḥanīfah*, vol. 2, pp. 83–84.

In a most daring and significant step for a principled stand, Imam A'ẓam prevented Al-Manṣūr's most trusted army chief, Ḥasan ibn Qaḥtubah, from proceeding to the battle-front against Al-Nafs al-Zakīyyah and Ibrāhīm. General Ḥasan's father, Qaḥtubah, was the person whose military skill, together with the political maneuvers of Abū Muslim of Khurāsān, helped in founding the Abbasid Empire. Ḥasan was installed in place of his father after his death and soon became the caliph's most trusted general. His stay in Kūfah, however, turned him into a great admirer of Imam Abū Ḥanīfah. Once he asked the Imam: 'You are aware of the sins I have committed during my tenure of service under al-Manṣūr. Do you think, there is any room for me now to be pardoned by the Lord?' The Imam replied: 'It depends on how sincerely you prove to Allah *subḥānahū wa ta'ālā* that you are truly repentant. For this you will have to be steadfast to the extent of preferring to be killed but not to kill innocent souls even if ordered by the ruler to do so, and you will have to solemnly pledge to the Lord that you will never repeat what you did in the past.' Ḥasan solemnly pledged before the Imam accordingly.

Shortly afterward, when the revolt by Al-Nafs al-Zakīyyah and Ibrāhīm started, al-Manṣūr ordered Ḥasan to crush the rebels. The general came to the Imam and sought his views. Imam A'ẓam told him: 'Now the time has come to test your penance. If you remain firm to your pledge with the Lord, your *tawbah* (repentance) will be intact. Otherwise, you will face the consequences of what you did in the past as well as of what you might do in future.' Ḥasan renewed his pledge before the Imam and went straight to al-Manṣūr and told him point blank: 'Amīr al-Mu'minīn, I will not go on this expedition. Whatever I have done to date in pursuance of your command, if it was in obedience to the Lord as well, then it is enough for me. But if it was in His disobedience, I am not willing to do more acts of sin.' Al-Manṣūr almost burst with anger at such a blunt response and ordered his arrest. Ḥasan's brother, Ḥamīd, then came forward and said: 'I have noticed a change in Ḥasan for about a year. It appears he has gone mad. I offer to go to this expedition.' Later, al-Manṣūr enquired from his close confidants about Ḥasan's contact with the eminent men of religion in Kūfah and he was informed that Ḥasan was a frequent visitor to Imam A'ẓam.[35]

The Imam's approach on the issue of revolt was in line with his considered opinion that if the revolt against a repressive rule is well-intentioned and righteous and if the chances of its success are bright, then the move is not only legitimate (*jā'iz*) but also obligatory. In fact, the Imam was not alone in his approach. His views were also shared by Imam Mālik. When Al-Nafs al-Zakīyyah rose in revolt, Imam Mālik was asked whether it was correct to side with another claimant to the caliphate while the yoke of allegiance to al-Manṣūr still lay on people's shoulders? He decreed that the oath of allegiance for the Abbasids was by compulsion and not by the people's free choice, and every oath, pledge, or divorce extracted by force is *ultra vires*. Due to this decree, the majority of people sided with Al-Nafs al-Zakīyyah and as a consequence the Abbasid governor of Al-Madinah al-Munawwarah, Ja'far ibn Sulaymān, sentenced Imam Mālik to a flogging that caused displacement of his arms from his shoulders.[36]

12.2.3. *The cornerstone of Islamic statecraft*

A Muslim ruler's allegiance to Allah and His Messenger (peace be upon him) and the popular approval of his rule through *al-bay'ah al-'ammah* are the two fundamental principles of Islamic statecraft that serve as its cornerstone. These principles were determined once for all during the golden era of *Al-Khulafā' al-Rāshidūn*. Imam Abū Ḥanīfah's detailed and scientific approach to its various dimensions was actually an elaboration of those very principles. Let us look at these principles in their practical form in the following glorious examples from the Golden Era of Islam.

Sayyidnā Abū Bakr in his first address following the popular oath of allegiance to him as the first caliph of Islam declared:

اَطِيعُونِى مَا اَطَعتُ اللهَ وَرَسُولَهُ، فَاِذَاعَصِيتُ اللهَ وَرَسُولَهُ فَلَا طَاعَةَ لِى عَلَيكُم.

[35] Al-Kardarī, vol. 2, p. 22.

[36] Al-Ṭabarī, *Tarīkh*, vol. 6, p. 160; Ibn Khallikān, *Wafayāt al-A'yān*, vol. 3, p. 285; Ibn Kathīr, *Al-Bidāyah wal-Nihāyah*, vol. 10, p. 84.

> Obey me so long as I obey Allah and his Messenger. But if I disobey Him and His Messenger, you are then bound by no oath of allegiance to me.[37]

The second caliph, *Sayyidnā* 'Umar, exemplified the same principle in his statement before the glorious assembly:

مَن بَايَعَ رَجُلاً مِن غَيرِ مَشوَرَةٍ مِنَ المُسلِمِينَ فَلَا يُبَايعُ هُوَ وَلَا الَّذِى بَايَعه تَغرَّةً اَن يُقتَلَا.

> He who takes oath of allegiance to someone without the Muslims' consensus, actually deceives himself and also the one in whose favour he is taking oath and thus makes himself and that person liable for killing.[38]

When Imam Ḥusayn (may Allah be pleased with him) rose against the established order of Yazīd, the majority of the Companions of the Prophet (peace be upon him) were alive and the eminent jurists from among the Tābi'ūn were also there. But none of them described Imam Ḥusayn's action as being contrary to the Qur'an and the Sunnah. Those who tried to dissuade him from the expedition did so on the following grounds: (i) the people of Kūfah were known for their lack of trustworthiness; (ii) practically, the success of his mission was extremely difficult; and (iii) that he was putting his life at stake along with the lives of those siding with him. In other words, the views of his well-wishers in the matter were exactly the same as was subsequently voiced by Imam Abū Ḥanīfah and which may be summed up as follows: 'The revolt against a wrong leadership is not in itself unlawful. But before launching such a revolt it must be carefully examined whether it is feasible to replace the corrupt system and establish a righteous order.'

Similarly, when 'Abd al-Raḥmān ibn al-Ash'ath revolted against the Umayyads during the tyrannical governorship of Ḥajjāj ibn

---

[37] Ibn Hishām, *Sīrat al-Nabīy*, vol. 4, p. 311; Ibn Kathīr, *Al-Bidāyāh wal-Nihāyāh*', vol. 5, p. 248.

[38] *Ṣaḥīḥ al-Bukhārī, Kitāb Al-Muḥāribīn.*

Yūsuf, senior jurists of the day, like Sa'īd ibn Jubayr, al-Sha'bī, Ibn Abī Layla and Abū'l-Bakhtarī rose along with him. Those who did not associate themselves with the uprising, however, did not describe it as unlawful. What Ibn Abī Layla and other scholars of the time said while addressing the forces of Ibn al-Ash'ath amply reflect the Islamic viewpoint on the question of revolt against an established order.

The views expressed by Ibn Abī Layla were as follows:

> O you who believe, if anyone of you sees the oppression and tyranny being perpetrated and evils being spread and he detests this at heart, he stands acquitted and absolved. If he boldly expresses his disapproval, he will get his reward and he is better than the first one. But the real go-getter to the right path and the one who has enlightened his heart from the radiance of faith is he who stands up against such people in order to hold aloft the banner of Allah's message and subdue the forces of tyranny. So, go ahead in your war against those who have turned the forbidden (haram) into the lawful (halal) and given rise to the wrong among the Muslim Ummah; those who are unmindful of truth and refuse to see it; those who act cruelly and do not take it as bad.

Al-Sha'bī said: 'Fight against them and do not for a moment think that it is something bad. To my knowledge, there is nobody in the world today who is worst than these people in tyranny and more unjust in decisions than these rulers. So, let there be no slackness in your campaign against them.' Sa'īd ibn Jubayr declared: 'Fight against these people, because they are repressive in government and rebellious in religion. They treat the weak with degradation and insult and let the regular prayers go waste.'[39]

12.2.4. *The subsequent change*

The precedent of the first century Hijrah and the views expressed by the great traditionists of the day laid the foundations for the legal brains of

[39] Al-Ṭabarī, *Tarīkh*, vol. 5, p. 163.

later years like Imam Abū Ḥanīfah, Imam Mālik and others, to build the legal and ethical structure of the concept of Islamic statecraft. Towards the end of the second century Hijrah, however, emerged the other viewpoint, which eventually became the viewpoint of the mainstream of *Ahl al-Sunnah*. This shift was due not to any weakness of the earlier stand, but because firstly, the oppressive rulers had left no way out for a peaceful change through popular consensus, and secondly because all attempts to change the regime through violent means successively produced results that were hardly desirable.

While the views of Imam Aʿẓam regarding permissibility of revolt against the Muslim ruler remained unchanged, the jurists of the Ḥanafī School subsequently followed the stance taken by the Traditionalist Group led by Imam Awzāʿī for the reasons explained above. By the end of the second century Hijrah, the jurists of *Ahl al-Sunnah wal Jamāʿah* virtually all came to the conclusion that the Islamic State's prevailing law and order situation under its autocratic rule demanded that a head-on collision with the authority in power be avoided, even though that authority itself might have been unlawful and enjoying no popular support and allegiance.

I personally believe, nevertheless, that the views adopted later were hardly in conformity with those held by the leading jurists and scholars of the first century Hijrah. It may not be out of place to mention here the pertinent point raised in this respect by a lady orientalist from England during the International Congress held in Lahore late in 1957. Her observation was that there was apparently no way out in Islam for amendments once a system of government was disturbed and derailed. In support of her viewpoint, she quoted the *Ashāʿirah* and jurists of the Ḥanafī School of later years, to prove that Islam permits only the raising of a lone, individual voice of truth but not a collective struggle for reform. We could furnish no answer to her observation other than what we know as Imam Aʿẓam's standpoint.

As for the Islamic state's right to quell an armed uprising, there are no two opinions about its being lawful. There is also nothing unlawful about rebels being killed in an open battle and their belongings being confiscated by the state. But would it be lawful for the state to dispense with the life and property of the entire population in an area under rebel control is entirely a different matter. I am personally of the view that such an extremist view cannot be described as juridically correct. Otherwise, what Yazīd did with the people of Al-Madīnah al-Mūnawwarah following the battle of Karbalā would naturally appear lawful and the strong reservations and condemnations expressed against such behaviour by the eminent Companions and their illustrious successors (Tābiʿūn) would be wrong.

13 The Message of the Martyrdom of Imam Ḥusayn*

Every year in Muharram, the first lunar month of the Hijrah calendar, millions of Muslims, both Shia and Sunni, express their sentiments of grief and sorrow over the martyrdom of *Sayyidnā* Imam Ḥusayn (may Allah be pleased with him). Unfortunately, however, very few of the mourners pay attention to the very purpose and objective for which the Imam laid down his life and sacrificed even the lives of his near and dear ones, including those of his family members. It is but natural to feel pain and express sorrow over the brutal killing of such a great man, his family members and close associates. Tragic incidents like these always evoke a deep sense of anger and grief. There is, nonetheless, no moral worth of such grief beyond its being a natural expression of love and sympathy for the martyr, his family members and relatives. The question, however, arises in this context: What makes the martyrdom of Imam Ḥusayn so different and great that the tragedy continues to evoke a wave of grief and sorrow even after the lapse of over 1,000 years? Had this martyrdom been for no great cause, there would have been no meaning and reason for this pall of gloom and grief to continue haunting the Muslim Ummah's conscience for so long simply because of our personal attachment to the Imam and his illustrious family. Frankly speaking, should we expect such demonstrations of a purely personal love to be of any worth in the eyes of the Imam himself? Had his own self been dearer to him than the objective he set himself to achieve, he would not have

* The article is based on an address that the author delivered at a special session held at the premises of a Shia leader in Lahore on 9 Muharram 1380 (Hijrah) to mark the tragedy of Karbalā and which was subsequently published in *Tarjumān al-Qur'ān* of July 1960 – Editor.

sacrificed his life for it. His glorious sacrifice itself is a proof of the fact that the objective before him was dearer to him than his personal life and the lives of his near and dear ones. If we do nothing, therefore, for that great cause, we should expect no appreciation from the Imam, nor any reward from the Lord on the Day of Judgment. Should we, then, remain content just to mourn this tragedy and hurl abuse and curses on his assassins?

Let us discover first what that great objective was. Did the Imam lay down his life for the sake of any claim he had over the Islamic State's 'crown and throne'? Nobody with even the least knowledge of the Imam's greatness of character and the nobility of his family would ever be guilty of attributing such a selfish motive to him. There is no reason or historic evidence to believe that the Imam and his illustrious family were instrumental in fomenting trouble and causing bloodshed among the Muslims just to get power for themselves. Who can falsify the witness borne out by the history of the full five decades, from the rule of the first caliph Hadrat Abū Bakr up to that of Amīr Muʿāwīyah? The illustrious record of the great family of Imam 'Alī shows that it never believed in infighting and bloodshed for the sake of power for itself or for any of its members. We are inevitably led, therefore, to accept the fact that at that particular juncture of Islamic history Imam Ḥusayn noticed signs of alarming change in the spirit, character and the socio-political order of the Islamic state and the society and he considered it essential to launch a relentless struggle to check this emerging dangerous trend. This struggle was not to instal himself in power but to save the crumbling edifice of the grand institution of the Islamic caliphate. To him, it was such an important task that even a fight to the last was not only lawful but obligatory.

What was that ominous change that needed immediately to be checked? Obviously, the people had not changed their religion. Everyone, including the rulers, believed as before in God, His Messenger and His Book. Nor was there any change in the Islamic state's constitution. The judiciary of the Umayyad Empire was handling cases strictly according to the injunctions of the Qur'an and the Sunnah, just as it used to do before their climb to power. In fact, there had been all along no change in the world of Islam's judicial system until the advent of the colonial rule in the eighteenth century. Some people take Yazīd's personal character as the sole reason behind the Imam's decision to dethrone him. Yet even if we consider Yazīd as the worst possible character, it is unthinkable that an extremely wise person, so well versed in Shariah and Islamic sciences like Imam Ḥusayn, would be impatient to the extent of rising in revolt to remove a bad person from power while the entire state system ran along the correct lines. Yazīd's person was, therefore, not the actual factor that impelled the Imam to take the ultimate step. A meticulous study of history makes it crystal clear that the iceberg of real change began showing its ugly tip with Yazīd's induction into power, first as the crown prince and then by his coronation. In effect this constituted a fundamental change in the Islamic State's governance, its character and objectives. Though the entire spectrum of this change and all its ramifications were not yet visible to the naked eye, anyone with insight and vision could see that the locomotive of Islam's socio-political order had changed track. It was this change of direction that the Imam noticed with great concern and he moved swiftly and resolutely forward to bring the train back to its right track, even at the cost of his life and the lives of his near and dear ones.

To exactly understand this point in its correct perspective, let us look at the basic characteristics of the Islamic constitution on which the entire system of the Islamic state had functioned during the previous forty years under the leadership of *Sayyidunā* Rasūl Allah (peace be upon him) and his Rightly-Guided Caliphs.[1] Then, we need also to look at the main features of the system of government that emerged with the induction of Yazīd as crown prince, the system that continued throughout the Umayyad and the Abbasid rules, and even afterwards; and how different it was from the illustrious model of *Al-Khilāfah Al-Rāshidah*. By a comparative study of the two systems, we can easily see on what track the 'train' of the Islamic socio-political order was running earlier and to which track it subsequently moved. From such a study, we can well understand why a person, brought up under the loving care and guidance of mankind's Greatest Benefactor

[1] For a detailed study of the subject, please see chapter 15 – Editor.

Sayyidnā wa Mawlānā (Our Guide, Master and Patron) Rasūl Allah (peace be upon him) and the best and noblest of parents, *Sayyidnā* 'Alī and *Sayyidah* Fātimah al-Zahrā', and in the company of the humanity's leading lights, the Companions of the Prophet (may Allah be pleased with them all), moved forward so resolutely to prevent the train from diversion to a wrong course? A dispassionate study alone can make it easy for us to understand why he did not bother about the consequences of confronting such a mighty train in order to keep it on the right track.

Allah's sovereignty is the most important and fundamental characteristic of Islamic statecraft. The concept can be summed up in one sentence as follows: *The state belongs to Allah, the people are His subjects, and the government is accountable to Him in all matters, including the subjects.* This is not a slogan but an article of faith for every Muslim, for the ruler as well as the ruled. The government of an Islamic state is not the master of its subjects nor are the subjects its bondsmen. The prime obligation of the Muslim rulers is to put the chain of Allah's obedience first round their own neck and then to enforce the rule of His Law on the people. Yazīd's elevation to the position of Crown Prince marked the turning point for the system of Islamic statecraft. It was the beginning of the order of kingship and the dynastic rule. The hallowed concept of Allah's supremacy was, thus, reduced to mere lip-service and a slogan and the Islamic concept of caliphate practically became a replica of the system that the worldly kings have always followed: The kingdom belonged to the king and his royal family and the king invested with the Divine Right to rule, which meant to disobey him was to disobey the Lord. His Majesty, every member of the royal family and close associates were also elevated above the law.[2]

---

[2] The evils of kingship and dynastic rule crept into the Islamic polity following the fall of *Al-Khilāfah Al-Rāshidah*, and the exposure of the Muslim Governors of Shām and Fāras to the splendours and luxuries of the courts of Caesars and Khusraus was the main factor responsible for that dereliction. In fact, *Sayyidnā* Rasūl Allah (Allah's peace and blessings be upon him) had forewarned the Ummah against the attractions and enticements of such worldly pleasures. The absence of the tight political and moral grip of the Rightly-Guided Caliphs subsequently led these evils to slowly and gradually overtake the system of Islamic polity and governance and the enthronement of Yazīd definitely proved a catalyst for the major derailment – Editor.

The basic objective of an Islamic state is to establish and promote the value-system ordained by Allah *subḥānahū wa taʿālā*, and to curb and crush the evil that displeases Him. But by following the course of kingship and dynastic rule, the principal objective of the state emerged as nothing beyond the conquest of lands, subjugation of peoples, collection of tariffs and taxes, and worldly leisure and pleasure. Very rarely did the Muslim kings devote their energies to serving the cause of Religion and spreading the Divine Message. They and their princes, senior officials and courtiers were responsible rather for spreading vice than virtue. The noble souls, who devoted their time and energies into promoting virtue and preventing vice and spreading the message of the Religion of Truth and Islamic learning, could rarely attract government support. They were instead exposed in most cases to such rulers' wrath and often remained behind bars; many even risked their lives to continue their mission. On the other hand, the negative impact of the lifestyle and policies of their majesties' governments, their officials and cronies, led the Muslim society to moral degeneration and social misconduct. The worst part of that scenario was that they even did not refrain for the sake of their own personal interests from creating hurdles in the way of Islam and its teachings. The ugliest manifestation of this was the imposition of *jizyah* on new Muslims during the Umayyad rule, while the tax was actually meant to be levied on non-combatant *dhimmīs* in return for guaranteeing protection to their life, property and honour.

The moving spirit of an Islamic state is love and fear of God, piety, and humaneness, and the head of the Islamic state and government of the past stood out as the most notable embodiment of these cherished ideals. The government functionaries, the judiciary, and the armed forces and their chiefs are similarly expected in an Islamic state to be motivated by this spirit, which they in turn instil into the whole of society. The derailment of the Islamic system of governance from the track of caliphate to that of kingship changed, however, the complexion of both the rulers and the ruled. The Muslim governments and their heads started following in the footsteps of the Caesars and

Khusraus, and their other worldly counterparts. Repression and tyranny replaced the rule of justice and fair play and the environment of piety and virtue was taken over by an atmosphere of perversity and profligacy, music and dance, lust and luxury. Politics gradually lost its link with morality. Instead of fearing God, rulers started frightening the ruled and instead of energizing the people's faith and conscience, they began purchasing their loyalty through perks and privileges.

That was the big change that could be noticed in the character, temperament, basic objectives and concept of the Islamic system of polity and governance under Yazīd. Similar changes of a crucial nature took place in the very fundamentals of the Islamic political order. Imam Ḥusayn embraced martyrdom in the way of his noble resolve to prevent transition from *Khilāfah* to monarchy. He knew full well that in the ideal Islamic political order, established by *Sayyidunā* Rasūl Allah (Allah's peace and blessings be upon him), *al-Khilāfah al-Rāshidah* was based on certain basic principles, which are seven in number and need to be discussed in detail. So let us do it in the paragraphs that follow.

13.1. The institution of *bay'ah* (pledge of support and allegiance)

Bay'ah, or the popular pledge of support and allegiance, is the first characteristic of the Islamic political order. In modern parlance *bay'ah* is similar to the voting system. It is the anchor-sheet that makes it incumbent on the government to be established only by the exercise of the people's free will. In the Islamic system of government no one is entitled to grab power through personal effort or by the use of force. Only the people have the power to select the best among themselves through mutual consensus and consultation and then hand over power to him. During the days of the Rightly-Guided Caliphs, *bay'ah* was the cause of a ruler's election to office and not the result of his elevation to that position. It was not possible then to achieve *bay'ah* by personal effort or manoeuvers, and the people were free to use their discretion in this regard. So long as one did not acquire a popular show of allegiance, one could not become caliph. Similarly, when the people's trust was lost, no one could cling to power. That is how each of the four Rightly-Guided Caliphs was inducted into power.

The stance of Amīr Mu'āwīyah, though an eminent Companion, unfortunately betrayed a deviation from the Islamic model of caliphate. That is the reason why he was not included among *Al-Khulafā' Al-Rāshidūn*. Yazīd's induction as his crown prince was the step that eventually turned that important principle of the Islamic system of governance and statecraft topsy turvy. It marked the beginning of the accursed system of dynastic monarchy and autocratic rule and conversion of the Islamic Caliphates into Muslim Empires. From the turning point of Yazīd's rule until now, the Muslim world has not been able to return to the golden system of the caliphate. From Yazīd onward, the Muslims found their rulers installed not through their free will, general consensus and consultation, but by the use of force, coercion, and manipulation. The institution of '*bay'ah* for power' was replaced by 'power for *bay'ah*' and the people were left with no choice but to either extend or withdraw their hand to reaffirm their allegiance (*bay'ah*). In fact, this vital institution could no longer be a precondition for the ruler to remain in authority. No one dared to refuse support and allegiance to a person seizing power, and once in power it was all too easy for him to formalize his rule through a coercive *bay'ah*. It was this act of coercive *bay'ah* that Imam Mālik and Imam A'ẓam ventured to challenge and consequently they were subjected to severe flogging and various oppressive methods during the reign of the Abbasid caliph al-Manṣūr.

13.2. Government through consultation (*shūrā*)

Government through consultation is the second fundamental principle of an Islamic state's political system. It is imperative for the government to consult in the affairs of state those men of learning, *taqwā* and vision, who enjoyed the people's trust. During the golden era of *Al-Khulafā' Al-Rāshidūn*, there was a Consultation Council (*Majlis al-Shūrā*), which we may call the counterpart of today's Parliament. This Council was not formally elected, but composed purely on merit. The members of *Majlis al-Shūrā* were not nominated for their political, ethnic, or dynastic affiliations. The caliphs nominated them due to no mundane considerations, nor with the hope of turning them into their 'yes men', fit to guard their narrow personal interests. Their selection was done exclusively on the basis of the unblemished record of their personal character, background of piety, uprightness and scholarship in religious disciplines. They were the select few from whom the caliphs sincerely looked forward to receiving the best counsel in the supreme interests of the state and the nation. They were expected to sincerely and selflessly contribute their considered views without any fear or favour and purely according to their knowledge, wisdom and the dictate of conscience. Nobody could even remotely think of them to misguide the government for their own sake or to win favours with those in authority. They were the outstanding members of the Islamic community, who alone would have won the popular vote had the system of adult franchise been in vogue in those days.

With the commencement of the monarchical rule, however, this well-respected *shūrā* system that had once enjoyed popular support and trust became a part of history. Those in power started ruling despotically and unchecked, and their princes, courtiers, sycophants, state governors and the armed forces' chiefs became members of their hand-picked councils. Their advisors then were those who, if put to popular vote, would have received the people's curses and disapproval instead of consent. Conversely, men of learning, scholarship, and piety, who enjoyed overwhelming respect and trust of the people, lost favour with the monarchs and were least trustworthy for them. We know, therefore, what the Umayyad and Abbasid rulers did with the great personalities of Islam, like Imam Abū Ḥanīfah, Imam Mālik, Imam Aḥmad ibn Ḥanbāl and so many others.

13.3. People's right to freedom of expression

The third article of the Islamic political order is the people's right to freedom of expression. Islam has declared *al-amr bi'l ma'rūf wal-nahy 'anil-munkar* as not just a right of every Muslim member of society individually but an obligatory duty as well for the state collectively. For the Muslim society and the state to run on correct lines, it is essential that the people's conscience and tongues be free; they must have the freedom to question the highest in the land about his lapses; and to speak the truth freely and fearlessly. During the days of the Rightly-Guided Caliphs, the people were not just guaranteed this basic right, but the caliphs took it as their duty and encouraged the people in discharging it. The members of their *Majlis al-Shūrā* were free to express their views, question things, and even to interrogate the caliphs not in their personal matters alone, which affected functioning of their office, but each and every member of the Muslim community also enjoyed that freedom. This right to freedom of speech was so sacrosanct that instead of being afraid of any reprisal on its exercise the people were rewarded. That was not a gift or *bakhshish* for the people by the caliph. It was a constitutional right guaranteed to them by Islam itself, which had to be respected, and the caliphs regarded it as their duty to ensure that freedom. To use this right in the best interest of the state and the people was mandatory for every Muslim, and caliphs took it as part of their official duty to keep the Islamic state's atmosphere always conducive for its discharge.

With the advent of monarchy, however, the people's conscience became captive and their tongues tied. The general principle, then, was either to keep one's mouth shut, or to open it only in praise of the ruler. Should someone be daring enough to risk speaking the truth and follow the dictates of his conscience, he knew that sooner or later he would either be killed or put behind bars. The state policy of repression and coercion gradually turned Muslim subjects into cowards and they became listless and opportunists. Those who did act according to their conscience and challenged those in authority became a rare commodity. Sycophants and flatterers had a field day, while the righteous and the upright had little to look forward to. The honest and better qualified gradually became disenchanted with the government, and the masses were left with no interest in the affairs of the state. The people cared the least about who ruled them and for how long. They never rose to defend those who were toppled, nor to welcome those who replaced them. Governments came and went, but the people remained silent spectators.

13.4. Accountability of the caliph and his government to God and His subjects

The fourth fundamental principle, closely inter-linked with the third, is the provision of accountability of the caliph and his government before God and His subjects. The hallowed record of the history of the Golden Days of Islam tells us how *Al-Khulafā' Al-Rāshidūn* remained restless day in and day out by the very thought of their being accountable to the Supreme Lord. As for their answerability to the people was concerned, they were always accessible and answerable to them. It was not their practice to permit only a member of *Majlis al-Shūrā* to raise a point of order to discuss something of public concern. They were available to their people five times a day in each congregation; on each occasion they were, thus, ready to face their questions and take action for redressal. Once a week, they rubbed shoulders with a much larger audience during the Friday congregation. They used the opportunity presented by the Friday sermon to apprise the people of matters of interest to them and the state and to listen to their grievances and complaints, if any. As part of their daily routine, the caliphs went on day-time and nightly 'meet-the-people' rounds of the city streets, public places, markets and residential sectors, with no bodyguards or trumpets heralding their arrival.

The doors of their 'Government House' (unostentatious personal mud-brick houses) remained open to anybody who wished to knock at their door. Everyone was thus free to raise any question of public, personal, or government interest and to receive an answer. This was not limited and formal but an open and full-time accountability, for which no separate institution was set up at government cost but it was held directly and publicly. They had taken over the reigns of authority through popular will and the people could remove them and bring in a new caliph any time they lost popular support. That is why they were never afraid of facing their *electorate* or of the risk of losing the highest position of authority in the land; nor did they ever bother to avert such an eventuality.

With the advent of kingship, however, that overpowering sense of accountability before the Lord and the people vanished into thin air. There might have remained a semblance of this insofar as the accountability to God was concerned. As for accountability to the people, nobody dared open his lips for complaint or protest before 'Their Majesties'. They always came to power by force and could be removed only through force. How could such rulers face their people, and who among the public was powerful enough to face them? Even when they offered Prayers it was never done shoulder to shoulder with the people, but within the well-guarded mosques of their massive castles, or surrounded by their trusted group of officials and bodyguards. Whenever they moved in public it was a pageantry, a royal cavalcade, with armed and mounted guards cordoning off their passage and crowds watching in awe from a distance [the normal spectacle we witness everywhere in our 'modern' times].

13.5. Financial integrity of the state and the government

The element of financial integrity of the state and the government is the fifth basic principle of the Islamic political order. The *Bayt al-Māl* of the Islamic caliphate was a sacrosanct institution as the Divine Treasury and repository of the people's trust. No amount of wealth came to it but through the right way and nothing went out of it but into the right channel. The caliph's right over the state treasury was only that much as sanctioned by the Book of God for an orphan's guardian from his ward's money. According to the injunctions in this regard, a guardian who is well off is to desist from claiming any remuneration from an orphan's money for the services and care rendered to him, while the one really in need is entitled to draw only the minimum possible. Allah *subḥānahū wa ta'ālā* says:

... وَمَن كَانَ غَنِيًّا فَلْيَسْتَعْفِفْ وَمَن كَانَ فَقِيرًا فَلْيَأْكُلْ بِٱلْمَعْرُوفِ ... ﴿٦﴾

If the guardian is rich, let him abstain entirely (from his ward's property); and if he is poor let him partake of it in a fair measure.[3]

The caliph was responsible to account for each and every penny spent from the *Bayt al-Māl* and every member of the Muslim community

[3] *Al-Nisā'* 4: 6.

was entitled to obtain a statement of account for the money spent. This Article too was followed by *Al-Khulafā' Al-Rāshidūn* to such an extent that their conduct became a model of honesty and sincerity of purpose for all times to come. The well off among the Righteous Caliphs [especially *Sayyidunā* 'Uthmān ibn 'Affān] received nothing by way of salary from the state treasury. In fact, they spent much on public welfare schemes out of their own pockets. As for those whose pockets did not allow them to devote their full time to the business of the state, they drew the bare minimum from the national exchequer, just enough to meet their most essential needs. Furthermore, the accounts of the state treasury were available for everyone to see and the caliphs were accessible all the time to satisfy anybody's query regarding the state's income and expenditure. Even a common man could rise up and publicly ask that the shawls received from Yemen were not large enough to make the long shirt *Amīr al-Mu'minīn* was wearing and how could he justify using the extra piece for his shirt?

When the institution of caliphate was replaced by monarchy, the treasury no longer belonged to God and His subjects, but was rather turned into a *Royal Purse*. The wealth that came to it, through fair means or foul, was spent the same way and none could challenge the authorities to account for their income and expenditure. The entire public exchequer became a banquet table from which everyone from the king down to his cronies and petty government functionaries gobbled whatever they could to their hearts' content. No state functionary considered for a moment that he had no licence to squander the national wealth at will.

13.6. Islamic Shariah, the supreme law of the land

The sixth fundamental article of the Islamic system of governance is the supremacy of the Shariah as the ultimate law of the land. No person is above the law, or has the right to bypass it. The law of the land is applicable equally to everyone from the caliph down to the common man. Justice is every citizen's prerogative and nobody enjoys any special privilege. The courts are free to dispense justice without fear or favour. The best model of this was provided by *Al-Khulafā' Al-Rāshidūn*. While enjoying more powers and authority than worldly kings, they themselves remained within the tight grip of the Divine Law. Neither their personal relationships or friendly ties could be of any benefit to anyone over and above the law, nor could their displeasure harm anyone in violation of the law. Even in case of any encroachment on their right, the Righteous Caliphs did not use the government machinery to punish the culprit but had to knock at the door of the Islamic court like an ordinary citizen, while in the case of a complaint against them, every citizen was free to seek justice and bring the caliph to court. Their governors and army commanders could also never think of being above the law, and no one would ever venture to influence a judge to obtain a favourable verdict. In short, nobody was powerful enough to transgress the law and escape the consequences.

The moment the caliphate was turned into kingship that article too became a thing of the past, and the law became captive of castle-politics. Not just the king, his princes, governors, government officials, and army commanders, but even the royal court's cronies, maid-servants, and page-boys emerged as part of a privileged class and were above the law. The people's property, life and honour lost their sanctity. There were double standards of justice, one for the weak and another for the powerful. The courts were always under pressure and a God-fearing judge who dared to dispense justice fearlessly had soon to face the consequences. Eventually, the situation came to such a pass that an eminent personality like that of Imam A'ẓam Abū Ḥanīfah preferred to be flogged than accept the royal offer to head the state's judiciary. He was brutally punished because of his refusal to be a tool in the hands of tyranny and, thus, invite divine wrath.

13.7. The rights and obligations of every citizen are guaranteed

The seventh and the last most important and much acclaimed principle of the Islamic political order is the state guarantee for the equality of rights and obligations of every citizen. This provision was also enforced effectively by the Righteously-Guided Caliphs, and it remained in force for some time even after them. Nobody enjoyed any distinction because of race, ethnicity, language, or place of origin. None was superior to anyone due merely to family, lineage or tribal affiliation. Every individual who believed in God and His Messenger (peace be upon him) enjoyed equal status and had the same rights and obligations. Any distinction that someone had over anyone was due only to his social conduct, piety, learning, and service to the people. When kingship replaced the caliphate the devils of parochialism, nepotism, and personal interest raised their ugly heads, the status of kings and their henchmen became superior to everyone else in the land. Their tribes enjoyed special status and bias of Arab over non-Arab soon replaced the spirit of harmony and Islamic brotherhood. Tribal rivalries emerged even among Arabs. History is witness to the great damage that this sad state of affairs caused to the body-politic of the Muslim Ummah, which has been reaping its bitter fruit ever since.

As already discussed, none can deny the historic fact that the change in the system of government from caliphate to kingship was instrumental in the cataclysmic changes which has haunted the world of Islam ever since. Yazīd's nomination as crown prince was definitely a disaster that marked the turning point and a beginning of those extremely damaging trends that ultimately turned the tide of Islamic history. His induction as the ruler of the sprawling Islamic Empire meant the introduction of the system of monarchy. Though it took some time for its evil effects to show up fully, anybody with insight could easily see which way things started moving and what was about to happen to those revolutionary reforms introduced during the glorious days of the caliphate. That was precisely the reason why the great Martyr of Karbalā rose to take an extremely bold step, though knowing full well the dire consequences of his action. He ignored the worst possible scenario of his uprising, because he considered no sacrifice too great in the way of meeting the greatest ever challenge that faced Islam and its system of governance.

14 The Islamic Movement and Social Change*

I am happy to be here at the world of Islam's global centre today to address this select gathering drawn from all over the Arab world on the auspicious occasion of Hajj. I would like to avail myself of this opportunity to explain the tasks that lie ahead and the things that are actually required to be done by those sincere in faith and talented in youth. I am going to try to make the best use possible of these precious and rare moments. Realizing that a similar opportunity may perhaps never be available to me again, I wish to lay bare my very heart to you so as to let you understand exactly the predicament that we are in today, its causes, and the measures and strategy I consider necessary to take for its redressal. فَلْيُبَلِّغِ الشَّاهِدُ الغَائِبَ[1] ('So, let those present transmit [the message] to those who are away.')

At the outset, let us understand that today the world of Islam is divided into two major segments. There is a part where the Muslims are in a minority and political power rests with non-Muslims. The second segment is that of Muslims in absolute majority, who also hold political power. Out of these two, the latter segment is naturally of greater importance and the Muslim Ummah's future obviously depends to a greater extent on the position the independent Muslim states lead or follow in matters of domestic and global significance. The former carries no less weight either, and has an importance of its own. The presence of co-religionists, those who believe in the same

* This is an adapted version of a speech delivered by Sayyid Mawdūdī in Arabic on the eve of the Hajj conference, organized at Makkah al-Mukarramah on 16 Dhū al-Ḥijjah 1382. The meeting was attended by a large number of young Muslims drawn from all over the Arab world. An article based on the speech was published subsequently in *Tarjumān al-Qur'ān*, 1963 – Editor.

[1] The quotation is from the Prophet (peace be upon him)'s address at the Mount of Mercy in Arafat during his Farewell Pilgrimage – Editor.

philosophy of life, faith and ideology, in every nook and corner of the globe, and that too in an overwhelming number, is definitely of immense help and strength for those who are in the field as champions and torch-bearers of the Islamic message and mission. Those under alien rule within their own home cannot be expected, however, to take steps which their counterparts in Muslim countries can take for the glory of Islam. It would be appropriate, therefore, to say that today Muslims everywhere are wistfully looking toward Muslim countries, from Indonesia and Malaya to Morocco, Nigeria and beyond, and the future of the world of Islam depends obviously on the future of these countries. Allah *subḥānahū wa taʿālā* is All-Powerful and, if He so Wills, the springs of His Infinite Bounties may gush forth out of bare rocks and deserts may bloom and turn into gardens. But that is something entirely different, and what we have been ordered to do is to resolutely gather our strength and strive the best we can to improve the situation.

14.1. The Muslim colonized mind and vision

To begin with, consider the premise that the future of the World of Islam is linked with the future of Muslim countries and let us examine the situation in which we find these countries today, and also the factors that led to their present predicament.

You may be well aware that Muslim countries have been under a long spell of intellectual stagnation, moral degeneration, and material backwardness. More or less, each country became an easy prey of Western imperialism. Beginning from the eighteenth century, the process of an all round decline and decay reached its lowest ebb during the earlier part of the twentieth century. Only a lucky few escaped political subjugation by the colonialists. Yet those too could remain free in name only, and due to the colonial powers' economic and socio-political grip, they were overtaken by a sense of terror and awe and became virtually spineless.

Among the most damaging consequences of colonial domination was our intellectual defeatism and moral degeneration. Had the colonial powers robbed us of everything, decimated us and killed our younger generation that would not have been a greater crime than the one they committed by thrusting upon us their system of education, their culture and civilization and the social and behavioural norms as its natural corollary. In every Muslim country that came under the imperialist stranglehold, their common policy had been to do away with its independent system of education. Wherever they could not fully succeed in this venture, they tried to leave no avenues for Muslim graduates to be of any worth in the social set up they devised for that country. They also made it part of their state policy to replace the local language as a medium of instruction and official language of the government. Instead, they introduced their own language in its place. Every imperialist power, whether British, Dutch, French, or Italian, followed the same policy line from East to West and succeeded in producing a generation of Muslims who were ignorant of Islam and Islamic teachings, were unaware of their faith and creed and had no knowledge of their own history and rich legacy of values and glorious traditions. On the other hand, the Muslim mind-set, viewpoints and perceptions were cast into the colonialist's mould. Successive generations naturally followed their predecessors and moved even further away from Islam, becoming more and more immersed in the colonialist's philosophy of life, civilization and culture. They considered it a matter of shame for themselves to talk to their own people in their native language and felt pride in conversing in the language of their colonial masters. While the imperialists were highly biased in favour of their Christian faith, our westernized elite felt ashamed of their being Muslims and it was a matter of fashion for them to publicly pose as rebels against their own religion. On the one hand were the intruders from the West, who held their outdated and decadent national traditions in high esteem, and on the other their native slaves, who felt pride in demeaning their own glorious traditions and values.

In spite of their life-long sojourn in Muslim countries, the imperialists never felt the need to adopt the local dress-code and values. Their native slaves, however, felt elated to mimic their masters' dress, lifestyle, dietary habits, eating and drinking manners, their cultural trappings and even their way of walking, talking and behaving. Everything originating from their own customs, traditions and values gradually became alien to them and worthy of contempt. Following in the footsteps of their imperial masters, they eventually consumed the ultimate dose of materialism, agnosticism and liberalism of the Days of Ignorance, and became ardent champions of materialism, narrow nationalism, moral depravity and promiscuousness. For them it was almost an article of faith that whatever came from the West was the absolute truth: one must follow that to pose as a progressive and whoever turned against it should be labelled as obscurantist and reactionary.

It was part of the imperialist powers' state policy to officially patronize the turncoats from among the natives – those immersed in Western culture and unaware of their Islamic moorings – and provide them with every avenue of promotion and progress in all walks of life. As a natural corollary of this, their diehard lackeys were inducted everywhere in positions closer to the seat of power and soon emerged as the eyes and ears of their colonial masters' civil and military establishments. They eventually moved on to acquire important status in local politics, became leaders of political movements, were elected to parliament as the 'people's representatives' and ultimately rose to dominate the Muslim countries' socio-economic life and the political scene.

When the people's struggle for independence started in the Muslim world, the westernized class of social elite at once seized the opportunity and jumped into the fray to lead the struggle. They enjoyed the blessings of their mentors as well, because they could speak the language of the colonizer, understood their mood, and had also a history of serving them. When eventually the Muslim countries started gaining independence, these imitators of the West emerged as successors to the colonial rulers in their respective countries. They climbed the ladder and occupied the seats of power with a predetermined agenda of continuing the same old policies and programmes of their masters in their countries' civil as well as military establishments.

14.2. The takeover by the neo-colonialists

There are certain significant features in the history of colonial rule and the Muslims' struggle for independence. In order to understand the whole scenario in its correct perspective it is imperative to keep in view some notable features of this crucial phase.

Firstly, throughout the history of colonial stranglehold, the imperialists could never succeed in turning the Muslim population en bloc away from their way of life. They did succeed in spreading misgivings about Islam and perverting people's manners and morals, and by imposing their own set of laws in place of the Shariah laws they could also succeed in paving the way for Muslims to lead their lives contrary to Islamic norms and values. They did not succeed, nonetheless, in turning the entire community into rebels against Islam. Even today, the Muslim common man remains everywhere as staunch a believer as before. The people may not have proper knowledge of Islam, but they do have their faith intact. They have a deep love for their religion and are not willing to barter it away for anything else. Their social conduct has been adversely affected, but no change could take place in their value-system and their standards of right and wrong, haram and halal. They may indulge in interest-based transactions, in felony and adultery, drink wine and commit similar other crimes for which Islam has imposed the severest of punishments, but nobody, except for an infinitesimal minority, would condone his unlawful acts as lawful. They may not give up their taste for music, dance and licence, but with the exception of a small group of fully westernized individuals, the majority of Muslims are not ready to accept this as part of their own culture. Generation after generation have lived under the dominance of Western laws, but nobody takes these laws as superior and the Shariah laws as outdated. A very small, though influential, section of westernized Muslims may be in favour of Anglo-Saxon laws, but the majority firmly believes in the superiority of the Islamic laws and are keen to see them enforced.

The strength of links between the people and the *'ulamā'* and religious scholars is the second significant feature of the present scenario. There is no priestly class in Islam and, therefore, the Muslims and their *'ulamā'* are more closely linked socially. Unfortunately, however, the religious leaders were deliberately kept outside the corridors of power for a long time. Due to their total isolation from mundane matters they now have little ability to lead the Muslim community politically, or to run the affairs of a Muslim state. This is why they could not emerge in any Muslim country as leaders of the freedom movement, nor could they become partners in government after independence. Their job in our social life has remained for a long time like that of the 'brake' for a 'motor car'. The 'driver' of the 'car' is the westernized class and the 'brake' has succeeded at least in impeding the car's speed to some extent. There are countries where this 'brake' too has become loose and consequently the vehicle is sliding headlong down the hill, although its drivers have the illusion of taking it up to some unknown heights.

The third aspect that must also be kept in mind is that the movement for independence was led everywhere in the colonially dominated world of Islam by that particular class of the neo-colonialists, but nowhere could they ever hope to mobilize the common man and inspire him to render sacrifice without appealing to his religious sensitivities. They had to appeal to them everywhere, without exception, in the name of Islam, the Messenger of Allah (peace be upon him) and the Book of God. They had to declare the struggle for independence as a war between Islam and *kufr*. It would not have been possible for them otherwise to obtain the massive support which they required. As was expected, the most hideous perfidy of the Islamic world's history today is that subsequent to assuming power the same elite class has turned away from their solemn pledge and now Islam is the prime target of their unabashed betrayal, in spite of the fact that they won the battle for independence in its name.

The fourth and last notable thing in this respect is that what the Muslim countries could achieve under the leadership of these people was political freedom. But the only difference between the erstwhile phase of slavery and this newly-gained freedom is that the reign of power has shifted from colonial masters to the neo-colonialists. This is why there has been no qualitative change and the same band of people with the same frame of mind and ideology continue ruling the roost and calling the shots even today. The system of education remains the same as was introduced by the imperialists. The laws enacted by them remain in force and further legislation is being made along the same pattern. The saddest part of the current scenario is that the Muslims'

Personal Law, which even the colonial powers did not dare lay their hands on, is now subject to slings and arrows in its own independent homeland. Instead of changing the pattern of the Muslim culture and social conduct according to the national ethos, which the imperialists had distorted to suit their purpose, our intellectually subjugated rulers are busy making them even more secularized and in conformity with the colonialist's standards. They can think of no better framework for our social life than the colonial model of nationhood. The way they are administering the Muslim states they are rending apart the Muslim nations from within and away from each other. They are intellectually close to atheism and wherever they are in a position to influence the Muslim youth, their mission remains to turn them away from Islam. They relish seeing the younger generation make fun of religion, the Messenger of Allah (peace be upon him) and the Day of Judgment. Steeped in a secular and liberal way of life themselves, their concerted efforts are to spread moral depravity and profligacy in a planned manner among the people. They masquerade as anti-imperialist, but the imperialists remain their hot favourites. In all that they do they mimic their spiritual *gurus* whose each and every act is a benchmark of right or wrong to their lackeys. The only difference between the past and present sets of rulers is that the colonialists from the West were the pioneers and their successors in the seats of power today are their blind followers. They cannot move even an inch away from the beaten track of their masters.

These are the four dominant features of the reality on the ground in the World of Islam today. As you evaluate the Muslim Ummah's predicament, it appears that every Muslim country is absolutely hollow from within. Each country is at war with the collective conscience of its own people. The Muslim community wants to return to Islam and its leadership is dragging them by force toward Westernization. The result is that nowhere does the Muslim community's heart throb in unison with their governments. For the governments to be stronger, the rulers' hands and the hearts of the ruled need to move in unison to rebuild the nation. Conversely, when there is a constant tug-of-war between the heads and the hearts, the body's entire strength is consumed by infighting and no headway is possible on the road to progress and prosperity.

14.3. Democracy in the garb of dictatorship

As the natural corollary to this state of affairs, dictatorships have emerged in Muslim countries one after the other. The tiny minority of the Westernized class that stepped into the shoes of their colonial masters know so well that if the system of government is based on the popular vote, they stand no chance of remaining in power any longer. The people, once given the freedom to exercise their choice, will naturally opt in favour of those who are closer to them emotionally, spiritually and in manners and morals, and the imperial legacy of dictatorship will, thus, gradually die a natural death. This is why our rulers are not willing to allow true democracy to take root in Muslim countries, although they have labelled their dictatorships as democracy to fool the world.

There is yet another alarming feature of the present scenario. Political leaderships of the Muslim world remained for some time in the hands of the colonized civilian rulers, who also ran the administration. Subsequently, however, the men in uniform realized that the civilian dictatorships drew sustenance from the military and, hence, they were better qualified to rule the land. This overpowering realization pushed the military junta into the arena and they have since been staging coups after coups and toppling civilian regimes. The armed forces are thus the biggest socio-political problem of the Muslim world today. To defend the state from foreign enemies is no longer their primary task. Instead, their principal objective is to conquer their own people and subjugate them by the use of the very weapons their people gave them to defend the country. The fate of Muslim countries is now being decided not through elections or parliaments, but by the army's general headquarters. In turn, the military too is nowhere unanimous on the question of leadership. Each officer remains on the lookout for an opportunity to conspire and eliminate his senior to step into his place. Whoever comes to the seat of power proclaims himself as the leader of a revolution, and when he goes he is declared a cheat and a traitor. From East to West, the Muslim communities have been reduced, by and large, to the position of mere spectators. They have no say in running the affairs of their own countries. 'Revolutions' brew without their knowledge in utter darkness and they come to know of them only when they have actually been staged. The warring military dictators have one thing in common: once in power, all of them display the same Westernized frame of mind and the same secular and materialistic approach.

14.4. Future prospects

There is, however, a ray of hope in the prevailing gloom and I can very distinctly see the glimmer of a pleasant turnaround. One such happy sign is the current trend of infighting among the champions of secularism and liberal ideologies, who are motivated so much by their narrow personal interests that they are virtually at each other's throats. Had they been united, their collective strength could have wrought disaster, God forbid. The devil is their patron-in-chief and the devil's machinations have always been weak.

Another very important factor and most healthy sign is the firmness of our people's faith. They are least inspired by their self-appointed leaders. Hence, it is not difficult to predict that the moment a dedicated group of righteous people, intellectually resolute, ideologically motivated and capable of leading, emerges, they are bound to dominate the socio-political arena in the long run, God Willing. That would be the time when the Muslim community will get rid of the type of leaders now at the helm of affairs everywhere in the length and breadth of the World of Islam.

14.5. Some words of advice to the youth

The real opportunity to do something great for Islam and the Muslim Ummah lies today with our youth, those who are well qualified in Western education and modern sciences and at the same time have their faith intact in Allah *subḥānahū wa taʿālā*, His Messenger (peace be upon him) and the Day of Reckoning. Those traditionally trained in religious disciplines can be their best comrades-in-arms morally, spiritually, and religiously. Though the latter category now lacks the qualities of leadership for the desired change, they can provide an effective support to the first category of pioneers who are definitely better qualified to be in the vanguard.

The need of the hour, therefore, is that this category of inspired youth should come forward and join the Islamic movement to discharge their responsibility for accelerating the process of socio-political change. I have the following words of advice to give them for guidance in their march forward.

(i) *Correct knowledge of Islam*

Our Western-educated youth is required first and foremost to seek the correct knowledge of Islam as provided by the Qur'an and the Sunnah. This will help them become as good a Muslim intellectually as they are emotionally. Then, they will be able to conduct the affairs of their community in a better way according to the Islamic injunctions and ideals.

(ii) *Self-development*

They are advised to reform their social conduct in such a manner that it practically conforms to the Islamic way of life, which they believe as right. They should always remember that contradiction in words and deeds sows the seeds of hypocrisy within man, and the people lose faith in such a person. Success depends entirely on sincerity and uprightness. Nobody can ever be taken as sincere and upright who says one thing and does something else. Contradiction within someone's way of life will never let him enjoy others' trust, nor will anybody be able to take him seriously. My sincere advice, therefore, to our younger generation, those committed to the cause of the Islamic *da'wah* (mission), is that they should try to do everything that they know as having been enjoined by the Qur'an and the Sunnah and strictly refrain from everything that they know is forbidden by their religion.

(iii) *Critical review of Western thought and culture*

Our educated youth then need to apply their intellectual potential and faculties of speech and writing to shatter the myth of the West's superiority by critically examining and exposing the inherent failings and weaknesses of the Western empirical paradigm. On the other hand, efforts should also be made, rationally and logically, to explain and elucidate the fundamentals of Islam as a way of life (*dīn*). This important task should be handled in such a manner that it may attract the modern mind as the most correct and comprehensive approach to life. The new generation must feel confident that Islam is the only panacea for all the ills plaguing human society everywhere. By becoming true Muslims and acting according to the tenets and fundamental principles of the Religion of Truth alone they can excel in all walks of life and successfully face the challenges of the time.

They should be firm in their belief that they are capable not only of catching up with the advanced nations of the world, but can even leave them far behind on the road to progress and prosperity. The more this task is done along the correct lines and on a wider scale, the more it would pave the way for grooming Islamic missionaries. These soldiers of Islam will thus continue to emerge in an ever-increasing number from every walk of life for ages to come. The Muslim Ummah will thus be able to gradually enrich its cadres of men, women, and children to a level that they may eventually attain positions of leadership in every walk of life and be able to run the affairs of Muslim countries according to the Islamic epistemic paradigm. So long as this process does not follow a gradual and natural process, it would be difficult for the Islamic revolution to take place, while no revolution happening through artificial means can ever be sustainable.

(iv) *The vanguard of the Islamic Movement*

The torch-bearers of the Islamic *da'wah*, who are trained in this way, will have to organize themselves into a well-knit group that we may call the *Islamic Movement*. They will have to be imbued with the essential ingredients of discipline, command and obedience (*al-sam'a wal-tā'ah*). Neither as individuals nor even collectively as disorganized groups can like-minded people serve as a cohesive and effective force for a healthy change. I am confident our well-disciplined and dedicated youth today will emerge tomorrow as the vanguard of this *Movement*, *Inshā'Allah* (God Willing).

(v) *Popular appeal*

To achieve their objective, the youth needs to propagate their message in such a way that people are gradually attracted towards their mission and thus able to educate themselves into the fundamentals of *dīn* and learn to differentiate between Islam and non-Islam. Simultaneously, efforts should also be made to reform public manners and morals and to close the flood gates of depravity and liberalism that godless leaderships have let loose over Muslim communities everywhere. No Muslim nation given to perversion and loose manners and morals has ever been fit to establish an Islamic state. The more the trend of disobedience to the Lord becomes a people's national characteristic, the more difficult it becomes for them to reform their society on the Islamic model.

(vi) ***Patience and sagacity***

Our Islamically-motivated youth should not be impatient in trying to reap the dividends of their struggle for an Islamic revolution. The objective before us requires a much more patient and sagacious approach. They are advised, therefore, take each and every step extremely carefully with sagacity and foresight. Before they take the next step, they should reassure themselves that they have consolidated the outcome of their first step. Progress made in haste is liable to be counter-productive. For example, there is a general impression that by joining hands with a godless leadership the target may become easy to reach and the objective easier to achieve. But practically speaking, the record of our experience shows that no positive outcome can be expected from such a 'marriage of convenience'. This is because those holding the reigns of power in their hands have their own agenda to pursue and those cooperating with them have to make compromises at each and every step until they are eventually reduced to the position of mere tools in the hands of the powerful.

(vii) ***No room for militancy and clandestine movements***

The last point I would like to stress in this respect is that every member of the *Islamic Movement* must necessarily curb the tendency to achieve their noble objectives through clandestine means or by the use of weapons. Something done in haste and with impatience is in fact worse in its outcome and counter-productive. A correct revolution is possible only through a popular movement. As dedicated missionaries of Islam, our youth should, therefore, spread their message openly;

try to reform minds and ideas on a massive scale; change people's perceptions; and conquer hearts through the weapons of love, good conduct and pleasing manners. The risks and challenges coming their way must be faced manly and with courage. A revolution thus staged, through an evolutionary process, will definitely be so strong and sustainable that no enemy ground or air power will be able to weaken it. A coup launched in haste through artificial means goes the way it comes.

These were the few words of advice I had to offer today at this blessed occasion to every sincere member of the *Islamic Movement*. I pray to Allah *subḥānahū wa ta'ālā* to be our Guide and Guardian and help us all in exerting correctly the best efforts we can for the supremacy of His *dīn*.

15 Why should Pakistan be an Islamic State?*

[Adapted version of a high profile discussion on a subject of vital national importance. Organized by the government and broadcast from Radio Pakistan, Lahore, on 18 May 1948, it was conducted by Mr Wajeehuddin, a senior government official – Editor.]

Q. 1 Before we start the discussion, let me begin by asking you what concept do you have in mind of a theocratic state?

A. 1 When a Muslim speaks of 'religion', he obviously means Islam. When I say that Pakistan has to be a 'religious state' I mean that it must be an Islamic state (and not a theocracy). It is a state based on the principles of socio-cultural values, traditions, law, politics and economy, given to us by Islam.

Q. 2 From this interpretation, it appears that you would like the reins of political power of this 'Islamic State' to remain within the hands of a certain section of religious scholars. Its job would be to conduct research and investigate political and administrative matters from an Islamic point of view, frame laws and resolve all state matters in light of Shariah injunctions! Now, the question arises as to who would be behind this group of scholars? As you are aware, our society is economically divided into various classes. Each class is on the lookout for a religious cover to sanctify its own attempts to reach the corridors of power for personal ends, and for this it would not mind exploiting people's religious sentiments. Our religious scholars

* *Nashri Taqrīren*, a popular collection of Sayyid Mawdūdī's radio talks (*Pakistan ko ek madh'habīriyāsat honā chāhiye*, pp. 104–115, [Lahore: Islamic Publications Ltd., June 1977]) – Editor.

cannot remain indifferent to and unconcerned with such class conflict. It is imperative for them either to side with popular forces, or align themselves with the capitalist and feudal class. In such a situation, the interpretations of the Qur'anic precepts would reflect the biased political notion of one group or the other. This may also lead to serious differences among religious scholars holding different political views; the economic tussle would take the form of an endless juristic debate; and the problems which call for urgent redress would end up lying in cold storage.

A. 2 The class conflict to which you are referring has actually emerged mainly due to the fact that under the centuries-old impact of un-Islamic trends our society today lacks the spirit of moral values and principles of social justice given to us by Islam. The materialistic approach, which divided other societies of the world into different classes and created among them a clash of interests and objectives, unfortunately poses a big threat now to our society as well. If the trend remains unchecked, it is bound to cause cleavages and head-on collision within our society, too. We have just passed through the horrific consequences of anti-Muslim riots and the wounds thus inflicted are still bleeding. We cannot let our people be exposed now to those alien ideologies and concepts which might cause turmoil and class conflicts within our own society in future and deprive us of the ability to live in peace until one class eliminates the other. Other communities may have accepted such concepts, perhaps because they do not have those principles of morality and social justice which prevent the growth and development of narrow selfish interests of different classes. Fortunately for us, we do have a social system that can save us from such threats. All that is required of us is to promote from amongst us those who have the necessary Islamic spirit and are capable of correct interpretation of the Islamic injunctions, uninfluenced by class biases or personal interests. We should then collectively accept, without any reservation, the interpretation offered to us through consensus or with a majority opinion. The whole nation ought to stand by those people without being led astray by this group or that group. The only criterion that we need to keep under consideration while electing those who are to run the affairs of government and the state is to ensure that they are of a reliable character and capable of correct interpretation of Islam. Pakistan thus needs no theocracy, but a system of government wherein Islam is supreme.[1]

Q. 3 Do you think sincerity and honesty are enough for evolving a political system? We have countless complex political and economic problems calling for serious thought. For example, should the means of production be left in private hands or nationalized? Should there be a one-party system or is it necessary for a democracy to have a multi-party system? Should labour have the right to protest and strike? If you hand over these and similar other tricky issues to religious leaders, you will find that they would arrive at no conclusion. The main reason for this is that the reconstruction of a state needs

---

[1] Due to time constraints, a detailed response regarding 'theocracy'was avoided. This point was, however, elaborated by Sayyid Mawdūdī in his book *Islamic Law and Constitution,* as follows:

> By the word 'vicegerency', your mind should not turn towards the Divine Right of kings, or to Papal authority. According to the Qur'an, the vicegerency of God is not the exclusive birthright of any individual or clan or class of people; it is the collective right of all those who accept and admit God's absolute sovereignty over themselves and adopt all laws and regulations. It says:
>
> *Allah has promised such of you as have become believers and done good deeds that He will most surely make them His vicegerent in the earth.*
>
> [*al-Mu'minūn* 24: 55]
>
> This concept of life makes the Islamic *Khilāfat* a democracy, which in essence and fundamentals is the antithesis of the Theocratic, the Monarchiacal and the Papal form of Government, as also of the present-day Western Secular Democracy.
>
> *Islamic Law and Constitution* (Lahore: Islamic Publications Ltd., March 1980), pp. 218–219) – Editor.

political insight and a sense of history and not just scholastic research and a theocratic approach. Don't you think, therefore, that instead of the scholars of *dīnīyyāt*[2] (Islamic Sciences), expert politicians and economists can provide better leadership in this respect)?

A. 3 When you say *dīnīyyāt,* you perhaps exclude *dunyawīyāt* (temporal matters) and hence your apprehension that scholars of Islamic sciences, whom you think are unaware of worldly matters, cannot resolve the state's political and economic problems. But to which way do you think we will move if we assign all issues concerning our civil and military administration, politics, and economy to the 'scholars of worldly matters' who are well-versed in Western theories and practices but have little knowledge of Islam? According to you, these people are better qualified to provide us leadership. But, I am afraid, such a leadership would land us in the same situation as faced today by most nations of the world – domestically in a situation of conflict among the narrow, self-centred, and class-based vested interests, and externally in a tug-of-war with selfish global forces. Don't you think it would be better to look up to those within our community who are equally well-versed in both the so-called temporal and the divine; who may have a good grasp over the teachings of the Qur'an and the Sunnah of the Prophet (peace be upon him) as also contemporary political and economic issues. Such people could be tasked to make pioneering efforts for the proper redress of the problems facing our fledgling Islamic state and arrive at viable solutions.

[2] An obvious pun is intended here. *Dīnīyyāt*, which literally means 'Islamic Sciences', is also the title of one of Sayyid Mawdūdī's earliest and most sought after publications. The booklet has been rendered in over two dozen languages. Its English version, by Prof Khurshid Ahmad, *Towards Understanding Islam*, has itself assumed the status of a classic and 'best seller' – Editor.

Q. 4 We are faced with yet another handicap. Often, we overlook the underlying spirit of religious injunctions and keep only their literal side in view. For example, the purpose behind the prohibition of interest was to prevent economic exploitation.[3] The situation has changed now. The difference between the lawful and the prohibited is now no longer valid.

A. 4 The handicap you have mentioned has always cropped up whenever a law has been taken at face value and its full import and spirit have been ignored. Such a problem sometimes emerges because of the lack of knowledge and insight and sometimes because of the people, who feel obliged to revolt against the spirit of the law but refrain from a formal change for the sake of saving face. The only thing that can save us from this awkward situation is the Muslim community's correct perception of Islam and the will to actually follow it in letter and spirit. When this happens, the community would elect only those from its midst for the interpretation and elucidation of the Islamic injunctions who are capable not only of understanding the literal meaning of the injunctions of the Qur'an and the Sunnah, but also of the full comprehension of their essence.

Q. 5 What would you say regarding the difference of views among religious seminaries and scholars in matters of Islamic significance in addition to their difference of opinion in matters of political interest? Don't you think these differences are great impediments for the formulation and functioning of an Islamic state's political and social strategy for the future?

---

[3] We may find detailed discussion on economic issues from an Islamic perspective in a number of books and articles contributed by Sayyid Mawdūdī. A compendium of his writings on the subject, compiled by Prof Khurshid Ahmad and translated and edited by the Editor, is now available in printed form in the Islamic Foundation's latest best-selling venture *First Principles of Islamic Economics*. The book offers an in-depth study of the fundamentals of Islamic Economics, including the question of *ribā*-free economy – Editor.

A. 5 The nature of these differences is exactly the same as that of our other differences and we can resolve them the way we resolve all other issues. There is no human society where you do not find different views on different issues. But such differences are never allowed to stand in the way of a society's onward march. The democratically established approach to resolving such differences is that the state's system is run according to the standpoint acceptable to the majority and the viewpoint of smaller segments is accommodated only to the extent permissible under the rules. We would strive hard to ensure that the State of Pakistan is established on the broad objectives and principles of Islam, which are acceptable to the majority of the country's Muslim population. There may remain, nevertheless, those who may not agree on various counts with the majority opinion. In that event, we would have to follow the same democratic approach as mentioned just now, or else it would be a very strange standpoint to opt for 'non-Islam' only because a few of us could not agree on 'Islam'.

Q. 6 Apart from the Muslims' internal differences, we also have to keep in mind the issue of religious minorities in Pakistan. How can you make them agree to Pakistan becoming a religious state and ensure their remaining loyal to it?

A. 6 This can be resolved like other differences among the State's Muslim majority. In a democracy, the country's system is evolved and run according to the stand taken by its majority. The minorities of the country are fully justified in demanding that their viewpoints on various national issues be also taken into consideration and that their basic human rights and personal laws be fully safeguarded. They are not entitled, however, to demand that the majority's opinion be changed for their sake. The vast majority of the people of Pakistan sincerely believe that their salvation lies in following the Islamic principles. Justice and common sense demand that they must have the right to let the country be governed according to the popoular vision and aspirations. The minority can ask the majority to safeguard its rights, but it has no right to demand the majority to opt for something else other than Islam to run the affairs of the state. As for the question of loyalty, the fact of the matter is that there is no relationship between allegiance and loyalty and the state being religious or secular. The matter of loyalty depends entirely on the level of justice, respect and magnanimity that a majority displays in its treatment of the minority. You cannot satisfy a minority by a show of civility only or even if you say to them: 'Look, we have gone to the extent of giving up our own religion for your sake and opted for a secular system.' The minority's interest lies in seeing justice being done to it and whether your attitude towards it is marked by a religious bias or by magnanimity and large-heartedness. Such an approach alone can eventually determine if the minority is willing to live as loyal citizens of the state or as an indifferent and displeased lot.

Q. 7 At the end of an extremely useful discussion, I would submit that a country's political system is a mirror of the customs and traditions, manners and morals and beliefs and aspirations of the people of that country. No system can be expected from the very start to be the flag-bearer of a particular philosophy or creed. If we try to do that, it would be an artificial and short-lived measure. If we are keen to build an Islamic state on ideological foundations, it would be appropriate first to inculcate the true Islamic spirit into the people of Pakistan. When religious traditions take root and Islamic values become ingrained in our national character, then alone can our political system automatically assume the Islamic complexion. To me it still appears a far cry as the people are not yet ready for an Islamic system.

A. 7 You are correct when you say that a country's political system reflects its people's moral and intellectual status. Now, if the people of Pakistan have a strong inclination towards Islam and a great desire is noticeable among them to move forward on the Islamic path, why then should their state not be a mirror of that popular aspiration and demand? You are also correct when you say that if we wish to make Pakistan an Islamic state, we would have to first inculcate within the countrymen a true Islamic spirit and awareness about the religion and the Islamic manners and morals. I, however, fail to understand why would you like the state itself to be exempted from taking an active part in such an effort. During the pre-14 August 1947 period, we were ruled by a non-Muslim authority. We were, therefore, unable then to get any assistance from the state, its organs and resources for the reconstruction of our nation and state on the Islamic model. In fact, the entire state machinery of the time had taken us, with all the power at its command, in a different direction and we had to strive hard in an extremely hostile environment to return to the Islamic way of life. Now that a political revolution has taken place, why should the people be faced with the basic question as to whether or not our Islamic Republic should embark on rebuilding the country on an Islamic model and play the pioneering role of an architect in this respect? Or should it follow the course of an indifferent and unconcerned spectator? Why should the people of Pakistan be left to alternately face the same position of hostility from the state and its organs and continue struggling for the revival of Islamic values in a situation as adverse as before? As the nation is engaged nowadays in framing the country's future system, we are keen, therefore, that Pakistan should emerge as an architect of the Islamic way of life and a role model in that capacity. If we succeed in realizing our dream it would be easier for the state, with all the resources and potentials at its command, to induce a moral and intellectual revolution in the lives of its people. When our society thus starts being transformed, Pakistan would begin gradually rising with the same degree as a truly Islamic state.

Biographical Outlines

Abū Ḥanīfah (Imam A'ẓam) (80/699–150/767): Abū Ḥanīfah al-Nū'mān ibn Thābit, reverently called Imam A'ẓam or the Great Leader, was a pioneer theologian, jurist, and founder of the most widely followed school of Islamic Law. His legal thought was marked by a high degree of reasoning and juridical insight. As an eminent Tābi'ī, he immensely benefitted by the knowledge and wisdom of some prominent Companions, like Anas ibn Mālik, 'Abd Allāh ibn Abī 'Awfā, Sahl ibn Sa'd and 'Amr ibn Wāthilah. Among his greatest contributions in the field of Islamic learning and law was the council he constituted to review and write down his opinions on legal issues. Consisting of around forty leading jurists of the time, some of whom were drawn from among his prominent pupils like Imam Abū Yūsuf, Imam Zufar and Imam Muhammad al-Sahybānī, the council reviewed the Imam's opinions on issues concerning almost every significant aspect of human life and activity. The number of such issues reached to the staggering figure of 1,290,000. This institutionalized arrangement reflected Imam A'ẓam's extreme care not to let an onerous task of documenting formal opinions on crucial issues of juridical significance be based entirely on his personal views and knowledge.

The Imam explained the guiding principle he always followed for his research in these words: 'I seek guidance from the Book of Allah in every issue that I handle. Then, I follow the Sunnah of Rasūl Allah (Allah's peace and blessings be on him). If the solution is not available there for an emergent issue, I seek help from the opinions of the Ṣaḥābah. If no clue is found even there, I have to follow the inductive method of *ijtihād*, the way other *mujtahidīn* have done, like Ibrāhīm, Sha'bī, Ibn Sīrīn and al-Atā." (*Tahdhīb al-Tahdhīb*, vol. 10, p. 451)

Those from the other schools of thought, who often criticized the *Ahnāf* for what they viewed as the Imam's excessive use of reason and *qiyās* (deduction by analogy), actually failed to correctly understand the research methodology of Imam A'ẓam, as he himself explained above. In fact, the same pattern of deduction and induction was followed more or less by the Mālikīyyah, Shawāfi' and even Ḥanābilah with the only difference that the number of juridical issues tackled by each one of them is too small as compared to those handled by Imam A'ẓam and his Sāhibayn (Associates) – Imam Abū Yūsuf and Imam Muhammad al-Sahybānī.

The Imam dominated the intellectual life of Iraq, then the cultural and civilizational nerve-centre of the world of Islam. In 120 AH/737 CE, following the death of his teacher Imam Ḥammād, he succeeded him as Dean of Iraq's *Madrasah Ahl al-Ra'y* (School of the Leaders of Public Opinion). In that capacity he was unanimously declared by the leading jurists of the time as *Faqīh Ahl al-Sharq* (Jurist of the Orient). He left behind a galaxy of disciples who were luminaries of the Islamic law, like Imam Abū Yūsuf; Imam Muhammad al-Sahybānī; Imam Zufar ibn al-Hudhayl (158/775); Dāwūd al-Atā' (165/781); Asad ibn 'Amr (160/806); and Ḥasan ibn Ziyād al-Lu'lu'ī (204/819); and among traditionists Imam 'Abd Allah ibn al-Mubārak (181/797). Imam A'ẓam's son, Ḥammād (named after the Imam's teacher Ḥammād), and his grandson Ismā'īl also rose to positions of eminence as the *qāḍī* of Basra and Raqqa.

Imam A'ẓam's notable treatise, *Al-Fiqh al-Akbar*, which literally means *The Greatest Knowledge*, is one of the earliest surviving and most significant texts on the fundamentals of the Islamic creed of *tawḥīd* and *risālah*. The narrative is held in high esteem due to the lucidity of its style and quality of scholarship that helps one improve his *'aqīdah* (fundamentals of Islamic faith). The work has been rendered in more than a dozen foreign languages including English and Urdu. Other works attributed to him include the epistle *Al-'Ālim wa'l-Muta'allim*'; *Al-Radd 'ala'l Qadarīyyah*; *Jami' Masānīd Abī Ḥanīfah* (*Compendium of Traditions recorded by Abū Ḥanīfah*), and *Al-Qaṣīdah Al-Nu'mānīyyah*, a poetic work dedicated to the life and achievements of *Sayyidunā* Rasūl Allah (peace be upon him).

Al-Ashā'irah: Also called Asha'rīyyah and Asha'rites, it stands out as an important theological school of the early fourth century Hijrah (tenth century CE). It marked a return to the pristine glory of the Qur'an and the Sunnah in response to the excessively rationalistic approach of the Mu'tazilah. The founder of the school, Abū al-Ḥasan 'Alī ibn Ismā'īl al-Ash'arī (260/873-4–324/935-6) of Basra was ninth in descent from the famous Companion Abū Mūsa al-Ash'arī and was one of the best pupils of Abū Ḥāshim al-Jubbā'ī, head of the Mu'tazilah school in Basra. The story about his moving away from his teacher's line of thought is quite revealing. It is reported that three times during the month of Ramadan he saw *Sayyidunā* Rasūl Allah (peace be upon him) in a vision commanding him to adhere to the true Tradition but not to abandon *'Ilm al-kalām*. His approach was thus a happy fusion of Tradition and rationalism.

Abu al-Ḥasan al-Ash'arī scientifically opposed the Mu'tazilites on the following extremely crucial points:

i. God's attributes are as eternal as His Person and He is a Knowing, Seeing and Speaking God and not merely an essence, as believed by the Mu'tazilah.
ii. Al-Ash'arī refused to accept the far-fetched Mu'tazilah interpretation of various Qur'anic expressions regarding God's 'Hand', 'Face' and 'Throne'. He brilliantly declared that while the Book of God meant nothing corporeal by such expressions, they were the attributes the precise nature of which is best known to the Lord alone.

iii. Against the Mu'tazilah view of the Qur'an being a creation of the Lord and hence not eternal, al-Ash'arī maintained that it was eternal because it was the Lord Almighty's Speech and not His creation.

iv. The Mu'tazilah were of the view that God could not be seen literally neither in this world nor in the Hereafter as that would imply His being corporeal, and limited. On the strength of the Prophetic Traditions, Imam al-Ash'arī stressed that the vision of the Lord Almighty 'which the *ahl al-Jannah* (people of Paradise) are going to be blessed with would be a reality, though none can understand the exact nature of that vision'.

v. As against the Mu'tazilah, al-Ash'arī and his school reaffirmed faith in God's Omnipotence: everything, good or evil, is willed by God alone and it is He Who has created the faculty of choice (*khiyār*) and acquisition (*kasb*) that enables man to do good or bad and thus earn reward or punishment for his act.

vi. The Mu'tazilah, according to their doctrine of *al-manzilah bayn al-manzilatayn* (intermission between two positions), held that a Muslim guilty of serious sin was neither believer nor unbeliever. Al-Ash'arī, however, strictly followed the true Islamic approach that a sinner remained a believer, though he was liable for the punishment of the Hereafter.

vii. Al-Ash'arī refused to rationally interpret, like the Mu'tazilites, various established terms of the Tradition, such as *al-Sirāt* (the Bridge), *al-Mīzān* (the Balance), and *al-Ḥawḍ* (the Basin).

Some of the eminent Ashā'irah personalities were: al-Bāqillānī (d. 403/1013), al-Samnānī (d. 444/1052), Imam Abū Ḥāmid Muhammad al-Ghazālī (d. 505/1111); al-Shahristānī (d. 548/1153), and Imam Fakhr al-Dīn al-Rāzī (d. 606/1210).

Al-Awzāʿī (al-Imām) (88/707–157/774): Abū ʿAmr ʿAbd Allah ibn ʿAmr al-Awzāʿī (with reference to his birthplace al-Awzāʿ, a suburb of Damascus) was an eminent traditionist and leading representative of the Syrian school of Islamic jurisprudence. Though with a limited appeal, he was a contemporary of Imam Abū Ḥanīfah and often differed from his approach in juridical matters. He is believed to have dictated the following books to his disciples: *Kitāb al-Sunan fi'l-Fiqh*, *Kitāb al-Masā'il fi'l-Fiqh*, and *Kitāb al-Siyar*. His book *al-Musnad* on Traditions was compiled later on.

Al-Dhahabī (Rabīʿ-II 675/October 1274–3 Dhū al-Qaʿdah 748/4 February 1348): Shams al-Dīn ʿAbd Allah Muhammad ibn ʿUthmān al-Dhahabī al-Shāfiʿī, born and buried in Damascus, was a prominent historian, Traditionist and scholar of the Science of the Profiles of the Narrators of Prophetic Traditions (*Fann Asmā' al-Rijāl*). He is also known as Ibn al-Dhahabī (son of the goldsmith), with reference to his father's profession. He is author of some best-known books on Islamic history and *Asma' al-Rijāl*, namely: (1) the voluminous *Ta'rīkh al-Islām*; (2) its abridged version *Al-Mukhtasar min Ta'rīkh al-Islām*; (3) *Tabaqāt al-Mashāhīr wa'l-Aʿlām*; (4) *Manāqib al-Imām Abī Ḥanīfah wa Sāhibayh*; (5) *Al-Iṣābah fi Tajrīd Asma' a'l-Ṣaḥābah* (based on *Usud al-Ghābah* of Ibn al-Athīr); (6) *Siyar al-Aʿlām a'l-Nubalā'*, the lexicographical works in Tradition; (7) *Tadh'hīb Tahdhīb al-Kamāl fi Asmā' l-Rijāl*; and (8) *Mizān al-Iʿtidāl fi Naqdi'l-Rijāl.*

Al-Ḥasan al-Basrī (al-Imām) (21/642–5 Rajab 110/728): Abū Saʿīd al-Ḥasan ibn Abī al-Ḥasan Yasār al-Basrī was an outstanding Tābiʿī scholar, jurist and preacher. During *Sayyidunā* ʿUmar al-Fārūq's rule, his father Peroz became a prisoner of war at the conquest of Maysān, a township between Basra and Wāsit. Peroz embraced Islam later on and settled in Al-Madinah al-Munawwarah as a freed slave of the eminent Companion Zayd ibn Thābit. He was then married to Khayyirah, a bondmaid also of Persian origin, whom *Ummu'l-Mu'minīn al-Sayyidah* Umm Salamah had freed on the birth of their son al-Ḥasan. Peroz thus became famous by his *kunyah* (nickname) Abū al-Ḥasan. The young al-Ḥasan had the honour of being brought up in the house of the *Ummu'l-Mu'minīn* and under her guidance. During his childhood, he had the opportunity to meet many eminent Companions of the Prophet (peace be upon him), who frequently visited the house to get educated in Ahadith. A glorious environment like that was bound to have a lasting impact on al-Ḥasan's personality and thus he emerged as an epitome of virtue, piety and devotion to Islam and Islamic learning. He is believed to have seen and benefitted from the knowledge of around seventy senior Companions who had taken part in the historic Battle of Badr. He was an ardent listener of the third caliph 'Uthmān's Friday sermons. A year after the Battle of Siffīn (36/657), he moved to Basra, where he remained till his death.

Al-Ḥasan studied in Basra, then the seat of Islamic learning, *'ilm al-Ḥadīth*, Islamic law, and Arabic language and rhetoric. Then he started teaching by delivering lectures on the sciences of the Qur'an, hadith and law. He also delivered sermons in the grand mosque of Basra and quickly became popular because of his powerful oration and lucidity of style. During 59–62 AH/670–673 CE, he took part in some military expeditions that led to the conquest of eastern Persia. Imam al-Ḥasan was a close friend of Caliph 'Umar ibn 'Abd al-'Azīz (60/680–20-25 Rajab 101/5-10 February 720), who loved him very much and often consulted him in matters concerning the administration of the Islamic state. He was installed as Judge of Basra in 102/720, a role he performed on a voluntary basis. Eminent scholars and traditionists of his time, like Abū Bardah, Abū Qatādah, Humayd and 'Awf, paid rich tributes to the Imam's scholarship, piety and frankness in matters concerning religion. He openly opposed the dynastic rule and the way of governance of the Umayyad Caliph Yazīd ibn 'Abd al-Malik. He also expressed anger against the Umayyad Governor of Iraq, Ḥajjāj ibn Yūsuf, when he embarked on rebuilding Wāsit by lavishly spending public money.

Al-Ḥasan did not leave much by way of written works, though some of his sermons and sayings have been partially preserved. However, he left an indelible mark in the annals of Islamic history as an icon for those who flocked to him to seek knowledge, take lessons in Prophetic Traditions and resolve juristic matters. The number of his disciples was in the hundreds, of whom some prominent ones were: 'Amr ibn 'Ubayd (d. 761), Imam Ayyūb al-Sakhtiyānī, the Arminian Christian Saint Farqad al-Sabakhī, who embraced Islam at the hands of Imam al-Ḥasan and Wāthil ibn 'Atā', the founder of the Mu'tazilah school that derived its name from the Imam's famous observation: '*itazalā 'annā*' (he has separated from us). Incidentally, Wāthil continued to claim his love, respect, and affiliation with the Imam, while the Ashā'irah had an equally eloquent claim on him as the true followers of his thoughts.

Imam al-Ḥasan is considered as the principal link to whom various Sufi chains attribute their affiliation. Abū Tālib al-Makkī in his *Qūtul-Qulūb* said: 'Al-Ḥasan was the Imam of the science of which we are representatives. We follow in his footsteps and seek light from the lamp lit by him.' (*Qūt*, vol. 1, p. 149) Famous Arab poet, al-Farazdaq, and literary figures, al-Jāhiz and al-Mubarrad, held the Imam in high esteem for the captivating eloquence and literary worth of his sayings and sermons. In his book *al-Kāmil*, al-Mubarrad extensively quoted the Imam's sayings as specimens of aphoristic expressions. Two such quotes are reproduced here:

حَادِثُوا هٰذِهِ القُلُوبَ فَإِنَّهَا سَرِيعَةُ الدُّثُور.

Reinvigorate the hearts for they soon become obsolete.

اِجعَلِ الدُّنيَا كَالقَنطَرَةِ تُجُوزُ عَلَيهَا وَلَا تعمُرُهَا.

Take this world like a bridge which you cross over but make it no home.

Ibn ʿAbd al-Barr (368/978–463/1072): Yūsuf ibn ʿAbd Allah ibn ʿ Abd al-Barr, also known by the nickname of Abū ʿUmar al-Nawavī al-Qurtubī was an eminent traditionist of the Mālikī school. His best known books include *Al-Istīʿāb fī Asmā' al-Ashāb*; *Al-Kāfī fī Madhāhib Mālik*; *Al-Maghāzī*; *Al-Tawḥīd limā fi'l-Muwaṭṭa' min al-Maʿānī wal Asānīd*; and *Al-Istidhkār li Madhāhib ʿUlāma' al-Amsār*.

Ibn Abī' al-ʿIzz al-Ḥanafī (731/1331–792/1390): ʿAlī ibn ʿAlī ibn Muhammad ibn ʿAbd al-Raḥmān ibn Abi'l-ʿIzz was an eminent jurist of the Ḥanafī school and a descendent of the celebrated warrior Sultān Salāh al-Dīn al-Ayyūbi, who was himself an expert of Ḥanafī law. Ibn Abī' al-ʿIzz was born in Damascus, stayed for a few years in Egypt and then returned to Damascus where he died. His major contribution was *Sharḥ al-ʿAdillah al-Ṭaḥāwīyyah*, a commentary on Imam al-Ṭaḥāwī's work (translated into English as *Commentary of al-Ṭaḥāwī*).

Ibn al-ʿArabī (Born in Seville, 468/1075–died in Fez, 543/1148): Abū Bakr Muhammad ibn ʿAbd Allah Al-Maʿāfirī, was a traditionist and scholar of Mālikī law from al-Andalus. He wrote many books on a variety of subjects, including hadith, *fiqh*, Qur'anic sciences, grammar and history. His well-known works are: *Tafsīr Aḥkām al-Qur'ān*; *ʿĀridat al-Ahwadhī*, a commentary on *Jāmiʿ al-Tirmidhī*; and *Al-ʿAwāsim min al-Qawāsim*, a history book exposing the Shia deviations.

Ibn al-Athīr: 'Ibn al-Athīr' was the family name that became prominent by the outstanding personalities of the three brothers of Iraqi origin who simultaneously rose to eminence in different fields of scholarship. Izzuddin Abu'l Ḥasan ʿAlī ibn Muhammad (4 Jumādā-I 555/13 May 1160–Shaʿbān or Ramadan 630/May-June 1233) was the second of the three scholar brothers. He is well-known for his famous book in history, *Kitāb al-Kāmil fi'l-Tārīkh*, and the most celebrated work in *Asmā' al-Rijāl*, the *Usud al-Ghābah fī Maʿrifat al-Ṣaḥābah* that gives detailed profiles of around 7,500 Companions of the Prophet.

Ibn al-Athīr's elder brother, Majd al-Dīn Abu'l-Sa'ādāt al-Mubārak ibn Muhammad (544/1149–29 Dhū al-Ḥijjah 606/24 June 1210), was a traditionist and an eminent grammarian. He is known for his books *Jami' al-'Usūl fi Aḥadīth al-Rasūl* and *al-Nihāyah fi Gharīb i'l-Ḥadīth.* The third brother, Diyā' al-Dīn Abu'l-Fath Nasr Allah ibn Muhammad (558/1163–29 Rabī'-II 637/28 November 1239), excelled in the field of history and literature. His books *Al-Mathal al-Sā'ir fi Adab il-Kitāb wa'l-Shā'ir* and *Al-Murassa' fi'l-Adabiyyāt* have remained equally popular among the students and scholars of Arabic arts and literature.

Ibn Ḥajar al-'Asqalānī (22 Shā'bān 773/28 February 1372–28 Dhū al-Ḥijjah 852/22 February 1449): Shaykh al-Islām Shihāb al-Dīn Abu'l Faḍl Aḥmad ibn Nūru al-Dīn 'Alī ibn Muhammad al-'Asqalānī al-Shāfi'ī was an outstanding scholar of the Science of Hadith, a prolific writer, historian and *Qāḍī al-Quḍāt.* He was born in Cairo, he became orphaned in childhood but being scion of an eminent trading family faced no financial hardship. He did not know exactly the origin of his family name, Ibn Ḥajar, while reference to 'Asqalān dated back to 587 (1191 CE) when Salāh al-Dīn al-Ayyūbī led an expedition to quell the insurgents there and had to evacuate eminent Muslim families of 'Asqalān and settle them in Cairo. Like his father, Nūru al-Dīn, who was a religious scholar and teacher of Tradition and law, Ibn Ḥajar had no interest in his family vocation of trade and commerce and devoted his entire life in the pursuit of knowledge, for which he frequently travelled to Palestine, Syria, Hijāz and Yemen. His principal academic association was with Cairo's *Khānqāh al-Baybarsīyyah* of which he was installed educational and administrative head on 3 Rajab 813/6 July 1410, a position he held for almost thirty-one years. Then he shifted his teaching activities to the *Dār al-Ḥadīth al-Kāmilīyyah.* He was also installed as a mufti at the *Dār al-'Adl,* an associate preacher and imam at al-Azhar and the Grand Mosque of 'Amr ibn al-'Ās. He finally took charge of the Muhammadīyyah Library where he compiled two catalogues of around 4,000 valuable manuscripts, one arranged alphabetically and the other topic-wise. His pupil, al-Shakhāwī, in his biography *Al-Jawāhir wal-Durrar fī Tarjumati Shaykh al-Islām Ibn Ḥajar* described him as an ideal Islamic scholar of hadith and a guide into various branches of knowledge.

Ibn Ḥajar's first publication was a collection of poems (*Qasā'id*) dedicated to the Prophet (peace be upon him). Among the best known of his works for which he has been universally acclaimed by scholars and students of Islamic Sciences are: (1) *Fatḥ al-Bārī*, the great commentary of Imam Bukhārī's *Al-Jāmi' al-Ṣaḥīḥ;* (2) *Ta'līq al-Ta'līq*, devoted to the *isnād* (chain of narrators) of *al-Jāmi' al-Ṣaḥīḥ*; (3) *Al-Isābah fī Tamyīzi'l-Ṣaḥābah*, offering authentic details about the lives of the Companions; (4) *Al-Dirāyah fī Muntakhab Takhrīj Aḥadīth al-Hidāyah*; (5) *Bulūgh al-Marām min Adillati'l-Aḥkām fī 'Ilm al-Ḥadīth*; (6) *Nukhbatu'l-Fikr fī Mustalah Ahli'l-Athr*; (7) *Tahdhīb al-Tahdhīb* (in 12 volumes); and (8) *Al-Durar al-Kāminah fī A'yān al-Mi'ah al-Thāminah,* containing biographical details of the notable Islamic personalities of the eighth century Hijrah (fifteenth century CE).

Ibn Ḥishām (d. 13 Rabī II 218/8 May 833): Abū Muhammad 'Abd al-Mālik ibn Ḥishām ibn Ayyūb al-Himyarī al-Basrī was born in Basra and moved to Fusṭāṭ (Cairo) where he died. Ibn Ḥishām was an outstanding scholar of genealogy and grammar, best known for his outstanding work *Sīrat al-Nabīy* on the life and achievements of *Sayyidunā* Rasūl Allah (peace be upon him). The book was his much-acclaimed edition of *Kitāb al-Sīrah* of Ibn Ishāq, one of the main authorities on the discipline of the Science of *Sīrah* and *Maghāzī* (Prophet's Biography and Expeditions). Ibn Ḥishām's edition is held in high esteem as one of the few authentic primary sources on the subject. He improved upon Ibn Ishāq's work by omitting some material that though authentic was not very relevant. He also provided more accurate versions of some popular early poems contributed in praise of the Messenger of Allah (peace be upon him), adding explanatory notes on difficult words and phrases used. This accounts for the great popularity of Ibn Ḥishām's edition.

Ibn Ḥishām also wrote another book, *Kitāb al-Tījān*, which is extant and which was a collection of antique tales and narratives from South Arabia and the Bible.

Ibn Kathīr (700/1300–Sha'bān 774/February 1373): Born in Basra and died in Damascus, 'Imād al-Dīn Ismā'īl ibn 'Umar ibn Kathīr was the best known historian and traditionist of Syria. He was influenced greatly by Imam Ibn Taymīyyah and his school. He received lessons in hadith from al-Dhahabī.

The most important of Ibn Kathīr's works were *Al-Bidāyah wa'l Nihāyah*, a monumental history of Islam in 14 volumes. The sources he drew upon for *Al-Bidāyah* (The Beginning) included the works of Ibn Jarīr al-Ṭabarī, Ibn al-'Asākir, Ibn al-Jawzī, Ibn al-Athīr and al-Dhahabī. For *Al-Nihāyah* (The End), his chief sources were *Al-Tārīkh* and *Al-Mu'jam* of al-Birzālī (d. 739/1338–9). In turn, this encyclopaedic work inspired later scholars like Ibn Ḥajar al-'Asqalānī, himself a great name in the science of hadith. His other well known publications include: (1) *Tafsīr al-Qur'ān al-'Azīm*, popularly known as *Tafsīr Ibn Kathīr*; (2) *Al-Sīrah al-Nabawīyyah*, a detailed biography of the Prophet; (3) *Kitāb al-Takmīl*, consisting of a catalogue of eminent traditionists; and (4) *Kitāb al-Jāmi'*, a remarkable compilation in alphabetical order of the Companions who had transmitted Ahadith.

Ibn Khaldūn (1 Ramadan 732/27 May 1332–25 Ramadan 808/16 March 1406): Universally acknowledged as a pioneer social scientist, Ibn Khaldūn's full name is Abū Zayd Walī al-Dīn 'Abd Al-Raḥmān ibn Muhammad. Born in Tunis and buried in Cairo, Ibn Khaldūn was scion of an Arab family of Hadramawt that moved to Seville and then settled in Tunis. He drew his surname from his great grandfather, Khālid al-Ḥadramī, whose nickname was Khaldūn. Ibn Khaldūn has been acclaimed as a polymath, or versatile genius, who was father of various scientific disciplines like historiography, the philosophy of history, sociology, demography, and modern economics. He was the most outstanding figure of the period of the Arabs' socio-political decline, who rose far above his age in his intellectual forays.

Ibn Khaldūn's earliest work was his autobiography *Al-Ta'rīf bi Ibn Khaldūn wa Rahlatuhū Gharban wa Sharqan* (commonly known as *Al-Ta'rīf*). Literally translated, the book means *Introduction to Ibn Khaldūn and His Journeys from West to East* and provides relatively a well-documented account of his life.

Before a brief study of his best known work, *Al-Muqaddimah*, it will be appropriate to mention his *Muqaddimat al-Muqaddimah*, which Ibn Khaldūn contributed as an 'Introduction'to the proper *Muqaddimah.* In this, he begins by defining history, which he expands to include the study of the whole human past, including its social, economic and cultural aspects. The study is based on the 'Criterion of conformity with reality' (*Qānūn al-Mutābaqah*).

Al-Muqaddimah, known in the West as *Prolegomenon* or Preface, was originally conceived as only an introduction to his 7-volume universal history, *Kitāb al-'Ibar*, which literally means *The Book of Lessons Drawn from History*. The *Introduction*, however, eventually proved to be a book in itself and a pioneering study of human civilization (*al-'Umrān al-Basharī*). *Al-Muqaddimah* is thus devoted to discuss the currents and cross currents of human history, its evolution and decline, which Ibn Khaldūn described as *'Ilm al-'Umrān* or the Science of Sociology and he called it 'an independent science' (*al-'ilm al-mustaqil bi-nafsihi*). His exposition is divided into six chapters of varying length: Chapter 1 is a general treatise on human society; Chapter 2 deals with rural society (*al-'Umrān al-Badawī*); Chapter 3 discusses different forms of government, states and institutions; Chapter 4 is devoted to the discussion of urban society and its civilizational cultures (*al-'Umrān al-Hadārī*); Chapter 5 describes industrial growth and economic affairs in general; and Chapter 6 is related to academic, literary, and cultural matters.

The wealth of ideas provided by *al-Muqaddimah* has enabled several specialists to find in it the early beginnings of a number of disciplines, related in particular to the new science that Ibn Khaldūn calls the Science of Sociology. The *Muqaddimah* has been translated into many European and Asian languages, and the famous French scholar, Robert Brunschvig, aptly said of Ibn Khaldūn: 'Just as he had no forerunners among Arab writers, so he had no successors or emulators in this idiom until the contemporary period.'

Ibn Khallikān (11 Rabiʿ II 608/22 September 1211–26 Rajab 681/30 October 1282): Aḥmad ibn Muhammad ibn Ibrāhīm ibn Khallikān al-Barmakī al-Shafiʿī was an outstanding biographer and jurist. Born in Irbil and died in Damascus, he was a contemporary of the famous historian Ibn al-Athīr and scholar Kamāl al-Dīn ibn Yūnus al-Subkī. During his visit to Egypt he was appointed deputy to the *Qāḍī'l-Quḍāt* of Egypt, Badr al-Dīn Yūsuf. In 659/1261, the Mamlūk Sultan Baybars appointed him *Qāḍī'l-Quḍāt* of Syria. His famous biographical directory *Wafayāt al-Aʿyān wa-Anbā' Abnā' al-Zamān* was intended by him to be a compendium of information on those great personalities of Islamic history about whom not much was available by way of authentic details. The long title of the book may be literally transated as follows: *Obituaries of Eminent Personalities and Profiles of Leading Figures of Their Times*. He, therefore, left out of the book those great figures about whose lives and achievements detailed information was already available, personalities like the Companions of the Prophet, Tābiʿūn, and *al-Khulafā' al-Rāshidūn*. Subsequently, he further improved and edited the book. Its translation also exists in Persian and Turkish.

Ibn Qayyim al-Jawzīyyah (7 Ṣafar 691/29 January 1292–13 Rajab 751/16 August 1350): Shams al-Dīn Abū Bakr Muhammad ibn Abī Bakr ibn Ayyūb al-Zarʿī was the son of the *qayyim* (rector) of al-Madrasah al-Jawzīyyah of Damascus and from that reference he became famous by the *kunyah* of Ibn Qayyim al-Jawzīyyah. Ibn Qayyim inherited the legacy of Islamic sciences from his father, Abū Bakr. He had the distinction of being the most famous pupil of the great traditionist and scholar Imam Ibn Taymiyyah. In 712 (1312), when the Imam took residence in Damascus, until his death in 728 (1328), Ibn Qayyim remained his devoted student and disciple. His long association with Ibn Taymiyyah elevated him to the coveted position of his successor and an outstanding jurist (*faqīh*) and scholar. Well versed in all disciplines of the time, like his teacher, he specially excelled in *tafsīr* (Qur'anic exegesis), hadith and *Uṣūl al-Fiqh* (Principles of Islamic Jurisprudence). He was imprisoned along with his teacher in the citadel of Damascus and was set free after the Imam's death, only to face opposition and hardship from the local *'ulamā*, who were deadly opposed to the Ḥanbalī approach of Imam Ibn Taymiyyah and Ibn Qayyim. He often differed from the rulings of the Damascus *Qāḍī' l-Quḍāt*, Taqī al-Dīn al-Subkī, of the Shāfi'ī school and had to face the consequences.

In addition to his immense contribution as a scholar and writer, Ibn Qayyim was also instrumental in editing, printing and publication – and thereby popularization – of Ibn Taymiyyah's masterpieces. Of his famous books, the following are held specially in high esteem and have remained popular ever since among the jurists, academicians and students of Islamic sciences: (1) *Zād al-Ma'ād fi Hudā Khayri'l 'Ibād*; (2) *I'lām al-Muwaqqi'īn*; (3) *Al-Ṭuruq Al-Ḥukūmīyyah fi'l-Siyāsat al-Shar'īyyah*; (4) *Shifā' al-'Alīl fi'l-Qaḍā'i wal-Qaḍari wal-Hikmati wa'l-Ta'līl*; (5) *Al-Kāfiyah al-Shāfiyah fi'l-Firqah al-Nājiyah*; (6) *Madārij a'l-Sālikīn*; (7) *Al-Wābil al-Ṣayyib*; (8) *Rawḍat al-Muḥibbīn wa Nuzhat a'l-Mushtāqīn*; (9) *Hidāyat al-Ḥayārā wal-Mu'aṭṭalah fi Ajwibati'l-Yahūd wa'l-Naṣārā*; and (10) *Al-Ṣawā'iqu'l-Munazzalah 'ala'l-Juḥamīyyah wal-Mu'aṭṭalah*.

Al-Jaṣṣās (Abū Bakr) (305/917–370/981): Aḥmad ibn 'Alī Abū Bakr al-Rāzī, better known as al-Jaṣṣās, was an eminent scholar of the Ḥanafī School. He received training in jurisprudence from 'Alī ibn al-Ḥasan al-Karkhī and excelled in the Islamic sciences under the guidance of the eminent scholars of his time. His pupils include some prominent names, like al-Qudūri and Abū Bakr Aḥmad ibn Mūsa al-Khwārazmī. The best known of his books are: (1) *Aḥkām Al-Qur'ān*; (2) *Kitāb al-Uṣūl*, which is a commentary on Imam Muhammad al-Shaybānī's *Al-Jāmi' Al-Kabīr*; and (3) a commentary on Imam al-Ṭaḥāwi's *Al-Mukhtaṣar fi'l-Fiqh*.

Al-Kardarī (d. 827/1424): Muhammad ibn Muhammad al-Kardarī, about whose life and works not much is available, is best known for his scholarly contribution on the life and achievements of Imam A'ẓam Abū Ḥanīfah, the 5-volume book *Manāqib Al-Imām Al-A'ẓam*.

Al-Khaṭīb al-Baghdādī (24 Jumādā II 392/10 May 1002-7–Dhū al-Ḥijjah 463/5 Sept 1071): Abū Bakr Aḥmad ibn 'Alī ibn Thābit ibn Aḥmad al-Shāfi'ī was an outstanding traditionist and historian. Son of the *khaṭīb* (preacher) of the grand mosque of the suburb of Baghdad, he himself became famous beyond the walls of Baghdad as al-Khaṭīb for his excellence in the art of preaching and knowledge of Islamic sciences. On completion of his studies at the hands of his father and other scholars of Baghdad, he travelled to various centres of Islamic learning of his time like al-Kūfah, Nishāpūr, Rayy and Isfahān. According to al-Dhahabī, his expertise in the science of Prophetic Tradition made him popular among the local *'ulamā'* who flocked to him to check the textual veracity of the Traditions they had collected before quoting them in their sermons and lectures. Al-Khaṭīb is best known for his encyclopaedic *Tarīkh Baghdād*, a compendium of scientifically arranged historical data in fourteen volumes regarding more than 7,800 scholars and eminent Islamic personalities, including women, connected with the socio-political and cultural life of Baghdad from the period extending from first century Hijrah to the year of his death (463 AH/1071 CE). Al-Khaṭīb's monumental work shows him more as a traditionist than a mere biographer. His chief concern was to make his *Tarīkh* a reference book for traditionists providing authentic data about the chain of transmitters (*isnād*) and *muḥaddithīn*. The book has established him as a great critical systematizer of the hadith methodology.

Khawārij: (sing. *Khārijī* also *Khārijites*): Literally meaning outsider, it is a derivative of the verb *khurūj* meaning to come out, to revolt. The term *Khārijī* was used for the first time for the conspirators who raised the bogeyman of avenging the murder of the Third Caliph 'Uthmān just to sow seeds of discord between the Fourth Caliph 'Alī and the governor of Syria, Amīr Mu'āwīyah, who was also related to Hadrat 'Uthmān. The conspiracy resulted in the internecine battle of Siffīn (Ṣafar 37/July 657). The same motley group of conspirators was earlier responsible for mutiny against the third caliph and his assassination while he was busy in reciting the Qur'an at home. That incident marked the beginning of the *Khārijī* conspiracy. The *Khārijī* ringleaders were external elements who infiltrated Madinah Munawwarah from outside and their actions confirmed they were either outside the pale of Islam or agents of Jewish conspirators against the flourishing Islamic caliphate. From that time onward, the group remained engaged in fomenting trouble on one pretext or the other in order to destabilize the established order.

Muslim historians are generally of the view that the masterminds of the *Khārijī* movement were Jews whose sole concern was to ignite revolt by capitalizing on internal dissent and exploiting some political/administrative weaknesses of the Muslim rulers. This is perhaps the reason why the *Khārijites* persistently claimed to be Islamic zealots motivated by a genuine urge for reform. Led by a lesser-known soldier of Kūfah, 'Abd Allah ibn Wahb, the group that earlier posed to be pro-'Alī, later challenged the Fourth Caliph on the pretext of avenging the death of 'Uthmān, which resulted in the Battle of Nahrawān (9 Ṣafar 38/17 July 658). The *Kharijīs* were routed in that battle and Ibn Wahb was killed. It did not root out the conspiracy, however, and one of his followers, 'Abd al-Raḥmān ibn Muljam, later on killed Hadrat 'Alī. The *Khawārij* continued their conspiracies during the Umayyad rule as well. At one time they planned to also kill Amīr Mu'āwīyah and the Governor of Egypt, 'Amr ibn al-'Ās, but did not succeed.

In later years, the *Khawārij* temporarily succeeded in controlling Kirmān, Fars, parts of the Eastern Umayyad Empire and also parts of eastern Arabia like Yamamah, Hadramawt and Yemen. They were led by a few gangsters, namely Abū Ṭālūt, Najdah ibn 'Āmir, and Abū Fudayk, till they were totally routed by al-Ḥajjāj ibn Yūsuf. It goes to al-Ḥajjāj's credit to completely quell this conspiracy and prevent further damage to the Islamic socio-political order of the time.

Ideologically, the *Khawārij* were non-conformists, who on the one hand opposed the Shia and on the other refused to recognize the legitimacy of the Third and Fourth Caliphs. They also regarded all non-*Khārijī* Muslims as apostates. While they showed extreme tolerance to non-Muslims, they believed in the principle of *isti'rād* or religious murder of non-*Khārijīs* who were opposed to them. One of their 'spiritual' leaders Yazīd ibn Abī Anīsah (founder of the *Yazīdīyah* group) believed that God will reveal a new Qur'an to a prophet among the Persians, who would launch a new religion for them as divine as Judaism, Christianity and Islam, and his followers would be no other than the Sābi'ūn mentioned in the Qur'an.

Al-Mas'ūdī (280/893–Jumādā-II 345/September 956): Abū al-Ḥasan 'Alī ibn al-Ḥusayn ibn 'Abdallah, known famously by his surname, al-Mas'ūdī with reference to his ancestor the eminent Companion 'Abdullūh ibn Mas'ūd, was a widely travelled historian, geographer, and scholar of the fourth century Hijrah (tenth century CE). Born and educated principally in Baghdad, he attended classes given by various eminent teachers of the day. He spent a year visiting Persia in 303/915. The next year he embarked on a journey of the Indo-Pak subcontinent, where he stayed at al-Mansūrah (Sindh) and also visited Multan. Then he left via the Indian coastal townships for Ceylon, travelling onward by ship to the China Sea region where it is not certain if he actually visited mainland China or not. Moving westward from there, he reached Zanjibar and then back into Oman. From 306 to 316 (918–926), he travelled to Iraq, Syria, Palestine, and Arabia. Next, he visited Armenia and the areas on the Southern coast of the Caspian Sea during 320–329 (932–940). From 330/941 onward he finally settled in al-Fusṭāṭ (Cairo), but frequently travelled between his hometown, Basra, Damascus, Alexandria and back to al-Fusṭāṭ.

His continuous travels were motivated not so much by his love for tourism but more by his instinctive quest for the unknown and a passion to gather first-hand knowledge about things which others might not have looked at that deeply. This is duly reflected in his writings as well. He wrote extensively, but unfortunately only a few of his around thirty-six books actually survived. However, the knowledge he gathered about peoples and places and tried to preserve in his books was sketchy and based on popular stories and folk tales, unlike the more analytical and scientifically documented accounts presented by his successor, al-Bayrūnī.

The best known of al-Mas'ūdī's books and the principal surviving work due to which he owes his reputation is *Murūj al-Dhahab wa Ma'ādin al-Jawāhir* (*The Golden Meadows and Mines of Jewels*). Written in 332/943 and revised twice, the compendium consists of five volumes, plus two volumes of index, for which he had recourse to no fewer than 165 written sources, including – in addition to the Arabic texts – translations of Plato, Aristotle and Ptolemy, as well as Arabic versions of the Pahlavi literature. The book is divided into two Parts, the first Part – roughly spread over two-fifths of the work – is devoted chiefly to generalities regarding the universe and information of an historical nature on non-Muslim peoples, including pre-Islamic Arabs. The contents include the 'sacred'history of humankind, from *Sayyidunā* Ādam up to *Sayyidunā* Rasūl Allah (peace be upon him), a survey of India including geographical data concerning its rivers and seas, China, the tribes of Turkey, a list of the kings of Mesopotamia, Persia, Greece, Rome, Byzantium, Egypt, and chapters on different races like Negroes, Slavs, Gauls and Galicians. Next come the calendars and the religious monuments of India, Persia and of the Sabaeans, and a summary of universal chronology. The second Part of the monumental work is devoted exclusively to the history of Islam from the golden days of the Prophet (peace be upon him), up to al-Mas'ūdī's own time.

According to al-Mas'ūdī, the book contains a summary of the studies he had presented in his earlier 30-volume compendium, *Kitāb Akhbār al-Zamān wa man Abādahū'l-Hidthān min al-Umam wa'l-Ajyāl al-Khāliyah wa'l-Mamālik al-Dāthirah* (332/943). This voluminous venture was undertaken as a book of universal history, but only its first volume remained intact and the rest is extant. If translated literally, the lengthy title throws light on the book's contents: *Chronicle of World History and of Those Lost in Time from Among Nations and Generations of the Past and the Countries of Antiquity*. Al-Mas'ūdī abridged the extraordinary work first in his book *Al-Kitāb al-Awsaṭ*, which also contained a supplement on points of detail, and then in a more systematic manner in his magnum opus, *Murūj al-Dhahab*.

Al-Mas'ūdī's fourth book, *Kitāb al-Tanbīh wal-Ishrāf*, composed around 344–345/955–956, is regarded as his last work and offers with greater precision essential points of the data contained in his earlier works concerning astronomical and meteorological phenomena and the history of Islam until the rule of al-Mutī'. The book also critically examines the works of some Christian authors, with the majority of whom he was personally acquainted. He also contributed some books, now extant, to highlight the virtues and glorious deeds of Imam

'Alī, *ahl al-Bayt* and the twelve Imams. These books lead one to believe that he was a Shia or *Imāmīyyah*. While al-Dhahabī saw him only as a Mu'tazilī, Imam Ibn Taymiyyah recognized his Shiism. Al-Mas'ūdī is known to have contributed another work, *Kitāb al-Intisār*, a refutation of *Khārijīism*.

Al-Māwardī (364/974–39 Rabī'-I 450/27 May 1053): Abu'l Ḥasan 'Alī ibn Muhammad ibn Ḥabīb al-Shafi'ī, born in Basra and died in Baghdad, was an eminent scholar of Islamic law, Tradition, politics and literature. According to Tāj al-Dīn al-Subkī, al-Māwardī became famous by his nickname with reference to his family trade in *mā' al-ward* (rose water). Of his fourteen books in the field of religion, politics, language, and literature, the following are the best-known: (1) *Kitāb al-Iqnā'*, the remarkably concise 40-page abridged version of his 4,000-page compendium of Shafi'ī law; (2) *Kitāb al-Ḥāwī fi'l-Furū'*; (3) *Kitāb Adab al-Qāḍī*, (two of the thirty sections of *Al-Ḥāwī*); (4) *Kitāb al-Aḥkām al-Sultānīyyah*, acclaimed as a classic work of public law and system of governance, also rendered in French in an edition that made al-Māwardī famous in the West; (5) *Kitāb Qawānīn al-Wizārah wa Siyāsat al-Mulūk*, a treatise in politics and statecraft; and (6) *Kitāb al-Amthāl wa'l-Ḥikam*, a collection 300 Traditions, 300 proverbs, and 300 selected verses.

Al-Muwaffaq al-Makkī (d. 568/1172): Abu'l-Mu'ayyad al-Muwaffaq ibn Aḥmad al-Makkī, a leading jurist of his time, is best known for his 27-volume biography, *Manāqib Al-Imām Al-A'ẓam Abī Ḥanīfah*, in which he scholarly portrayed the outstanding features of Imam Abū Ḥanīfah's personality and his legal acumen.

Mu'tazilites: The *Mu'tazilah* movement of speculative dogmatism was founded in Basra in the first half of the second century Hijrah/eighth century CE by Wāṣil ibn 'Aṭā' (d. 131/748). It subsequently became an important intellectual movement till the emergence of the *Ashā'irah*. The term emerged from what Imam Ḥasan al-Baṣrī observed regarding his pupil Wāṣil when he differed with him on some points of intellectual debate: *I'tazala 'annā'* (He separated himself from us). The infinitive *i'tizāl* denotes a position of neutrality in the face of opposing views. Wāṣil, and his lieutenant 'Amr ibn 'Ubayd, both disciples of Imam al-Ḥasan al-Baṣrī, led an intellectual movement which had a political undertone as well. The *Mu'tazilah* were generally hostile to the Umayyads and showed a cautious approach towards the Shia. They can legitimately be called 'rationalist' theologians and appeared to have been influenced to some extent by fragments of Greek philosophy. In the realm of ethics, they held that man was capable of knowing by his reason alone that which was morally good or evil and the Revelation could only confirm what reason guided him to. They believed, nonetheless, that reason was not capable of making man aware of everything that was evil (forbidden) or matters which were obligatory, and the Revelation alone could reconfirm that.

For a detailed overview of the speculative dogmatism of the *Mu'tazilites* see *al-Ashā'irah* (pp. 173–175).

Al-Sarakhsī (d. 490/1096): Abū Bakr Muhammad ibn Aḥmad ibn Abī Sahl al-Sarakhsī was an eminent jurist of the fifth century Hijrah (eleventh century CE), who dedicatedly worked in Transoxania (*Mā warā' al-Nahr*) to promote its rich Ḥanafī tradition. He produced a number of works, the most important being *Kitāb Al-Mabsūt*, *Sharḥ al-Siyar al-Kabīr*, and the book on *Uṣūl al-Fiqh*. In *Al-Mabsūt*, al-Sarakhsī explained and expanded Imam Muhammad al-Shaybānī's exposition of Ḥanafī law in a manner that makes it a remarkable contribution to the juristic literature. His *Sharḥ* is a commentary on Imam Muhammad's *Kitāb al-Siyar al-Kabīr*. Al-Sarakhsī's scholarly contribution established him as an outstanding Ḥanafī jurist. Not much is available, however, by way of authentic details about his personal life and even the date of his death has been mentioned variously as 480/1090 and 500/1106.

Sayyid Mawdūdī (1321/1903–1399/1979): Born in Aurangabad, India, Sayyid Abul A'lā Mawdūdī is considered as one of the leading scholars and religious revivalists of contemporary history. In 1927, he published his first major work, *Al-Jihād fi al-Islām* (*War and Peace in Islam*), which established him at once as a writer of stranding at the age of twenty-seven. In 1933, Mawdūdī founded a monthly journal, *Tarjumān al-Qur'ān*, which was to serve as the main platform for his ideas. In Lahore in 1941 he founded the Jamā'at-e-Islami, which was soon to emerge as the world of Islam's major revivalist movement. The movement was led by him until 1972 and it aimed at challenging the socio-political order of the day and upholding the cause of Islam. After the creation of Pakistan in 1947, he was a leading figure in getting the 22-point Objectives Resolution of 1951 adopted by the country's religious scholars, which defined the fundamental principles of the Islamic State and which eventually came to form part of the Constitution of the Islamic Republic of Pakistan. Between 1948 and 1964, Sayyid Mawdūdī's struggle often saw him in and out of jail, but nothing could deter his resolute march forward on the road to Islamic revivalism.

Sayyid Mawdūdī's intellectual and ideological contribution was immense. He wrote more than eighty books and tracts, which covered a wide variety of subjects, including *tafsīr*, Sīrah, law, history, politics, economics, and social sciences. His magnum opus, *Tafhīm al-Qur'ān* (1972–1974), in six volumes, remains the most widely read commentary of the Qur'an. It has also been rendered in English and is popularly known as *Towards Understanding the Qur'ān*. His other notable works include: (1) *Pardah* (*Hijab and the Status of Women in Islam*, 1939/1972); (2) *Islam aur Dabt-i-Wilādat* (*Birth Control: Its Social, Political, Economic, Moral and Religious Aspects*, 1951/1968); (3) *Islamī Riyāsat* (*Islamic Law and Constitution*, 1952/1960); (4) *Tajdīd-o-Ihyā'-i-Dīn* (*A Short History of the Revivalist Movement in Islam*, 1952/1963); (5) *Shahādāt-i-Ḥaqq* (*Witness Unto Mankind*, 1957/1986); (6) *Islam aur 'Adl-i-Ijtimā'ī* (*Islam and Social Justice*, 1963); (7) *Khilāfat-o-Mulūkiyat* (*Caliphate and Monarchy*, 1967);

and (8) *Qur'ān kī Chār Bunyādī Istilāhen* (*Four Key Concepts of the Qur'an*, 1969/2006). Some of his works on Islamic economics include: (9) *Sūd* (*Interest*, 1948–1952); (10) *Mas'alah-i-Milkīyat-i-Zamīn* (*The Question of Land Ownership*, 1950); and (11) *Ma'āshīyat-i-Islam* (*First Principles of Islamic Economics*, 1970–2011).

For an overview of his life and thought and for a comprehensive bibliography of his writings, one may consult the collection of articles edited by Prof Khurshid Ahmad and Dr Zafar Ishaq Ansari, *The Islamic Perspectives* and *Studies in Honour of Sayyid Abul A'lā Mawdūdī* (Leicester, 1980).

Al-Sha'rānī (897/1492–12 Jamādā-I 973/5 December 1565): 'Abd Al-Wahhāb ibn Aḥmad al-Sha'rānī was a scholar and a moderate Sufi of the Shādhilīyah tradition and a prolific writer on various religious subjects. He was brought up and educated in Cairo and also died and was buried there in a *zawīyah* (the tomb beneath the cupolaed mosque) built for him. Al-Sha'rānī's works include his autobiography, *Latā'if al-Minan*, a lengthy account of the graces bestowed upon him by the All-Mighty; and *Al-Yawāqīt Wa'l-Jawāhir* in which he rendered the great mystic Muhyi'l-Dīn Ibn al-'Arabī's complicated ideas in a simplified way.

Kitāb al-Mizān al-Kubrā was al-Sha'rānī's most unique contribution in *fiqh* in which he aimed at unification of the four *madhāhib* (schools), or at least to highlight their commonalities, and stressed the need to close the gaps between them. According to him, the founders of these schools were *awliyā'* Allah (close to the Lord) and they had much in common with hardly any real differences among them, which only their *muqallidīn* (followers) often exaggerated.

Al-Shahristānī (479/1086–548/1153): Abū 'Abdallah Tāj al-Dīn al-Fath Muhammad ibn 'Abd al-Karīm was born in Shahristān, a town in the Khurāsān province in Persia, though not much is known about his personal life. He travelled to Nishāpūr to study and then went to Baghdad for further training in Islamic sciences, where he taught for three years at the prestigious *al-Nizāmīyyah* school. He returned afterwards to Persia to serve under Sanjar, the Saljūq ruler of Khurāsān, as Deputy of his Chancellery. He spent his last days in his native town where he died and was buried. From his life, al-Shahristānī appeared to some as an *Imāmī Shī'ah.* This impression was, however, incorrect because of his education at the hands of *Ash'arī* teachers and his teaching career at *Al-Madrasah al-nizāmīyah*, an essentially *Ash'arī* institution of learning. His works display a richness and originality of philosophical and theological thought which contributed in making him an outstanding author of his time.

Al-Shahristānī's magnum opus, *Kitāb al-Milal wal-Nihal* (*The Book of Sects and Creeds*) was a monumental work of religious studies with a systematic and scientific approach. The UNESCO-sponsored French translation of the book (1986–1993) made him famous among Western scholars. His other works include: (1) *Nihāyat al-Aqdām fī 'Ilm al-Kalām* (*The End of Steps in the Science of Theological Scholasticism*), dealing essentially with the limitations of this science; (2) *Mafātīh al-Asrār wa-Masābīh al-Abrār* (*The Keys of Mysteries and Lamps of the Righteous*), a commentary on surah (*Al-Baqarah* and *'Āl 'Imrān*; surahs 2 and 3) with an introductory chapter on the Qur'an; (3) *Muṣāra'ah al-Falāsifah*, a critique of Ibn Sīnā (Avicenna); and (4) *Al-Majlis*, a discourse delivered to the *Ithnā 'Asharī* Shia audience.

Al-Shawkānī (1173/1760–1255/1839): Muhammad ibn 'Alī ibn Muhammad ibn 'Abdullah al-Shawkānī was born in a Zaydī Shia Muslim family of Hijrat al-Shawkān, near Sana'a in Yemen, the place from which he derived his surname. He later adopted the Sunni Salafi ideology. He was a spirited writer and an authority to whom scholars of the day often turned for details of Islamic law. He was also a mufti from whose *fatāwa* the people of Yemen benefitted immensely. Shawkānī was opposed to *taqlīd* (unquestioning adoption of the legal decisions of a particular person or school) and considered himself a *mujtahid* or a juristic expert duly qualified to take independent decisions in matters of legal significance. Some of his well known works are: (1) *Tafsīr Fath al-Qādir*; (2) *Nayl al-Awṭār*; and (3) *Irshād al-Fuḥūl*, a book on *Usūl al-Fiqh*.

Al-Ṭabarī (Ibn Jarīr) (224/838–319/923): Born in Amol, Tabaristān, 20-kilometres south of the Caspian Sea, his full name is Abū Ja'far Muhammad ibn Jarīr al-Ṭabarī. He is one of the earliest most prominent Persian historians and commentator of the Qur'an. He studied initially at Rayy (Rages) for five years under Abū 'Abd Allah Muhammad ibn Ḥumayd al-Rāzī, who had taught in Baghdad and then returned to his native Rayy. Ibn Jarīr studied under him, specially his well known work on the Sīrah of *Sayyidunā* Rasūl Allah (*peace be upon him*), before leaving in the prime of his youth for Baghdad, the Islamic world's greatest seat of learning and the cultural hub of the time, with a keen desire to seek knowledge from Imam Aḥmad ibn Ḥanbal. Incidentally, the Imam had died before his arrival and so he travelled to Kūfah and Basra and then returned to Baghdad. His urge to know more about Islamic sciences took him to Syria, Palestine, Egypt, Beirut and Hijaz. He remained a bachelor and engaged in reading, writing and teaching. He died in Baghdad on 17 February 923.

Imam al-Ṭabarī's voluminous corpus, *Tarīkh al-Rusul wa'l Mulūk*, better known by its abbreviated name *Tarīkh al-Ṭabarī*, presents a detailed account of human history since the earliest of times, in light of the data revealed in the Qur'an, till the year 915 CE (a few years before his death). His second most celebrated book is *Jāmi' al-Bayān fi Ta'wīl i'l-Qur'ān*, known by its abbreviated title *Tafsīr Ibn Jarīr al-Ṭabarī*. It took him seven years to complete this great exegesis, which is spread over 3,000 pages. Scholars like Jalāl al-Dīn al-Suyūtī and al-Baghawī largely relied on *Tafsīr al-Ṭabarī* for their commentaries. *Tahdhīb al-Āthār*, a book on the Traditions transmitted by the Ṣaḥābah, was his other great work, which, however, remained incomplete.

Al-Ṭabarānī (260/873–360/971): Abu'l Qāsim Sulaymān ibn Ayyūb ibn Muṭayyir al-Ṭabarānī was one of the most important traditionists of his age. He is said to have begun his studies in hadith at the age of thirteen, with his education spanning his native Syria, Iraq, Hijaz, Yemen and Egypt. His travels in pursuit of knowledge lasted for about thirty-three years. His teachers in Tradition included Abū Zur'ah al-Dimashqī, Imam al-Nasa'ī, and Imam Abū Ja'far Muhammad ibn Jarīr al-Ṭabarī. Al-Ṭabarānī is known especially for his three works on hadith: (1) *Al-Mu'jam al-Kabīr 'ala Asmā'l-Ṣaḥābah*; (2) *Al-Mu'jam al-Awsaṭ fi Aḥadīth al-Afrād wa'l-Gharā'ib*; and (3) *Al-Mu'jam al-Saghīr*. Some of his other works include: (4) *Kitāb al-Du'ā*; (5) *Kitāb al-Manāsik*; (6) *Kitāb al-Sunnah*; (7) *Kitāb al-Nawādir*; and (8) *Kitāb Dalā'il 'il-Nubūwwah.*

Al-Ṭaḥāwī (Al-Imām) (239/853 or 229/844–6 Dhū al-Qa'dah 321/31 October 933): Abū Ja'far Aḥmad ibn Muhammad ibn Salāma ibn 'Abd al-Malik al-Azdī al-Ṭaḥāwī (with reference to his place of birth, Taḥā in Upper Egypt), was a great exponent of Ḥanafī law and also an eminent traditionist. He received his early education at the hands of his maternal uncle, Abū Ibrāhīm Ismā'īl ibn Yahyā al-Muzanī, who was one of the eminent pupils of Imam al-Shāfi'ī. Al-Ṭaḥāwī also received from him a copy of the manuscript of Imam al-Shāfi'ī's *Musnad.* Subsequently, he travelled to Shām where he spent some time with the *Qāḍī'l-Quḍāt*, 'Abd al-Ḥamīd ibn Ja'far al-Ḥanafī. From there he travelled in pursuit of knowledge to al-Quds, Ghazzah and 'Asqalān. On his return, he became associated with the *Qāḍī'l-Quḍāt* of Egypt, Muhammad ibn 'Abduhū. It was during these fruitful interactions with the Ḥanafī jurists and scholars that al-Ṭaḥāwī was inspired with the comprehensiveness of Ḥanafī law and became its ardent follower.

Though essentially a *faqīh* (jurist), Imam al-Ṭaḥāwī extensively narrated Prophetic Traditions to support his legal stance. His commentaries and analysis offer admirable arguments that promote harmony between hadith and Ḥanafī law, and remove any apparent conflict between the two. Among the best known of his over two dozen books on law, Tradition, and history are: (1) *Al-Sharḥ* (*Commentary*) on Imam Muhammad's *al-Jāmi' al-Kabīr* and *al-Jāmi' al-Saghīr*; (2) *Al-Mukhtasar fi'l-Fiqh*; (3) *Ikhtilāf al-Fuqahā'*; (4) *Aḥkām al-Qur'ān*; (5) *Ma'ānī'l-Āthār*; (6) *Mushkil al-Āthār* (four volumes); (7) *Al-Shurūṭ al-Kabīr*; (8) *Al-Shurūṭ al-Awsaṭ*; (9) *Al-Shurūṭ al-Saghīr*; (10) *Manāqib Abī Ḥanīfah*; (11) *Al-Nawādir al-Fiqhīyyah*; and (12) *al-Risālah fi Uṣūli'l-Dīn*.

Among the more prominent of Imam al-Ṭaḥāwī's pupils were the noted traditionist Abi'l Qāsim Sulaymān ibn Ayyūb al-Ṭabarānī, 'Abd al-'Azīz ibn Muhammad, who later became a *Qāḍī* of Egypt, *al-Qāḍī* Ibn Abi'l-'Awwām, Maslamah ibn al-Qāsim al-Qurṭubī, and 'Abd Allah ibn 'Alī al-Dāwūdī.

Al-Yāfi'ī (698/1298–768/1367): Abū As'ad ibn 'Alī ibn 'Uthmān al-Shāfi'ī was a religious scholar and Sufi. He was born in Yemen, where he subsequently became a disciple of Sufi al-Shaykh 'Alī al-Ṭawāshī, to whom he remained close till his death. In 718/1319, he moved to Makkah Mukarramah to make it his home in life and his place of rest after death. He completed his education in Islamic sciences with the Haram scholar *al-Qāḍī* Radī al-Dīn al-Ṭabarī. He lived the life of an ascetic and frequently shuttled between the Haramayn of Makkah Mukarramah and Madinah Munawwarah. He also travelled to al-Quds, Damascus and Egypt, not to seek education but meet the local Sufis. He was a devout *Ash'arī* and resolutely combated *Mu'tazilī* rationalism. His major works are: (1) *Mir'āt al-Jinān wa 'Ibrat al-Yaqẓān* (a biographical compilation in four volumes, based on the data taken from Ibn al-Athīr, Ibn Khallikān, and al-Dhahabī); (2) *Rawḍat al-Rayahīn fi Hikāyāt al Ṣāliḥīn*, containing details of the lives and spiritual qualities of around 500 Sufis and Darwishes; and (3) *Marham al-'Ilal al-Muḍillah fi'l Radd 'alā A'immati'l-Mu'tazilah*, a treatise against the speculative dogmatism of the *Mu'tazilīs*.

Index